CIMA

MANAGEMENT LEVEL

PAPER F2

ADVANCED FINANCIAL REPORTING

EXAM PRACTICE KIT

FOR EXAMS IN 2015

BPP LEARNING MEDIA

First edition 2015

ISBN 9781 4727 1393 3
e-ISBN 9781 4727 2057 3

British Library Cataloguing-in-Publication Data
A catalogue record for this book
is available from the British Library

Published by

BPP Learning Media Ltd
BPP House, Aldine Place, 142/144 Uxbridge Road
London W12 8AA

www.bpp.com/learningmedia

Printed in the United Kingdom by Polester Wheatons

Hennock Road
Marsh Barton
Exeter
EX2 8RP

Your learning materials, published by BPP Learning
Media Ltd, are printed on paper obtained from
traceable, sustainable sources.

Contents

                                                                        Page

Using the Kit

Question and Answer index   iv
Using your BPP OT Kit   v
The Objective Test exam   v
Learning Objectives   vi

Passing F2

Tackling OTQs   viii
Demonstrating your understanding of F2   ix

Questions and answers

Questions   3
Answers   95

Mathematical tables and exam formulae   169

Question and Answer index

		Page number	
		Question	**Answer**
CIMA F2 Assessment			
1	Sources of long-term finance	3	95
2	Cost of capital	4	96
3	Financial instruments	7	98
4	Leases	9	100
5	Provisions, contingent liabilities and contingent assets	11	102
6	Deferred taxation	14	104
7	Share-based payments	16	107
8	Revenue and construction contracts	19	109
9	Basic groups	22	111
10	Associates and joint arrangements	25	113
11	Changes in group structures	27	115
12	Indirect control of subsidiaries	31	118
13	Foreign subsidiaries	34	120
14	Consolidated statement of changes in equity	37	123
15	Consolidated statements of cash flows	40	126
16	Related parties	44	129
17	Earnings per share	46	131
18	Ethics	48	133
19	Analysis of financial performance and position I	52	136
20	Analysis of financial performance and position II	54	138
21	Analysis of financial performance and position III	56	141
22	Analysis of financial performance and position IV	59	144
23	Analysis of financial performance and position V	62	146
24	Analysis of financial performance and position VI	65	148
CIMA F2 Further Question Practice			
25	Mixed Bank 1	68	149
26	Mixed Bank 2	71	152
27	Mixed Bank 3	74	154
28	Mixed Bank 4	77	156
29	Mixed Bank 5	80	158
30	Mixed Bank 6	83	160
31	Mixed Bank 7	86	162
32	Mixed Bank 8	89	164

Using your BPP OT Kit

One of the key criteria for achieving exam success is question practice. There is generally a direct correlation between candidates who study all topics and practise exam questions and those who are successful in their real exams. This Kit gives you ample opportunity for such practice throughout your preparations for your OT exam.

All questions in your exam are compulsory and all the component learning outcomes will be examined so you must **study the whole syllabus**. Selective studying will limit the number of questions you can answer and hence reduce your chances of passing. It is better to go into the exam knowing a reasonable amount about most of the syllabus rather than concentrating on a few topics to the exclusion of the rest.

Practising as many exam-style questions as possible will be the key to passing this exam. You must do questions under **timed conditions**.

Breadth of question coverage

Questions will cover the whole of the syllabus so you must study all the topics in the syllabus.

The weightings in the table below indicate the approximate proportion of study time you should spend on each topic, and is related to the number of questions per syllabus area in the exam.

F2 Financial Management	
Syllabus topics	**Weighting**
A Sources of long-term finance	15%
B Financial reporting	60%
C Analysis of financial performance and position	25%

The Objective Test exam

The Objective Test exam is a computer based assessment, which is available on demand at assessment centres all year round.

Objective Test exams in each level can be taken in any order, but candidates must pass all the OT exams for a level before they can sit the Integrated Case Study Exam for that level.

Each exam lasts for 90 minutes and the pass mark is 70%.

Results are available shortly after the test has been completed, and the results will include feedback.

The exam will be made up of different types of questions, including:

Question Type	Explanation
Multiple choice	Standard multiple choice items provide four options. 1 option is correct and the other 3 are incorrect. Incorrect options will be plausible, so you should expect to have to use detailed, syllabus-specific knowledge to identify the correct answer rather than relying on common sense.
Multiple response	A multiple response item is the same as a multiple choice question, except more than one response is required. You will normally (but not always) be told how many options you need to select.
Drag and drop	Drag and drop questions require you to drag a "token" onto a pre-defined area. These tokens can be images or text. This type of question is effective at testing the order of events, labelling a diagram or linking events to outcomes.

BPP
LEARNING MEDIA

Question Type	Explanation
Gap fill	Gap fill (or "fill in the blank") questions require you to type a short numerical response. You should carefully follow the instructions in the question in terms of how to type your answer – e.g. the correct number of decimal places.
Hot spot	These questions require you to identify an area or location on an image by clicking on it. This is commonly used to identify a specific point on a graph or diagram
Drop-down list	Drop-down lists follow the same principle as multiple choice questions, in that you need to select one option from a pre-defined list. This can be used in conjunction with a gap-fill question: for example, you may be asked to key a numerical answer into a gap-fill box and then select an explanation for the approach you've taken from a drop-down list.

Learning Objectives

The table below has been prepared by CIMA to help you understand the abilities that CIMA is seeking to assess.

Learning objective	Verbs used	Definition	Example question types
1 Knowledge			
What you are expected to know	• List	• Make a list of	MCQ
	• State	• Express, fully or clearly, the details of/facts of	MCQ
	• Define	• Give the exact meaning of	MCQ
2 Comprehension			
What you are expected to understand	• Describe	• Communicate the key features of	Multiple Response
	• Distinguish	• Highlight the differences between	Multiple Response
	• Explain	• Make clear or intelligible/state the meaning or purpose of	Drop down list
	• Identify	• Recognise, establish or select after consideration	Hotspot
	• Illustrate	• Use an example to describe or explain something	Drop down list
3 Application			
How you are expected to apply your knowledge	• Apply	• Put to practical use	Multiple response
	• Calculate/ compute	• Ascertain or reckon mathematically	Number entry
	• Demonstrate	• Prove the certainty or exhibit by practical means	Hotspot
	• Prepare	• Make or get ready for use	Drag and drop
	• Reconcile	• Make or prove consistent/ compatible	Drop down list
	• Solve	• Find an answer to	Number entry
	• Tabulate	• Arrange in a table	Drag and drop

BPP
LEARNING MEDIA

Learning objective	Verbs used	Definition	Example question types
4 Analysis			
How you are expected to analyse the detail of what you have learned	• Analyse	• Examine in detail the structure of	Multiple response
	• Categorise	• Place into a defined class or division	Drag and drop
	• Compare & contrast	• Show the similarities and/or differences between	Hotspot
	• Construct	• Build up or complete	Drag and drop
	• Discuss	• Examine in detail by argument	Multiple response
	• Interpret	• Translate into intelligible or familiar terms	Multiple response
	• Prioritise	• Place in order of priority or sequence for action	Drop down list
	• Produce	• Create or bring into existence	Drag and drop
5 Evaluation			
How you are expected to use your learning to evaluate, make decisions or recommendations	• Advise	• Counsel, inform or notify	Multiple response
	• Evaluate	• Appraise or assess the value of	Multiple response
	• Recommend	• Propose a course of action	Multiple response

In your CBA, questions will be set which test up to the cognitive level of the verb in the component learning outcome in each paper's syllabus, so this means they will test up to level 5 verbs where the learning outcome permits this.

CIMA will limit the number of lower level questions in the exam – so that students will not be able to achieve the pass mark solely based on correctly answering knowledge and comprehension questions. Higher level questions, requiring candidates to demonstrate application, analysis and evaluation skills must be answered correctly for the pass mark to be reached.

Passing the F2 Objective Test exam

Tackling OTQs

- Read, and **re-read the question** to ensure you fully understand what is being asked.

- When starting to read a question, especially one with a lengthy scenario, **read the requirement first**. You will then find yourself considering the requirement as you read the data in the scenario, helping you to focus on exactly what you have to do.

- **Do not spend too much time on one question** - remember you should spend 1½ minutes, on average, per question

- If you cannot decide between two answers – look carefully and decide whether for one of the options you are making an unnecessary assumption – **do not be afraid of trusting your gut instinct**

- **Do not keep changing your mind** – research has shown that the 1st answer that appeals to you is often the correct one

- Remember that marks are awarded for correct answers, and marks will not be deducted for incorrect answers. Therefore **answer every single question**, even ones you are unsure of.

- Always submit an answer for a given question even if you do not know the answer - **never leave any answers blank**

- **Pace yourself** - you will need to work through the exam at the right speed. Too fast and your accuracy may suffer, too slow and you may run out of time. Use this Kit to practice your time keeping and approach to answering each question.

- If you are unsure about anything, remember to **ask the test administrator** before the test begins. Once the clock begins ticking, interruptions will not be allowed

- Remember to **keep moving on!** You may be presented with a question which you simply cannot answer due to difficulty or if the wording is too vague. If you have only approximately 90 seconds per question, and you find yourself spending five minutes determining the answer for a question then your time management skills are poor and you are wasting valuable time.

- If you finish the exam with time to spare, use the rest of the time to **review your answers** and to make sure that you answered every OTQ

Demonstrating your understanding of F2

The F2 examiner will expect you to demonstrate the following:

Knowledge	You will need to demonstrate solid, specific knowledge in each of the syllabus areas.
Calculations	Calculations are an important part of this exam. Make sure you learn the formulas by heart, through repeated practice. It's important (especially when it comes to ratios) that you learn the formulas as provided in this Study Text.
Explanation	Questions may require you to select the correct definitions and make inferences in a short scenario, based on your understanding of the topics. The need to apply your knowledge to the circumstances in the scenarios – even in an OT exam – is important at this level.

All OTQs in all the exams are worth the same number of marks, both in this Kit and in the real exam. However, this is an approximate guide: some OTQs are very short and just require a factual selection, which you either know or you don't, while others are more complex, which will inevitably take more time. Note that the real exam will be balanced such that the 'difficulty' of the exam will be fair for all students – the OTQs in this Kit have also been balanced in a similar way.

Using the solutions and feedback

Avoid looking at the answer until you have finished a question. It can be very tempting to do so, but unless you give the question a proper attempt under exam conditions you will not know how you would have coped with it in the real exam scenario.

When you do look at the answer, compare it with your own and give some thought to why your answer was different, if it was.

If you did not reach the correct answer make sure that you work through the explanation or workings provided, to see where you went wrong. If you think that you do not understand the principle involved, work through and revise the point again, to ensure that you will understand it if it occurs in the exam.

Objective test questions

1 Sources of long-term finance

1.1 **Which THREE of the following statements are true?**

A   Bonds and shares are both securities which can be traded in the capital markets.

B   Holders of both bonds and shares will have a right to a cash payment from the issuing entity.

C   Both bonds and shares will normally be redeemable at any point in time.

D   The ability to sell bonds on the capital markets enhances their attractiveness to bond holders.

E   Bond holders will normally be paid a fixed return known as the coupon rate.

1.2 **Complete the following sentences below by writing in the correct narrative from the list provided.**

Ordinary shares carry voting rights and [   ] to any declared dividend. They are a [   ] form of finance from the company's perspective.

Picklist for narratives

entitlement
no entitlement
flexible
risky

1.3 **A bank loan that restricts the recipient of the loan by placing limits on their ability to borrow in future, is said to contain which ONE of the following?**

A   A positive loan covenant.

B   A fixed charge.

C   A floating charge.

D   A negative loan covenant.

1.4 **Which ONE of the following statements about obtaining a full stock market listing is NOT correct?**

A   Compliance costs are likely to increase, but better public profile and access to funds benefit the business.

B   All else being equal the value of the business is likely to be unaffected.

C   It allows owners to realise their investment.

D   It increases the liquidity of the shares for shareholders.

1.5 **Which THREE of the following are most likely to be associated with a bond issue?**

A   Underwriters are paid a fee for guaranteeing that the bonds will be purchased.

B   The company issuing the bonds reduces its reliance on bank lending.

C   Interest costs are often lower than an equivalent bank loan because the bonds can be sold by investors.

D   Finance can be raised more quickly than an equivalent bank loan.

E   Underwriters will guarantee to the investors that the company can pay the interest on the bond.

1.6 **Which of the following statements are true in respect of raising equity finance using a rights issue?**

A   If an entity is not listed on a stock market it cannot initiate a rights issue.

B   A rights issue will be at the existing market price of an entity to avoid a dilution in its share price.

C   A rights issue is when equity shares are available to be purchased by institutional shareholders only.

D   A rights issue allows shareholders the right to ensure that their existing shareholding is not diluted.

1.7 **A convertible bond will not normally contain which ONE of the following features?**

  A   A low coupon rate.
  B   The obligation to convert into shares at the expiry of the bond.
  C   Debt covenants.
  D   The entitlement to redeem the bond at its par value.

1.8 **According to the creditor hierarchy, list the following from high risk to low risk (from the viewpoint of the investor):**

  I   Ordinary share capital
  II   Preference share capital
  III   Trade payables
  IV   Bank loan with fixed and floating charges

  A   I,II,III,IV
  B   I,III,II,IV
  C   IV,III,II,I
  D   IV,II,III,I

1.9 **Which ONE of the following is an advantage of an offer for sale compared to a placing?**

  A   Lower issue costs.
  B   A higher issue price.
  C   Speed.
  D   No dilution of control.

1.10 **Rank the following from highest risk to lowest risk from a company's perspective.**

  I   Preference shares
  II   Convertible bonds
  III   Redeemable bonds
  IV   Ordinary shares

  A   II,III,IV,I
  B   III,I,IV,II
  C   II,III,I,IV
  D   IV,I,II,III

2 Cost of capital

2.1 **Complete the following sentences below by writing in the correct narrative from the list provided.**

The post-tax cost of debt for a convertible bond is the [   ] of the relevant cash flows associated with it. The relevant cash flows are the market value [   ] of now, the annual interest payments [   ] tax and the higher of the redemption value of the bond in the future or the anticipated share price if conversion occurs.

Picklist for narratives

internal rate of return
net present value
the shares
after
before
the bond

2.2 A company has just paid an ordinary dividend of 20 cents per share; as a result the shares are trading at $5.30.

If dividend growth is expected to be 4% per annum what is the company's cost of equity to the nearest whole number?

A   6%
B   7%
C   8%
D   9%

2.3 Mex Tex Co has the following capital structure.

	$m
80 million ordinary shares of 50c	40
Reserves	240
11% bonds	30
	310

The bonds are irredeemable and are trading at their par value. The company's rate of tax is 40%.

Mex Tex's cost of equity has been estimated at 18% per annum. The current market price per share is $1.00 ex div.

The company's weighted average cost of capital, for investment appraisal purposes, is?

A   14.4%
B   14.9%
C   17.0%
D   16.3%

2.4 Company B has a 2% convertible bond that is redeemable in 5 years time at a premium of 10% to its par value of $100 or convertible into 20 shares. B's share price is currently $4 and is expected to rise by 10% per year. The rate of corporate income tax is 25%.

Which TWO of the following are cash flows that will be used to calculate the cost of B's convertible bonds?

A $2 \times (1-0.25)$
B   100
C   128.8
D   110

2.5 Alpha Co has $250 million of 4% bonds in issue. This debt was originally issued at its par value of $100 and is now trading at 125% of this value. Alpha pays 25% tax.

Calculate Alpha's post tax cost of debt:

[   ] % to one decimal place.

2.6 X Co has a policy of increasing its dividend at a rate of 10% per year. X Co's shares are currently trading at $4.20 cum div, and a dividend payment of $0.20 is due to be paid.

Using the dividend growth model, the cost of equity for X Co is:

[   ] % (to one decimal place)

2.7 The price of a company's share is currently $40 ex div. The last dividend that has been paid is $3.00 per share.

If the company's cost of equity is 10% pa, what is the implied constant annual dividend growth rate?

A   2.33%
B   2.50%
C   7.50%
D   10.00%

2.8 Extracts from the statement of financial position of Drum Co are as follows.

	$m
6% irredeemable bonds	800
Ordinary shares of 25 cents	100
Reserves	1,000

The shares have a market value of $5 each and the cost of equity is 9%. The bonds have a market value of $105.0. Tax is 25%.

What is the weighted average cost of capital of Drum Co?

A   6.0%
B   6.1%
C   7.1%
D   7.6%

2.9 **Which TWO of the following are advantages of convertible bonds compared with a bank loan?**

A   Lower interest payments.

B   Tax relief on interest payments.

C   The possibility of lower cash repayments at the end of the term of the debt.

D   The ability of the company to convert the bonds into shares if interest repayments become a problem.

2.10 FX has 6% irredeemable debentures in issue which are currently quoted at 90% of their nominal value of $100. FX pays tax at a rate of 25%.

The post-tax cost of debt of these irredeemable debentures is:

A   4.1%
B   4.5%
C   6.7%
D   5.0%

3 Financial instruments

3.1 HJ has provided YT with a loan of $10,000 over five years with 6% annual interest payments in arrears, however YT is in financial difficulty and HJ has agreed to restructure the loan repayments.

Under which of the following circumstances would HJ recognise an impairment of the loan?

1   YT repays the full $10,000 two years after the original due date, but does not make any of the 6% interest payments.

2   YT repays the full $10,000 on the original due date, but does not make any of the 6% interest payments.

3   YT repays the full $10,000 on the original due date and makes all of the interest payments on time but at a new lower 4% interest rate.

4   YT repays the full $10,000 two years after the original due date and makes all of the interest payment on time at 6%, but does not pay interest in the extended two years.

A   Options 2 and 3
B   Options 1 and 4
C   Options 1, 2 and 3
D   Options 1, 2, 3 and 4

3.2 **Describe the appropriate accounting treatment, as required by IAS 39 *Financial instruments: recognition and measurement* for gains and losses on financial assets classified as 'held for trading'.**

A   These assets are held at cost and gains and losses will only be recognised on disposal of the assets.

B   These assets are held at amortised cost and the effective interest on the assets will be recognised in profit or loss over the term of the asset.

C   These assets are restated to fair value and gains and losses are recognised in other comprehensive income.

D   These assets are restated to fair value and gains and losses are recognised in profit or loss.

3.3 Z issues 6% redeemable preference shares on 31 December 20X3.

Which one of the following statements is true?

A   The issue is classified as equity because shares certificates are issued.
B   The dividend payable on these shares will be included in the statement of changes in equity.
C   The issue will be recorded by debiting investment and crediting bank.
D   The dividend payable will be included in Z's finance cost as a period expense.

3.4 On 1 January 20X1 Instrument issued 290,000 $100 zero-coupon bonds for $66 each. Issue costs amount to $22,200 in total. The redemption value of the zero-coupon bonds is slightly higher than the net issue proceeds, which give rise to an implicit annual rate of interest of 5%.

What will be the carrying value of the bonds as at 31 December 20X1 (to the nearest $)?

$ [   ]

3.5   W Co issued 1,500 convertible bonds on 1 January 20X7. The bonds have a 2 year term and are issued at par with a face value of $500 per bond. Interest is payable annually in arrears at a nominal annual interest rate of 5%. Each bond is convertible at any time up to maturity into 200 common shares.

When the bonds were issued the prevailing market interest rate for similar debt without conversion options was 7%.

The 2 year 7% simple and cumulative discount factors are 0.873 and 1.808 respectively.

What is the value of the equity component of the bond on 1 January 20X7 (to the nearest $)?

$ [   ]

3.6   PZG purchased a 2% holding in equity shares in a listed company, FJK. PZG's intention is to hold this investment for the long term.

How should this financial asset be initially classified and subsequently measured in accordance with IAS 39 *Financial instruments: recognition and measurement*?

A   Held for trading; fair value through profit or loss.
B   Held to maturity, amortised cost.
C   Available for sale; fair value through profit or loss.
D   Available for sale; fair value with gains or losses in other comprehensive income.

3.7   GZP purchased a small holding in shares in a listed company, ANG. GZP's intention is to realise this investment within a few months when seasonal fluctuations in its business make a cash shortfall probable.

How should this financial asset be initially classified and subsequently measured in accordance with IAS 39 *Financial instruments: recognition and measurement*?

A   Held for trading; fair value through profit or loss.
B   Held for trading; fair value with gains or losses in other comprehensive income.
C   Available for sale; fair value through profit or loss.
D   Available for sale; fair value with gains or losses in other comprehensive income.

3.8   LU issued a debt instrument on 1 January 20X4 at its nominal value of $4,000,000. The instrument carries a fixed coupon interest rate of 6%, which is payable annually in arrears. Transaction costs associated with the issue were $200,000. The effective interest rate applicable to this instrument has been calculated at approximately 8.4%.

The liability for this instrument at 31 December 20X4 will be calculated as follows:

Complete the calculation of the financial liability as at 31 December 20X4 by writing in the correct figures.

Liability $
Opening balance   [   ]

Plus: finance cost   [   ]

Loss: interest paid   (X)
Closing balance   (X)

3.9 Casablanca issued 3,000 6% convertible bonds on 1 April 20X4. The bonds have a 3-year life and were issued with a face value of $100 per bond. Interest is paid annually in arrears and each bond is convertible any time up to maturity into 50 ordinary shares.

At 1 April 20X4 the market interest rate for similar debt without the conversion option was 9%. The 9% three year simple and compound discount factors are 0.772 and 2.531 respectively.

What was the value of the equity component in the bond on issue (to the nearest $)?

A $300,000
B $231,600
C $45,558
D $22,842

3.10 EM acquired a debt instrument on 1 January 20X3 at its nominal value of $2,000,000. The instrument carries a fixed coupon interest rate of 7%, which is receivable annually in arrears. Transaction costs associated with the acquisition were $20,000.

The journal entry that initially records the instrument is:

A   DR Investment $1,980,000
    CR Bank $1,980,000

B   DR Investment $2,000,000
    DR Profit or loss $20,000

C   DR Investment $2,020,000
    CR Bank $2,020,000

D   DR Investment $1,980,000
    DR Profit or loss $20,000
    CR Bank $2,000,000

4 Leases

4.1 Alpha enters into a lease for an aircraft which has a fair value of $270,000 at the inception of the lease. The terms of the lease require Alpha to pay 10 annual rentals of $37,000 in arrears. The interest rate implicit in the lease is 10%. The present value of the 10 annual rentals of $37,000, discounted at the interest rate implicit in the lease, is $237,000. The terms of the lease indicate that Alpha has substantially all of the risks and rewards of ownership.

Applying the provisions of IAS 17 to this lease, the amount to be added to Alphas's non-current assets in respect of the aircraft is:

A $nil
B $237,000
C $270,000
D $370,000

4.2 A company leases a building for five years under a operating lease. Lease payments are $3,000 per month in arrears, but as an incentive to take on the lease the company has been given the first 6 months rent free.

What will be the total charged to profit or loss for the second year of the lease?

A $36,000
B $32,400
C $39,600
D $33,000

4.3   On 1 January 20X7 ED purchased a machine on a finance lease with a $6,000 deposit and then two payments of $7,080 made on 31 December 20X7 and 20X8.

The machine had a cash price of $18,000 and the interest rate implicit in the lease is 12%.

How much is the finance charge in the profit or loss for the year ended 31 December 20X7?

$ [   ]

4.4   An asset is hired under a finance lease with a deposit of $30,000 on 1 January 20X1 plus 8 six monthly payments in arrears of $20,000 each. The fair value of the asset is $154,000. The finance charge is to be allocated using the sum-of-the-digits method.

What is the finance charge for the year ending 31 December 20X3?

A $7,000
B $8,000
C $10,000
D $11,000

4.5   **Which TWO of the following statements describe an acceptable accounting treatment for a finance lease transaction in the accounts of the lessee?**

A   DR Asset (with total payable under the lease).
B   DR Asset (with the fair value of the leased asset).
C   CR Lease liability (with the present value of the minimum lease payments).
D   DR Statement of profit or loss (with the total finance charges arising under the lease).

4.6   On 1 January 20X0, Armitage hires a computer on an operating lease. The lease is for 4 years and under the terms of the contract an initial payment of $130 is due followed by 4 annual payments in arrears of $420 per annum.

What is the hire charge expense for the year ended 31 December 20X0 (to the nearest $)?

A $453
B $420
C $550
D $130

4.7   A company leases some plant on 1 January 20X4. The cash price of the plant is $9,000, and the company leases it for four years, paying four annual instalments of $3,000 beginning on 31 December 20X4.

The company uses the sum-of-the-digits method to allocate interest.

What is the interest charge for the year ended 31 December 20X5?

A $900
B $600
C $1,000
D $750

4.8   CS acquired a machine, using a finance lease, on 1 January 20X4. The lease was for a five-year term with rentals of $20,000 per year payable in arrears. The cost price of the machine was $80,000 and the implied interest rate is 7.93% per year.

Using the actuarial method, calculate the non-current lease liability figure required by IAS 17 *Leases* to be shown in CS's statement of financial position at 31 December 20X5 (round your answer to the nearest $).

$ [   ]

4.9   GH has leased an item of plant. Under the terms of the lease GH will pay $280,000 a year for the next five years. The plant has a fair value of $1,000,000 at the inception of the lease and is expected to have an economic useful life of 10 years from that date. The plant has been modified to suit the specific manufacturing needs of GH. At the inception of the lease GH had no intention of using the asset beyond the five year term, although there is an option to purchase the asset at the end of the term at a value significantly less than fair value.

Which of the following factors indicates that the lease could be a finance lease?

Choose one or more:

A   The lease term is not for the majority of the plant's useful life.

B   The minimum lease payments are likely to cover the fair value of the plant at the inception of the lease.

C   GH has no intention of keeping the plant for its estimated economic useful life.

D   The plant would need to be modified to be used by another entity.

E   There is an option to purchase the plant at significantly less than fair value in 5 years' time.

4.10   CF enters into a four year operating lease on 1 January 20X6 with payments of $50,000 per year, however no payments are required in 20X6.

What should appear in the financial statements as at 31 December 20X7?

	Rental in the profit or loss	Deferred income in the statement of financial position
A	Nil	Nil
B	$50,000	Nil
C	$37,500	$37,500
D	$37,500	$25,000

---

5 Provisions, contingent liabilities and contingent assets

5.1   **Which one of the following transactions would be acceptable as a provision under the terms of IAS 37?**

A   XYZ decided to reorganise a manufacturing facility during November 20X1 and commissioned a consulting engineer to undertake a feasibility study. A provision of $2 million for the reorganisation was created at 31 December 20X1.

B   In January 20X2, ABC contracted with a training company to provide essential training for its workforce to be carried out in January and February 20X2. A provision for the necessary expenditure was created in its accounts at 31 December 20X1.

C   CDE was ordered by its local authority in October 20X1 to carry out an environmental cleanup in 20X2 following pollution from one of its factories.

D   FG acquired RST and provided for likely future operating losses at the date of acquisition amounting to $250,000.

5.2 Mulroon Co, a publishing company, is being sued for $1 million in a libel action in respect of a book published in January 20X0.

On 31 October 20X0, the end of the reporting period, the directors believed that the claim had a ten per cent chance of success. On 30 November 20X0, the date the accounts were approved, the directors believed that the claim had a thirty per cent chance of success.

In the financial statements to 31 October 20X0 the amount which should be provided is:

A   nil
B $100,000
C $300,000
D $1,000,000

5.3 Fonex sells mobile phones with a 12-month warranty. Any defects arising during that period are repaired free of charge. It has been estimated that in any given year 5% of phones sold will require minor repairs and 3% will require major repairs. If all the phones sold in 20X3 required minor repairs the total cost would be $3m. If all the phones sold in 20X3 required major repairs the cost would be $7m.

What amount of warranty provision should be included in the statement of financial position of Fonex as at the end of 20X3?

A $360,000
B $440,000
C $800,000
D $400,000

5.4 **Which TWO of the following statements per IAS 37 are correct?**

A   An entity should not recognise a contingent liability in the statement of financial position.

B   A provision must be recognised when an entity has a present obligation (which must be a legal obligation) as a result of a past event, it is probable that a transfer of economic benefits will be required to settle the obligation and a reliable estimate can be made of the amount of the obligation.

C   An entity should only recognise a contingent asset if it is more likely than not that a present obligation exists at the balance sheet date. An entity may choose whether or not to discount a provision, but the decision must be applied consistently.

D   If discounting is used the compounding back of the liability over time should be recognised as an interest expense.

E   IAS 37 allows entities to prudently 'build up' provisions to replace machinery in future over a number of years, where this is the management's intention.

5.5 D prepares its accounts to 30 September each year. During the year to 30 September 20X2 the engineering division was being sued for damages relating to a faulty product it manufactured. Independent consultants have prepared a report that confirms that the product was faulty but this was partly due to the failure of a component that was manufactured by C. The damages are estimated at $1 million and the level of contributory negligence of C is considered to be 40%.

How should the above be shown in the financial statements for the year ended 30 September 20X2?

A   Provision of $1 million liability and an asset of $400,000 (40%) shown separately on the statement of financial position.

B   Disclosure of a contingent liability and no disclosure of the contingent asset as it is not virtually certain.

C   Disclosure of a contingent liability and disclosure of the contingent asset as it is probable that they will have to pay out and reclaim 40%.

D   A provision of $1 million and disclosure of the contingent asset.

5.6 Provisions for restructuring a business are to be recognised (in accordance with IAS 37) only when an entity has an obligation to carry out the restructuring.

An obligation arises when an entity:

A   Makes the decision to restructure.
B   Announces the main features of the restructuring plan to those who will be affected by it.
C   Completes the restructuring.
D   Is first invoiced for restructuring costs.

5.7 **Which ONE of the following would be valid grounds for a provision?**

A   A company has decided to close down a division and has estimated the restructuring costs.

B   A law comes into force which means that by the end of the following year a company will have to install safety guards on its machinery and the cost involved has been reliably estimated.

C   A company has moved its offices out of London but is tied into the lease of the London building for another 6 months and is not permitted to sublet it to another tenant.

D   An ex-employee is suing the company for wrongful dismissal. It is almost certain that damages will have to be paid but the amount is uncertain.

5.8 Cactus is facing a legal claim from a customer regarding a faulty product. The total amount being claimed is $3.6 million and it is estimated by lawyers that the customer has a 75% chance of being successful.

What amount, if any, should Cactus provide in respect of this claim in accordance with IAS 37 *Provisions, contingent liabilities and contingent assets*?

A $3.6 million
B $2.7 million
C $0.9 million
D   No amount should be provided

5.9 ER organise music festivals throughout Europe. In September 20X3 there was accident at a concert and one of the main performers was injured. This performer is pursuing a lawsuit, claiming that the safety equipment provided by ER was faulty and that ER was responsible for the accident. The lawsuit was filed in November 20X3 and at the year-end ER's legal advisors advised that ER was likely to lose the case although at that time no reliable estimate of the likely payout could be made.

Which of the following statements is TRUE in respect of this scenario?

A   The lawsuit has not concluded at the reporting date and so no disclosures about the accident are required to be included in ER's financial statements at 31 December 20X3.

B   A probable future outflow of economic benefit will result from this lawsuit and so a provision should be recorded in ER's statement of financial position at 31 December 20X3.

C   There is a probable outflow of economic benefit but the timing and amount is uncertain and so a contingent liability be included in ER's financial statements at 31 December 20X3.

D   There is a probable outflow of economic benefit but the timing and amount is uncertain and so no disclosure is necessary as at 31 December 20X3.

5.10 GT incurs a present obligation on 31 December 20X5 in relation to the restoration of a piece of machinery which expects to settle in five years' time for $400,000. The appropriate discount rate is 8%.

The 8% five year simple discount factor is 0.681.

The journal entry to record the event for the year ended 31 December 20X5 will be:

Complete the table showing the journal entry by writing in the correct narratives and figures.

	Account reference	$
Dr		
Cr		

6 Deferred taxation

6.1 A company purchased some land on 1 January 20X1 for $300,000. On 31 December 20X8 was revalued to $500,000. Income tax is at 30%. No tax allowances have been granted on this land.

Complete this statement of financial position extract as at 31 December 20X8.

	$
Property	500,000
Deferred tax liability	
Revaluation surplus	

6.2 Taxco bought a machine on 1 October 20X2 for $600,000. The machine attracted writing down tax allowances at 25% on the reducing balance. Depreciation was 10% on the straight-line balances.

Assuming a rate of income tax of 30%, calculate the deferred tax liability (to the nearest $) as at 30 September 20X4.

$ [   ]

6.3 **In accounting for deferred tax, will the following items can give rise to temporary differences (select yes or no)?**

		Yes	No
A	Differences between accounting depreciation and tax allowances for capital expenditure	☐	☐
B	Expenses charged in the statement of profit or loss and other comprehensive income but disallowed for tax	☐	☐
C	Revaluation of a non-current asset	☐	☐
D	Unrelieved tax losses	☐	☐

6.4 **Which THREE of the following are examples of assets or liabilities whose carrying amount is always equal to their tax base?**

A   Accrued expenses that will never be deductible for tax purposes

B   Accrued income that will be taxed on a receipts basis

C   Accrued expenses that have already been deducted in determining the current tax liability for current or earlier periods

D   Accrued income that will never be taxable

E   An allowance for doubtful debts where tax relief is granted when the debt goes bad

F   Intangible asset relating to development costs which are granted tax relief when paid

6.5 An item of equipment cost $60,000 on 1 April 20X6. The equipment is depreciated at 20% per annum on a reducing balance basis.

50% tax allowances are awarded in the first year and 25% reducing balance thereafter. The relevant tax rate is 30%.

Complete the journal entry below in relation to deferred tax for the year ended 31 March 20X8 by writing in the correct account references and amount.

	Account reference	Amount in $
Debit		
Credit		

6.6 A property was bought for $600,000. It was revalued to $800,000 in the current financial year. Accumulated depreciation on the property to date is $220,000. The appropriate rate of company income tax to use is 30%.

Which of the following options is correct if the company was not planning to sell the property in the future?

A   A deferred tax liability would still be necessary on the revaluation gain as the property will generate taxable income in excess of the depreciation allowed for tax purposes.

B   No deferred tax liability would be necessary in relation to the revaluation gain as there will be no future taxable gain, however the amount would need to be disclosed as unprovided in the accounts.

C   No deferred tax liability would be necessary in respect of the revaluation gain as there will be no future taxable gain; nor would the amount need to be disclosed in a notes to the accounts.

D   Deferred tax would be recognised in respect of the difference between cumulative depreciation and cumulative tax allowances but not in respect of the revaluation gain.

6.7 H Co buys machinery costing $200,000 and depreciates it over its expected useful life of 10 years on a straight-line basis. For tax purposes the machinery is depreciated at 25% per annum (straight line). The tax rate is 20%.

What will be the deferred tax expense or income in the fifth year of the life of the plant?

(Put a minus sign before any income eg –1,000).

$ [ ]

6.8 **Which ONE of the following is does NOT give rise to a temporary difference for tax purposes?**

A   Tax losses.
B   Tax-allowable depreciation.
C   Sale of a non-current asset.
D   Interest capitalised in a jurisdiction where tax relief is granted on interest when it is paid.

6.9 F has made losses of $4m to the year ended 31 December 20X7. The tax regime allows F to carry forward and utilise any losses against future profits. It is expected that F will make profits of $5m next year. F pays tax at 28%.

Complete the following sentence by writing in the correct narrative from the list provided:

As F is expected to make [＿＿＿＿＿＿＿] in the future, a deferred tax [＿＿＿＿＿＿＿] of $ [＿＿＿＿＿＿＿] million can be recorded in the financial statements for the year ended 31 December 20X7.

Picklist for narratives

profits
losses
asset
liability
1.12
1.4

6.10 BC has a deferred tax liability related to non-current assets of $450,000 in the statement of financial position as at 31 December 20X6. At 31 December 20X7 the carrying amount of these assets is $1.9m and the tax base is $1.3m.

BC pays tax at 30%.

The journal entry to record the deferred tax for the year ended 31 December 2075 will be:

Complete the table showing the journal entry by writing in the correct narratives and figures.

	Account reference	$
Dr		
Dr		

---

7 Share-based payments

7.1 A company grants 500 cash share appreciation rights to each of its 800 employees on 1 January 20X5, vesting on 31 December 20X7, on condition that they remain in its employ until that date. The fair value of each share appreciation right is $4.20 on 1 January 20X5 and $4.30 on 31 December 20X5. At 1 January 20X5 the company estimated that 620 employees would remain employed until the vesting date, adjusted to 610 at 31 December 20X5 as more employees had left than anticipated.

How much should be recognised as an expense in respect of the share appreciation rights for the year ended 31 December 20X5?

A $0
B $437,167
C $1,311,500
D $1,281,000

7.2 ABC Inc granted 500 share options to each of its 8 directors on 1 April 20X5, which will vest on 31 March 20X7. The fair value of each option at the grant date is $12, and all are anticipated to vest on 31 March 20X7.

What is the accounting entry in the financial statements for the year ended 31 March 20X6?

A   Dr Expense $24,000, Cr Equity $24,000.
B   Dr Expense $48,000, Cr Liability $48,000.
C   Dr Current Assets $24,000, Cr Liability $24,000.
D   Dr Equity $48,000, Cr Expense $48,000.

7.3 PT granted 1,000 share options to each of its 400 employees on 1 January 20X4, with the condition that they continue to work for PT for 4 years from the grant date. The fair value of each option at the grant date was $5.

25 employees left in the year to 31 December 20X4 and at that date another 60 were expected to leave over the next three years.

The journal entry required to record the charge to PT's profit or loss for the year ended 31 December 20X4 in respect of the share options will be:

Use the drop down boxes to complete the table.

	Account reference	$
Debit	Profit or loss	
Credit		

7.4 **Complete the sentence by writing one of the following options into the space:**

estimate
policy
transaction
period

Any changes in estimates of expected number of employees being entitled to receive share based payment is treated as a change in accounting [   ] and recognised in the period of the change.

7.5 V grants 80 share appreciation rights to each of its 600 employees on 1 January 20X8 providing they remain in employment with V for the next two years.

In 20X8 12 employees leave and it is expected that a further 7 will leave in 20X9. In 20X9 a further 15 leave. On 31 December 20X9 457 employees exercise their rights.

The fair value of the rights and the intrinsic values at the dates of exercise are shown below:

1	January	20X8	FV	$12.50		
31	December	20X8	FV	$12.90		
31	December	20X9	FV	$13.20	Intrinsic value	$11.00

What is the journal required to record the transactions in the year ended 31 December 20X9?

		$
A	Dr Liability	305,292
	Dr Staff costs	96,868
	Cr Cash	402,160
B	Dr Liability	177,300
	Dr Staff costs	224,860
	Cr Cash	402,160
C	Dr Liability	177,300
	Cr Staff costs	177,300
D	Dr Staff costs	576,600
	Cr Liability	174,500
	Cr Cash	402,160

7.6   On 1 January 20X4 PN grants 1,000 share options to each of its 300 employees providing they remain in employment for 2 years from the grant date. The options may be exercised within a year of the end of the vesting period at an option price of $6.10. The current fair value of the option is $1.40 and the expected fair value in two years' time is $2.40 (adjusted for the possibility of forfeiture in both cases). At 31 20X4, 20 employees had left and it was estimates that the another 15 would leave in the year ended 31 December 20X5.

Under IFRS 2 *Share-based Payments*, how much expense would be recognised in profit or loss for the year ended 31 December 20X4?

A   None
B $185,500
C $196,000
D $318,000

7.7   On 1 May 20X5, More Shares Plc grants 25 share appreciation rights to each of its 3,500 employees, on the condition that each employee remains in service until 30 April 20X8. 55% of the rights are expected to vest on 30 April 20X8. The fair value of each right on 30 April 20X6 is $18, and their intrinsic value on that date is $12.

What is the accounting entry in the financial statements for the year ended 30 April 20X6?

A   Dr Current Assets $866,250, Cr Liability $866,250.
B   Dr Expense $288,750, Cr Liability $288,750.
C   Dr Expense $288,750, Cr Equity $288,750.
D   Dr Expense $433,125, Cr Cash $433,125.

7.8   During its financial year ended 31 January 20X6, TSQ issued share options to several of its senior employees. The options vest immediately upon issue.

Which ONE of the following describes the accounting entry that is required to recognise the options?

A   DEBIT the statement of changes in equity   CREDIT liabilities
B   DEBIT the statement of changes in equity   CREDIT equity
C   DEBIT the statement of profit or loss   CREDIT liabilities
D   DEBIT the statement of profit or loss   CREDIT equity

7.9   **Which THREE of the following statements concerning share based payments are true?**

A   Vesting conditions must be fulfilled before the share options can be granted.

B   The spreading of the share based payment expense reflects the period over which the company expects the employees to stay in employment.

C   Vesting conditions must be satisfied for the other party to become entitled to receive the share based payment.

D   The share based payment expense is spread over the vesting period to reflect the value of the goods or services consumed over that period.

E   A minimum period of service for an employee is an example of a vesting condition.

7.10   **Which TWO of the following statements are true?**

A   When measuring a cash settled share based payment, the fair value used in the calculation is adjusted at each period end.

B   When calculating the expense, the expected number of leavers at the grant date is used and never adjusted.

C   The expense is spread over the exercise period for cash settled transactions.

D   The company must create an asset to represent the amounts payable under a cash settled scheme.

E   The fair value of the option at the grant date is used to calculate the cost of equity settled transactions.

8 Revenue and construction contracts

8.1 ES develops bespoke software solutions for entities operating in the banking sector. ES has invoiced a customer an agreed fixed fee of $5 million, comprising $4 million for the development of the software and $1 million for service and support of the software over the 24-month support period.

EMS should:

A Recognise the revenue associated with the development of the software but defer recognition of the revenue from the support services until the end of the 24-month support period.

B Recognise the revenue associated with the development of the software and recognise the revenue from the support services evenly over the 24- month support period.

C Defer recognition for the entire amount of the agreed fixed fee revenue until the 24-month support period is concluded as that is when the significant risks have been transferred to the customer.

E Recognise the full amount of the agreed fixed fee revenue on invoice since the main risk has been transferred and the amount of revenue can be reliably measured.

8.2 On 31 March 20X7, DT received an order from a new customer, XX, for products with a sales value of $900,000. XX enclosed a deposit with the order of $90,000.

On 31 March 20X7, DT had not completed credit referencing of XX and had not despatched any goods. DT is considering the following possible entries for this transaction in its financial statements for the year ended 31 March 20X7.

Which of the following would be the correct accounting entry to record the transaction with XX for the year ended 31 March 20X7?

A Dr Cash $90,000, Dr Trade receivables $810,000; Cr Revenue $900,000
B Dr Trade receivables $900,000; Cr Revenue $900,000
C Dr Cash $90,000; Cr Revenue $90,000
D Dr Cash $90,000; Cr Deferred income $90,000

8.3 The position of a construction contract at 30 June 20X6 is as follows.

	$
Contract price	900,000
At 30 June 20X6	
Costs to date	720,000
Estimated costs to completion	480,000
Progress payments invoiced and received	400,000
Percentage complete	60%

What figures should appear for this contract in the financial statements for the year 30 June 20X6, according to IAS 11 *Construction contracts*?

A SPLOCI: Revenue $540,000; Cost of sales $840,000
 SOFP: Trade receivables $140,000

B SPLOCI: Revenue $40,000; Cost of sales $720,000
 SOFP: Nothing

C SPLOCI: Revenue $540,000; Cost of sales $840,000
 SOFP: Gross amounts due from customers $20,000

D SPLOCI: Revenue $540,000; Cost of sales $720,000
 SOFP: Trade receivables $140,000

8.4 BL started a contract on 1 November 20X4. The contract was scheduled to run for two years and has a sales value of $40 million. At 31 October 20X5, the following details were obtained from BL's records:

	$m
Costs incurred to date	16
Estimated costs to completion	18
Percentage complete at 31 October 20X5	45%

Applying IAS 11 *Construction contracts*, how much revenue and profit should BL recognise in its statement of profit or loss and other comprehensive income for the year ended 31 October 20X5 (round your answer to 1 decimal place)?

Revenue = $ ☐ m

Profit = $ ☐ m

8.5 **Which two of the following accounting entries correctly record progress payments invoiced and revenue recognised in respect of a construction contract?**

A   Dr trade receivables, Cr revenue.

B   Dr trade receivables, Cr amounts due from customers.

C   Dr bank, Cr amounts due from customers.

D   Dr amounts due from customers, Cr revenue.

E   Dr bank, Cr revenue

8.6 EJ publishes trade magazines and sells them to retailers. EJ has just concluded negotiations with a large supermarket chain for the supply of a large quantity of several of its trade magazines on a regular basis.

EJ has agreed a substantial discount on the following terms:

- The same quantity of each trade magazine will be supplied each month;
- Quantities can only be changed at the end of each six month period;
- Payment must be made six monthly in advance.

The supermarket paid $150,000 on 1 September 20X7 for six months' supply of trade magazines to 29 February 20X8. At 31 October 20X7, EJ had supplied two months of trade magazines.

How should the above transaction be recorded in the financial statements of EJ for the year ended 31 October 20X7?

A   Dr Trade receivables $150,000; Cr Revenue $150,000

B   Dr Cash $150,000; Cr Revenue $150,000

C   Dr Cash $150,000; Cr Deferred income $100,000, Cr Revenue $50,000

D   Dr Cash $150,000; Cr Deferred income $150,000

8.7 OC signed a contract to provide office cleaning services for an entity for a period of one year from 1 October 20X8 for a fee of $500 per month.

The contract required the entity to make one payment to OC covering all twelve months' service in advance.

OC received $6,000 on 1 October 20X8. Assume that the outcome of the contract can be reliably estimated.

How much revenue should OC recognise in its statement of profit or loss and other comprehensive income for the year ended 31 March 20X9?

A $6,000

B $3,000

C $1,500

D $500

E   None

8.8   HH has agreed to provide services over a two year period for a total contract price of $200,000. In the first year costs incurred are $60,000 and 45% of the work has been completed. The contract has not progressed as expected and HH is unsure of the final outcome of the contract, however the costs incurred are expected to be recovered.

How much revenue should be recognised by HH at the end of the first year?

$ [   ]

8.9   HS, a contractor, signed a two year fixed price contract on 31 March 20X8 for $300,000 to build a bridge. Total costs were originally estimated at $240,000.

At 31 March 20X9, HS extracted the following figures from its financial records:

	$'000
Contract value	300
Costs incurred to date	170
Estimated costs to complete	100
Progress payments received	130
Value of work completed	165

HS calculates the stage of completion of contracts using the value of work completed as a proportion of total contract value.

Which of the following are the correct figures for revenue and profit in relation to this contract to be recognised in HS's statement loss and other comprehensive income for the year ended 31 March 20X9?

A   Revenue: $188.9m; Profit $18.9m

B   Revenue $165m; Profit $33m

C   Revenue $130m; Profit $30m

D   Revenue $165m; Profit $16.5m

8.10   HS, a contractor, signed a two year fixed price contract on 31 March 20X8 for $300,000 to build a bridge. Total costs were originally estimated at $240,000.

At 31 March 20X9, HS extracted the following figures from its financial records:

	$'000
Contract value	300
Costs incurred to date	170
Estimated costs to complete	100
Progress payments invoiced and received	130
Value of work completed	165

HS calculates the stage of completion of contracts using the value of work completed as a proportion of total contract value.

Which of the following correctly shows how the contract should be recorded in the statement of financial position of HS as at 31 March 20X9?

A   Gross amounts due from customers (asset): $56.5m

B   Gross amounts due to customers (liability): $23.5m

C   Gross amounts due from customers (liability): $73m

D   Gross amounts due from customers (liability): $56.5m

9 Basic groups

9.1 MN acquired 80% of the equity shares in LK on 1 January 20X6. The consideration for the acquisition consisted of the following: Cash of $1,200,000 paid on 1 January 20X6;

Cash of $500,000 paid on 1 January 20X8 (a discount rate of 7% was applied to value the liability in the financial statements of MN); and

The transfer of 750,000 shares in MN with a nominal value of $1 each and an agreed value on the date of acquisition of $2 each.

The best estimate of the fair value of the consideration to be included in the calculation of goodwill arising on the acquisition (to the nearest $'000) of LK is:

A $2,387,000
B $3,137,000
C $3,186,000
D $3,200,000

9.2 AB owns 80% of the ordinary share capital of CD, its only subsidiary.

In the year ended 31 December 20X3 CD has total comprehensive income of $238,000. A fair value adjustment at acquisition results in additional depreciation of $8,000 in the year ending 31 December 20X3. Goodwill on the acquisition of CD was impaired by $10,000 in the year to 31 December 20X3 and $12,000 in the previous year.

The group policy is to measure non-controlling interest at fair value at the acquisition date.

The share of total comprehensive income attributable to the non-controlling interest for the year ended 31 December 20X3 is:

A $41,600
B $43,200
C $44,000
D $47,600

9.3 In the year ended 31 December 20X1 S, an 80% owned subsidiary of P, sold P some goods for $1,000,000 at mark up of 25%.

P had sold half of these goods by the year end.

Which FOUR of the following statements are true about that year's consolidated statement of profit or loss?

A   Revenue will need to be reduced by $1,000,000 to reflect the intra-group trading.

B   Revenue will not need to be adjusted to reflect the intra-group trading.

C   Cost of sales will need to be reduced by $1,000,000 to eliminate the intra-group purchase.

D   Cost of sales will not need to be reduced to reflect the intra-group purchase.

E   Cost of sales will need to be increased by $100,000 to remove the unrealised profit from closing inventory.

F   Cost of sales will need to be reduced by $125,000 to remove the unrealised profit in closing inventory.

G   Non-controlling interest will need to be adjusted to reflect the unrealised profit in closing inventory.

H   Non-controlling interest will not need to be adjusted to reflect the unrealised profit in closing inventory.

9.4 **Which ONE of the following options would affect the calculation of the fair values of the subsidiary's net assets at the date of acquisition?**

A Changes to the assets and liabilities as a result of the post-acquisition intentions or actions of the acquirer.

B The existence of contingent liabilities in the books of the subsidiary at the acquisition date.

C Provisions for post-acquisition reorganisation costs anticipated by the acquirer at the acquisition date.

D Post-acquisition losses anticipated by the acquirer at the acquisition date.

9.5 On 1 July Mole plc acquired 80,000 of Ratty Ltd's 100,000 $1 ordinary shares for $450,000. At that date Ratty Ltd's shares were trading at $3.75.

At the acquisition date Ratty Ltd had retained earnings of $165,000 and the fair values of the net assets were approximately equal to fair value, with the exception of one building which had a fair value of $80,000 in excess of its carrying amount.

It is the policy of the Mole Group to value the non-controlling interest at full (fair) value, for which the share price at acquisition is the best estimate.

What is the goodwill arising on acquisition?

$ [   ]

9.6 ZA acquired 75% of the 2 million issued $2 ordinary shares of PJ on 1 January 20X2 for $3,700,000 when PJ's retained earnings were $1,770,000. ZA has no other subsidiaries.

The carrying value of PJ's net assets was considered to be the same as the fair value at the date of acquisition with the exception of PJ's non-depreciable property. The book value of these assets at acquisition was $1,890,000 and their fair value was $2,200,000.

Property, plant and equipment of ZA and PJ were included in there individual financial statements at 31 December 20X3 at a net book value of $16,000,000 and $1,750,000 respectively.

Property, plant and equipment will be included in the consolidated financial statements of the ZA group at 31 December 20X3 at a value (to the nearest $'000) of:

$ [   ]

9.7 ZA acquired 75% of the 2 million issued $2 ordinary shares of PJ on 1 January 20X2 for $3,700,000 when PJ's retained earnings were $1,770,000. ZA has no other subsidiaries.

The carrying value of PJ's net assets was considered to be the same as the fair value at the date of acquisition with the exception of PJ's non-depreciable property. The book value of these assets at acquisition was $1,890,000 and their fair value was $2,200,000.

Property, plant and equipment of ZA and PJ were included in their individual financial statements at 31 December 20X3 at a net book value of $16,000,000 and $1,750,000 respectively.

The group policy is to measure non-controlling interest at fair value at the acquisition date. The fair value of the non-controlling interest in PJ was $1,140,000 on 1 January 20X2.

An impairment review performed on 31 December 20X3 indicated that goodwill on the acquisition of PJ had been impaired by $100,000. No impairment was recognised in the year ended 31 December 20X2. The retained earnings of PJ at 31 December 20X3 were $2,400,000.

The goodwill that will be recorded in non-current assets of the ZA group as at 31 December 20X3 is:

A $540,000
B $660,000
C $760,000
D $970,000

9.8   ZA acquired 75% of the 2 million issued $2 ordinary shares of PJ on 1 January 20X2 for $3,700,000 when PJ's retained earnings were $1,770,000. ZA has no other subsidiaries.

The carrying value of PJ's net assets was considered to be the same as the fair value at the date of acquisition with the exception of PJ's nondepreciable property. The book value of these assets at acquisition was $1,890,000 and their fair value was $2,200,000.

Property, plant and equipment of ZA and PJ were included in their individual financial statements at 31 December 20X3 at a net book value of $16,000,000 and $1,750,000 respectively.

The group policy is to measure non-controlling interest at fair value at the acquisition date. The fair value of the non-controlling interest in PJ was $1,140,000 on 1 January 20X2.

An impairment review performed on 31 December 20X3 indicated that goodwill on the acquisition of PJ had been impaired by $100,000. No impairment was recognised in the year ended 31 December 20X2. The retained earnings of PJ at 31 December 20X3 were $2,400,000.

The retained earnings of PJ to be included in the consolidated retained earnings of the ZA group at 31 December 20X3 will be:

A $397,500
B $473,000
C $530,000
D $630,000

9.9   ZA acquired 75% of the 2 million issued $2 ordinary shares of PJ on 1 January 20X2 for $3,700,000 when PJ's retained earnings were $1,770,000. ZA has no other subsidiaries.

The carrying value of PJ's net assets was considered to be the same as the fair value at the date of acquisition with the exception of PJ's nondepreciable property. The book value of these assets at acquisition was $1,890,000 and their fair value was $2,200,000.

Property, plant and equipment of ZA and PJ were included in their individual financial statements at 31 December 20X3 at a net book value of $16,000,000 and $1,750,000 respectively.

The group policy is to measure non-controlling interest at fair value at the acquisition date. The fair value of the non-controlling interest in PJ was $1,140,000 on 1 January 20X2.

An impairment review performed on 31 December 20X3 indicated that goodwill on the acquisition of PJ had been impaired by $100,000. No impairment was recognised in the year ended 31 December 20X2. The retained earnings of PJ at 31 December 20X3 were $2,400,000.

Which THREE of the following statements are TRUE in respect of the non-controlling interest to be included in the consolidated statement of financial position of the ZA Group for the year ended 31 December 20X3?

A   25% of AB's post-acquisition earnings will be debited to it.
B   It will be included at its fair value on acquisition plus share of post-acquisition earnings of AB.
C   It will be included as a separate component of equity.
D   25% of the impairment in the goodwill arising on acquisition will be debited to it.
E   It will be included in the non-current liabilities of the ZA Group.

9.10   On 1 January 20X2 C purchased 60% of the equity share capital of E for a total cash price of $50 million. The total net assets of E were $60 million. However, the net assets of E were believed to have a fair value to the C Group of $65 million in total. The directors of C considered that a group reorganization would be necessary because of the acquisition of E and that the cost of this would be $5 million. This reorganisation was completed by 31 August 20X2.

It is group policy to measure non-controlling interests at fair value at acquisition. The fair value of the non-controlling interest in E on 1 January 20X2 was $30 million.

What is the amount of goodwill to be recognised on consolidation (round your answer to the nearest $ million)?

$ [   ] million

10 Associates and joint arrangements

10.1   EF, in addition to its other holdings, acquired a 30% stake in the 100,000 $1 ordinary shares of SR on 1 January 20X1 for $50,000. At acquisition, SR's retained earnings were $22,000.

During the year ended 31 December 20X4, SR sold goods to EF for $10,000 at a margin of 20%. As at 31 December 20X4, a quarter of these goods had been sold on to third parties.

The retained earnings of the EF Group (excluding SR) and SR at 31 December 20X4 were $390,000 and $90,000 respectively. The investment in SR was impaired by $2,920 by 31 December 20X4.

Calculate the consolidated retained earnings of EF Group (incorporating SR) at 31 December 20X4.

The consolidated retained earnings of EF Group (incorporating SR) at 31 December 20X4 are:

$ [   ]

10.2   Monty plc acquired 30% of the share capital of Tiger Ltd for $75,000 on 1 July 20X8. Monty plc was able to exercise significant influence over Tiger Ltd. During the year to 30 June 20X9 Tiger Ltd made a profit after tax of $270,000 and paid a dividend of $50,000. At 30 June 20X9, the investment in the associate was considered to be impaired by 10%.

What amount will appear in the consolidated statement of financial position of Monty Ltd at 30 June 20X9 in respect of its investment in Tiger Ltd?

$ [   ]

10.3   IFRS 11 *Joint Arrangements* classifies joint arrangements as either joint operations or joint ventures.

Which TWO of the following statements are true?

A   A joint venture is always structured through a separate vehicle.
B   A joint operation is never structured through a separate vehicle.
C   A joint operation does not need a contractual arrangement.
D   A joint venture must have a contractual arrangement.

10.4   IFRS 11 sets out the accounting treatment required for joint arrangements.

Which TWO of the following statements are true in respect of this accounting treatment?

A   Joint ventures must be equity accounted.

B   Joint operations must be equity accounted.

C   Joint ventures are accounted for by including the investor's share of assets, liabilities, income and expenses as per the contractual arrangement.

D   Joint operations are accounted for by including the investor's share of assets, liabilities, income and expenses as per the contractual arrangement.

10.5 **The objective of IFRS 12 *Disclosure of interests in other entities* is to require entities to do which one of the following ?**

  A   Disclose information that enables users to evaluate the nature of, and risks associated with, interest in other entities and the effect of those on financial position, performance and cash flows.

  B   Eliminate intragroup transactions in the consolidated financial statements.

  C   Evaluate the performance of all investments made by the entity, including those accounted for under IAS 39.

  D   Consolidate subsidiaries, equity account for associates and joint ventures and disclose investments in joint operations or unconsolidated structured entities.

10.6 On 1 January 20X4 Herring, a company with subsidiaries, acquired 25% of Kipper for $650,000, when Kipper's retained earnings were $720,000. At 31 December 20X4 Kipper had retained earnings of $1,600,000 and Herring recognised an impairment loss of $300,000 in respect of its investment in Kipper.

  What amount will be shown as investment in associate in the consolidated statement of financial position of Herring as at 31 December 20X4?

  A $870,000
  B $570,000
  C $350,000
  D $830,000

10.7 Holly owns 35% of Hock, its only associate. During the year to 31 December 20X4 Hock made a profit for the year of $721,000. This included sales of $240,000 to Holly, on which Hock made a gross profit margin of 40%. 30% of these goods were still held in inventory by Holly at 31 December 20X4.

  Holly considers its investment in Hock to have suffered a $20,000 impairment during the year.

  At what amount should 'share of profit of associate' be stated in the consolidated statement of profit or loss of Holly for the year ended 31 December 20X4?

  A $235,270
  B $225,150
  C $222,270
  D $218,750

10.8 **Which TWO, according to IFRS 11 *Joint arrangements*, are the characteristics of a joint operation?**

  A   The parties with joint control have rights to the assets and obligations for the liabilities of the joint venture.
  B   The parties with joint control have rights to the net assets of the arrangement.
  C   The arrangement is never structured through a separate entity.
  D   The arrangement is contractual.

10.9   On 30 June 20X3, Sugar entered into an agreement with two other investors to establish a new entity, Spice. All three investors subscribed for one third of the equity shares in Spice and each share carries one vote. All three investors appointed two representatives to the six-member board of directors of Spice. All key policy decisions require the agreement of five of the six board members. A contractual agreement gives the three investors rights to the net assets of Spice.

Which THREE of the following statements are correct in relation to the treatment of the investment in Spice in the consolidated financial statements of Sugar for the year ended 30 September 20X3?

A   Spice will be treated as a joint venture simply because the three investors hold one third of the shares each.

B   Spice will be treated as a joint venture in this case, but only because of the requirement that key policy decisions require the consent of at least five of the directors.

C   Sugar should account for its share of Spice's assets, liabilities, expenses and revenue in its own financial statements

D   Sugar should equity account for Spice in its consolidated financial statements

E   In Sugar's own financial statements, the investment in Spice should either be held at cost or in accordance with IAS 39

10.10   SD owns 80% of the equity share capital of N. In the year to 31 December 20X9, N obtained a long term loan from a financial institution. To secure a competitive borrowing rate, SD guaranteed the loan. On 31 December 20X9, N showed no signs of financial distress.

Which ONE of the following statements in respect of SD's individual financial statements is true?

A   N is showing no signs of financial distress and therefore there is no need to disclose details of this arrangement.

B   There is no need to disclose details of this arrangement as the entities are part of the same group and their liabilities will be combined.

C   To enable users to evaluate the risk of SD guaranteeing its subsidiary's borrowings, this arrangement should be disclosed.

D   This arrangement constitutes a contingent liability in the individual financial statements of SD.

11 Changes in group structures

11.1   GH acquired a 10% investment in LM on 1 April 20X0 for $1,600,000.

On 1 January 20X3, GH acquired an additional 60% of the 10 million $1 equity shares of LM at a cost of $10,350,000, when the retained earnings were $4,800,000. The fair value of the original 10% investment was $2,000,000 at 1 January 20X3. The fair value of the non-controlling interest at 1 January 20X3 was $5,400,000.

The value of goodwill arising on the acquisition of LM will be recorded in the consolidated statement of financial position as at 31 December 20X3 at:

A $950,000
B $1,990,000
C $2,550,000
D $2,950,000

11.2 Funny Inc acquired 3.2 million of the 4 million issued share capital of Peculiar on 1 October 20X4, and 6 million of the 8 million issued share capital of Strange on 1 March 20X5.

Funny sold 2.8 million shares in Strange on 30 June 20X7.

Extracts from the statement of profit or loss for the year ended 31 December 20X7 are as follows:

	Funny $'000	Peculiar $'000	Strange $'000
Revenue	30,000	32,000	28,000

What is the revenue to be included in the consolidated statement of profit or loss for the year ended 31 December 20X7?

A $76,000,000
B $81,600,000
C $61,200,000
D $66,100,000

11.3 JL acquired 8 million of the 10 million issued share capital of DP on 1 October 20X1 for $14.8 million, when the balance on retained earnings was $6 million. On 30 September 20X8 JL sold 25% of its holding for $4.4 million.

Non-controlling interests at acquisition was measured at the proportionate share of net assets. Goodwill on acquisition was recognised as 70% impaired by the disposal date.

An extract from the statement of financial position of DP as at 30 September 20X8 is as follows:

	$'000
Share capital	10,000
Retained earnings	8,900
	18,900

What is gain or loss on disposal / adjustment to parent's equity to be included in the financial statements for the year ended 30 September 20X8?

A $500,000 adjustment to parent's equity.
B $470,000 gain to profit or loss for the year.
C $620,000 adjustment to parent's equity.
D $20,000 gain to profit or loss for the year.

11.4 On 1 July 20X1, SP acquired 75% of the 1 million ordinary shares in MN for $6 million. Goodwill of $1 million arose on the acquisition. SP measures non-controlling interests at acquisition at their proportionate share of the subsidiary's net assets.

On 31 December 20X8, SP disposed of part of its shareholding in MN for $4 million, retaining a 40% interest. The net assets of MN on 1 July 20X8 were $8.5 million and MN made a profit of $800,000 in the year ended 30 June 20X9 (no dividends were paid or declared by MN in that year). As at 31 December 20X8 the fair value of a share in MN was $10.10.

Non-controlling interests in MN at 31 December 20X8 amounted to $2.225 million.

What is the profit or loss on disposal that will be included in the consolidated statement of profit or loss of SP for the year ended 30 June 20X9?

A $3,675,000 loss
B $365,000 profit
C $615,000 profit
D $1,365,000 profit

11.5 TR holds 100% of the shares in CV at the beginning of the year, but then disposes of 70% of the shareholding three months into the year.

Which THREE of the following statements are true in the above scenario?

A An adjustment is required to TR's equity to reflect that there is no change in substance

B The non controlling interest is increased to 30%

C The results of CV are consolidated for the entire year

D The remaining 30% shareholding is revalued to fair value

E CV is consolidated into the statement of profit or loss for the first three months of the year

F CV appears as an investment in an associate in the statement of financial position at the year end

11.6 On 1 September 20X6, BLT held 60% of the ordinary share capital of its only subsidiary CMU. The consolidated equity of the group at that date was $576,600, of which $127,000 was attributable to the non-controlling interest. BLT measures non-controlling interests at acquisition at their proportionate share of the subsidiary's net assets.

On 28 February 20X7, exactly halfway through the financial year, BLT paid $135,000 to buy a further 20% of the ordinary share capital of CMU. In the year ended 31 August 20X7 BLT's profits for the period were $98,970 and CMU's were $30,000. It can be assumed that profits accrue evenly throughout the year.

What is the adjustment to parent's equity as a result of BLT's acquisition of further shares in CMU?

A $68,500 debit
B $68,500 credit
C $2,000 debit
D $2,000 credit

11.7 PQ acquired 80% of ST's 100,000 $1 shares on 1 January 20X2 for $600,000 when the reserves of ST were $460,000. It is group policy to measure non-controlling interests at fair value at acquisition. The fair value of the non-controlling interests in ST at acquisition was $150,000.

On 1 June 20X6 PQ disposed of half of its holding in ST for proceeds of $750,000. At that date, the ST's reserves were $710,000. The remaining holding (fair value $700,000) is to be dealt with as an associate.

Goodwill in ST of $190,000 arose on acquisition. No impairment has been necessary.

Calculate the group profit or loss on disposal of ST to be shown in the consolidated accounts for the year ended 31 December 20X6.

A $650,000 profit
B $600,000 profit
C $750,000 profit
D $100,000 loss

11.8 On 1 January 20X4, Geranium acquired 60% of the equity share capital of Rose for $5 million. At that date, the net assets of Rose were $8 million.

On 1 July 20X9 Geranium sold half of its holding in Rose for $4.5 million. The fair value of the remaining shareholding in Rose on 1 July 20X9 was also $4.5 million. No impairment of the remaining investment was deemed necessary at 31 December 20X9.

The capital and reserves of Rose at 31 December 20X9 are shown below:

	$'000
Share capital ($1 ordinary shares)	5,000
Retained earnings at 1 January 20X9	6,500
Retained profit for the year ended 31 December 20X9	2,000
	13,500

At what amount should the investment in Rose be shown in the consolidated statement of financial position of the Geranium group at 31 December 20X9?

A $2,500,000
B $2,800,000
C $4,800,000
D $5,500,000

11.9   S acquired a 10% investment in Y for $3,200,000 in 20X7. On 31 December 20X9 S acquired an additional 60% of the 10 million $1 equity shares of Y for $20,000,000. The fair value of the original 10% investment was $4,000,000. The non-controlling interest in Y was measured at its fair value of $11,000,000 at 1 December 20X9. S has no other investments.

Which of the following THREE statements are true in respect of S?

A   Goodwill will be calculated at both acquisition dates and the total presented in the consolidated financial statements of S.

B   The non-controlling interest will be initially recognised on 31 December 20X9.

C   The goodwill included in the consolidated financial statements will relate solely to the 60% acquisition of Y's shares.

D   Goodwill is initially calculated at 31 December 20X9 and will include the fair value of the original 10% holding in Y.

E   Goodwill and non-controlling interests are recognised only when S controls Y.

11.10 V acquired 60% of the equity shares of H several years ago and chose to measure the non-controlling interest (NCI) in H at its proportionate share of net assets.

On 31 December 20X6 V acquired a further 20% of H's equity shares for $3,000. At that date the net assets of H were $14,000.

The accounting entry to record the acquisition of the additional 20% investment in H in the group financial statements is:

A   Dr Bank $3,000
     Cr NCI $2,800
     Cr Group retained earnings $200

B   Dr NCI $2,800
     Dr Profit for the year $200
     Cr Bank $3,000

C   Dr NCI $2,800
     Dr Group retained earnings $200
     Cr Bank $3,000

D   Dr NCI $3,000
     Cr Bank $3,000

12 Indirect control of subsidiaries

12.1 Owen acquired 90% of the equity shares in Sassoon on 1 January 20X5 when the retained earnings of Sassoon and Thomas were $200,000 and $80,000 respectively. Sassoon had acquired 60% of the equity shares in Thomas on 1 January 20X4 when the retained earnings of Thomas were $40,000.

Non-controlling interests is measured at fair value at acquisition. The fair value of non-controlling interests in Sassoon and Thomas on 1 January 20X5 was $44,000 and $75,000 respectively.

There has been no impairment of goodwill since acquisition.

Extracts from the statements of financial position at 31 March 20X8 are shown below:

	Owen $'000	Sassoon $'000	Thomas $'000
Investment in Sassoon and Thomas	400	100	
Other net assets	1,000	250	150
	1,400	350	150
Share capital	500	100	50
Retained earnings	900	250	100
	1,400	350	150

What is the amount of goodwill to be included in the consolidated financial position of the Owen Group as at 31 March 20X8 (to the nearest $'000)?

$'000 [   ]

12.2 D has owned 80% of the equity shares of E since 1 January 20X2. E has owned 60% of the equity shares of F since 1 January 20X0. The retained earnings of F at 31 December 20X9 stood at $30 million. The retained earnings of F stood at $12 million on 1 January 20X0 and $14 million on 1 January 20X2.

Ignoring goodwill, what is the amount of F's retained earnings that should be included in the consolidated retained earnings of D group at 31 December 20X9?

A $10.8 million
B $9.6 million
C $8.64 million
D $7.68 million

12.3 HT owns 60% of the equity share capital of G. G owns 80% of the equity share capital of P. The profits for the year for G and P were $6,000 and $10,000 respectively. There are no other entities in the HT group.

The profit attributable to non-controlling interest that will be reported in the consolidated profit or loss of HK will be:

A $2,400
B $4,400
C $7,200
D $7,600

12.4 AB owns 60% of the issued ordinary share capital of CD. CD owns 60% of the issued ordinary share capital of EF.

Which ONE of the following statements is correct?

The effective interest of AB in EF is:

A 20%
B 24%
C 36%
D 60%

12.5 T purchased 70,000 ordinary shares in Y for $240,000 on 1 December 20X7 when the retained earnings of Y were $80,000 and the fair value of the non controlling interest was $45,000. Y had $1 ordinary share capital of 100,000.

Y purchased 50,000 of the ordinary shares in K for $160,000 on 31 December 20X8. At that time, K had $1 ordinary share capital of 80,000. At 31 December 20X9 Y and K had retained earnings of $180,000 and $90,000 respectively.

During 20X9 the goodwill in Y had been impaired by $25,000.

The non controlling interest of Y to be included in the consolidated statement of financial position for the year ended 31 December 20X9 is:

A $19,500
B $27,000
C $67,500
D $75,000

12.6 P acquired 60% of the equity share capital of B on 1 January 20X4.

B acquired 70% of the equity share capital of G on 1 June 20X4.

Which THREE of the following statements in respect of the consolidated financial statements of the P Group for the year ended 31 December 20X4 are true?

A   G will be equity accounted because P has an effective interest of 42% in G.

B   100% of the trade receivables balances of both B and G will be included in the statement of financial position.

C   The consolidated profit or loss will include 100% of the revenue of G earned in the seven months to 31 December 20X4.

D   P controls both B and G and both will be consolidated as subsidiaries as at 31 December 20X4.

D   70% of the post-acquisition retained earnings of G will be included within consolidated reserves.

12.7 The FG group of entities comprises FG and its subsidiaries, HI and JK.

FG acquired 80% of HI's ordinary shares on 31 December 20X1, when the reserves of HI stood at $10,000,000, and the reserves of JK stood at $7,600,000.

HI acquired 75% of JK's ordinary shares on 31 December 20X0, when the reserves of JK stood at $7,000,000.

At 31 December 20X4, HI's reserves stood at $12,200,000, and JK's reserves stood at $10,600,000.

There have been no other acquisitions and disposals in the group, and no impairments of goodwill or intra-group trading adjustments have been recorded.

How much profit has been added to consolidated reserves in the FG group in respect of the investments in HI and JK between acquisition and 31 December 20X4?

A $3,560,000
B $3,920,000
C $4,010,000
D $4,460,000

12.8 S purchased 90% of the ordinary share capital of D and D purchased 75% of the ordinary share capital of F; both transactions occurred several years previously.

The following extract is taken from the statements of financial position of S, D and F at 31 December 20X7:

	S	D	F
	$	$	$
Current assets	230,000	180,000	160,000
Current liabilities	190,000	70,000	110,000

During 20X7 S made sales of $60,000 to D at a mark up of 20%, D held half of these items in inventory at the year end.

F showed a current liability due to D of $12,000 at the year end, but D was recognising a current asset of $18,000 in respect of the same transaction, the difference was due to cash in transit.

The current assets in the consolidated statement of financial position are:

A $542,000

B $547,000

C $552,000

D $553,000

12.9 BV acquired its 75% interest in YH for $480,000 on 1 January 20X2. YH acquired its 80% of JM's 300,000 $1 ordinary shares for $320,000 on 1 January 20X3.

The net assets of YH and JM were:

	1 Jan 20X3	1 Jan 20X2
	$	$
YH	400,000	480,000
JM	360,000	450,000

BV elected to measure the non-controlling interest in YH and JM at acquisition at fair value. The fair value of the non-controlling interest in YH at 1 January 20X2 was $150,000. The fair value of one equity share in JM at 1 January 20X3 was $1.10.

Goodwill in the consolidated statement of financial position for JM only as at 31 December 20X5 is:

$ ☐

12.10 YH purchased 75% of the ordinary shares of SW on 31 December 20X6. SW purchased 70% of the ordinary shares of LP on 1 July 20X7 and YH purchased 8% of the ordinary shares of LP on the same date.

Complete the sentences by writing in the correct numbers from the list provided.

In order to calculate the consolidated retained earnings of the YH group ☐ % of the post acquisition reserves of LP are consolidated. To calculate the non controlling interest in LP in the consolidated statement of financial position an NCI percentage of ☐ % is used.

Picklist for numbers

60.5

52.5

78

70

47.5

22

30

39.5

13 Foreign subsidiaries

13.1 VW reports in A$ and has an 80% interest in its subsidiary XY whose functional currency is B$.

It translates the subsidiary's statement of profit or loss and other comprehensive income using the average rate for the period. The net assets (equity) of XY are B$6,510,000 as at 31 December 20X3 (B$4,557,000 as at 31 December 20X2).

XY made a profit for the year of B$1,674,000 and paid a dividend of B$372,000 on 31 August 20X3. There was no other comprehensive income.

Relevant exchange differences are:

31 December 20X2	A$/B$1.4
31 August 20X3	A$/B$1.55
31 December 20X3	A$/B$1.6
Average for 20X3	A$/B$1.5

What are the exchange differences on net assets and profit to be reported in other comprehensive income in the consolidated statement of profit or loss and other comprehensive income of the VW Group for the year ended 31 December 20X3?

A   A $49,800 loss.
B   A $62,250 loss.
C   A $54,250 loss.
D   A $302,250 loss.
E   A $49,800 gain.

13.2 Z, an entity based in the USA, presents its financial statements in US dollars. On 1 January 20X8, Z purchased 80% of the ordinary share capital of B. B's functional currency is the Euro (€) and the 80% investment cost €20 million. The fair value of the net assets of B at the date of acquisition was €19 million. The fair value of the non-controlling interests at 1 January 20X8 was €4.2 million. There has been no impairment in goodwill since acquisition. Z measures non-controlling interests at fair value at acquisition.
The relevant exchange rates are as follows:

1 January 20X8	$1: €0.64
31 December 20X8	$1: €0.74
Average for 20X8	$1: €0.68

What is the value of goodwill that will appear on the consolidated statement of financial position of Z as at 31 December 20X8?

A $6,486,000
B $7,027,000
C $7,500,000
D $8,125,000

13.3 AB reports in $. On 1 April 20X7, it acquired an 80% interest in EF. EF operates in Country C whose currency is the Crown. Net assets of EF as at 1 April 20X7 were 391,680 Crowns and 489,600 Crowns as at 31 December 20X7, the reporting date. Profit for the period 1 April to 31 December 20X7 is 97,920 Crowns and is to be translated at the average rate. There was no other comprehensive income and no dividends were paid. Assume that no goodwill arose on the acquisition. Exchange rates are as follows:

1 April 20X7	$/Crowns 1.8
31 December 20X7	$/Crowns 1.6
Average for the period	$/Crowns 1.7

What is the total effect of this acquisition on group reserves at 31 December 20X7?

A $70,720
B $88,400
C $57,600
D $46,080

13.4 IAS 21 explains two currency concepts:

- The functional currency
- The presentation currency.

Which of the following statements about the presentation currency are true?

Select one or more:

A It is the currency of the entity's primary economic environment.
B It is the currency of the year end financial statements.
C It is the currency that mainly influences the entity's sales prices.
D The entity may choose which presentation currency to use.

13.5 **Complete the sentence below by writing in the correct narrative from the list provided.**

When a foreign subsidiary has a different functional currency to the presentation currency of the group financial statements, [   ] assets and liabilities of the subsidiary must be translated at the

[   ] , income and expenses at the [   ] rate and exchange differences should be reported in [   ] .

Picklist of narratives

monetary
non-monetary
all
opening rate
closing rate
average rate
profit or loss
other comprehensive income

13.6 ST, an entity that reports in $, owns 100% of the issued share capital of WX, a company incorporated in Country B where the currency is the Blop.

Extracts from the statement of profit or loss for the year ended 31 December 20X5 are as follows:

	ST	WX
	$	Blops
Revenue	12,000	28,050

WX sells goods to ST on 12 September for 5,700 Blops.

Rates of exchange for the period have been as follows:

- Average rate for 20X5 $1 = 3.75 blops
- 12 September 20X5 $1 = 3.8 blops
- 31 December 20X5 $1 = 4 blops

What is the most appropriate figure for revenue to be included in the consolidated statement of profit or loss for the year ended 31 December 20X5?

A $17,980
B $18,055
C $17,960
D $19,480

13.7 Parent has three overseas subsidiaries.

I   is 80% owned. A does not normally enter into transactions with Parent, other than to pay dividends. It operates as a fairly autonomous entity on a day to day basis although Parent controls its long term strategy.

II   is 100% owned and has been set up in order to assemble machines from materials provided by Parent. These are then sent to the UK where Parent sells them to third parties.

II   is 75% owned and is located in France. It manufactures and sells its own range of products locally. It negotiates its own day to day financing needs with French banks.

Which of the subsidiaries are likely to have a different functional currency from Parent?

A   I and II
B   I and III
C   II and III
D   All three subsidiaries

13.8 Rat acquired 75% of equity shares of Mole, a foreign operation, on 1 January 20X5, when its reserves were 220,000 units. The fair value of Mole's net assets was considered to be the same as the book value at acquisition. Summarised statements of financial position of the two entities at 31 December 20X6 are shown below:

	Rat	Mole
	$'000	Unit'000
Investment in Mole	350	-
Other assets	3,550	1,260
	3,900	1,260
Share capital ($1/Unit1 ordinary shares)	1,000	500
Reserves	1,900	460
	2,900	960
Liabilities	1,000	300
	3,900	1,260

	Unit=$1
1 January 20X5	2.0
31 December 20X5	2.5

It is group policy to measure non-controlling interests at their proportionate share of net assets at acquisition. Total cumulative exchange losses on goodwill as at 31 December 20X6 are $16,000. There has been no impairment of goodwill since acquisition.

What are consolidated reserves at 31 December 20X6 (to the nearest $)?

$ [   ]

13.9 YH prepares its financial statements in dollars. YH acquired 80% of the equity share capital of OP on 1 January 20X3. OP operates in country L, which has the Ludd as its currency. OP sources the majority of its raw materials locally and is subject to local taxes and corporate regulations. The current workforce is recruited locally, although the majority of its sales are to customers in other countries. During the year OP secured a four-year term loan from a bank in L to fund its own capital investment requirements.

Which of the following statements are TRUE?

Select ALL that apply.

A   OP is a subsidiary of YH and should therefore select the dollar as its functional currently because the entities are part of a group.

B   The functional currency of OP will be determined by the currency that dominates the primary economic environment in which OP operates.

C   The functional currency of OP will be the dollar as the majority of the sales revenue is generated outside of L.

D   OP operates autonomously and raises its own finance which indicates that its functional currency should be Ludd.

E   OP must adopt the Ludd as its presentational currency.

13.10 SG acquired a controlling interest in TH on 1 April 20X7, paying 3 million shillings (TH's functional currency) for 700,000 of TH's issued share capital of 1,000,000 1 shilling ordinary shares. TH's reserves at the date of acquisition were 1,500,000 shillings.

Rates of exchange were:

1 April 20X7 1$ = 5 shillings

31 March 20X8 1$ = 4 shillings

Non-controlling interest is measured at fair value at acquisition. The fair value of the non-controlling interest in TH on 1 April 20X7 was 1.2 million shillings.

Calculate goodwill on acquisition (assuming no impairment has taken place) in respect of the TH acquisition for inclusion in the SG group's statement of financial position at 31 March 20X8 (round your answer to the nearest $'000).

$'000 [ ]

14 Consolidated statement of changes in equity

14.1 SP has a 75% subsidiary, AX and a 30% associate CR. In the year to 31 December 20X9 the companies paid the following dividends:

	$
SP	1,000,000
AX	400,000
CR	200,000

What total amount will appear in the consolidated statement of changes in equity of the SP group at 31 December 20X9 in respect of dividends paid?

A $1,000,000

B $1,100,000

C $1,160,000

D $1,400,000

14.2   JK owned 70% of GH's equity shares on at 31 December 20X2. JK purchased a further 20% of GH's equity shares on 31 December 20X3 for $520,000, when the existing non-controlling interest (NCI) in GH was measured at $759,000.

Write in the correct amounts in respect of the additional purchase or use BLANK in order to reflect the impact on the consolidated statement of changes in equity for the JK Group for the year ended 31 December 20X3.

Extract from the consolidated statement of changes in equity for JK Group for the year ended 31 December 20X3:

	Attributable to equity holders of the parent	Non-controlling interest
	$000	$000
Balance at the start of the year	3350	650
Comprehensive income for the year	1280	150
Dividends paid	(200)	(30)
Adjustments to NCI for additional purchase of GH shares	☐	☐
Adjustments to parent's equity for additional purchase of GH shares	☐	☐

14.3   P acquired 80% of S on 1 January 20X1. For the year ended 31 December 20X3, the total comprehensive income for P and S respectively was $200,000 and $100,000. During December 20X3, S sold goods to P for $15,000 at a margin of 20%. One third of these goods had been sold to third parties by the year end.

What figures should be reported in the consolidated statement of changes in equity for total comprehensive income attributable to the owners of the parent and to the non-controlling interests?

A   TCI for owners of parent   TCI for non-controlling interests
       $285,000 $20,000

B   TCI for owners of parent   TCI for non-controlling interests
       $277,600 $19,400

C   TCI for owners of parent   TCI for non-controlling interests
       $300,000 $20,000

D   TCI for owners of parent   TCI for non-controlling interests
       $278,400 $19,600

14.4   **Which THREE of the following would appear in a line of its own in a consolidated statement of changes in equity?**

A   A gain on revaluation of a property
B   Profit for the year
C   Issue of share capital
D   Other comprehensive income for the year
E   Total comprehensive income for the year
F   Dividends

14.5 AA owns 80% of its subsidiary BB. In the year ended 31 December 20X4, AA issued 500,000 shares for $2.00 per share. The nominal value of each share is 50 cents.

How should this share issue be recorded in the consolidated statement of changes in equity of the AA group for the year ended 31 December 20X4?

A   As an increase to the 'equity attributable to the owners of the parent' of $250,000

B   This is an intragroup transaction which cancels on consolidation so will not appear in the consolidated statement of changes in equity

C   As an increase to the 'equity attributable to the owners of the parent' of $1,000,000

D   As a decrease of $800,000 to the 'equity attributable to the owners of the parent' and of $200,000 to the 'non-controlling interests'

14.6 On 1 September 20X6, BLT held 60% of the ordinary share capital of its only subsidiary CMU. The consolidated equity of the group at that date was $576,600, of which $127,000 was attributable to non-controlling interests.

On 28 February 20X7, exactly halfway through the financial year, BLT bought a further 20% of the ordinary share capital of CMU for $80,000. In the year ended 31 August 20X7 BLT's profits for the period were $98,970 and CMU's were $30,000. No dividends were paid in the year and there was no other comprehensive income or share issue. It can be assumed that profits accrue evenly throughout the year. Non-controlling interest was measured at the proportionate share of net assets at acquisition.

Write in correct amounts in respect of the additional purchase or use 'BLANK' in order to reflect the impact on the consolidated statement of changes in equity for the BLT Group for the year ended 31 August 20X8.

BLT GROUP STATEMENT OF CHANGES IN EQUITY FOR THE YEAR ENDED 31 AUGUST 20X7

	Attributable to the owners of the parent $	Non-controlling interest $
Balance at 1 September 20X6	449,600	127,000
Total comprehensive income	119,979	9,000
Adjustment to NCI for additional purchase of CMU shares		
Adjustment to parent's equity for additional equity for additional purchase of CMU shares		

14.7 **Which FOUR of the following statements about the consolidated statement of changes in equity are true?**

A   Adjustments to equity as a result of subsidiary to subsidiary step acquisitions or disposals are not included in the consolidated statement of changes in equity

B   It is a primary statement required by IAS 1 *Presentation of financial statements*

C   The total comprehensive income for the year line comes from the ownership reconciliation in the consolidated statement of profit or loss and other comprehensive income

D   It reconciles equity from the prior year's consolidated statement of financial position to equity from the current year's consolidated statement of financial position

E   Movements in equity in the year include consolidated total comprehensive income, share issues and dividends paid

F   Subsidiaries must be excluded from the consolidated statement of changes in equity

G   Associates must have their own column in the consolidated statement of changes in equity

14.8 LK acquired a 75% stake in SW several years ago when the reserves of SW were $350,000. The share capital and share premium of LK are $1,000,000 and $200,000 respectively.

Reserves of LK and SW on 1 January 20X5 stood at $4,500,000 and $500,000 respectively.

What is the 'equity attributable to the owners of the parent' at 1 January 20X5 for inclusion in the consolidated statement of changes in equity of the LK group for the year ended 31 December 20X5?

$ [   ]

14.9 **Which of the following statements is TRUE in relation to the dividends line in the consolidated statement of changes in equity?**

A   It includes the group share of dividends received from subsidiaries and associates

B   It includes dividends paid by the parent and dividends paid by the subsidiary to its external shareholders

C   It includes represents dividends paid by the parent and dividends paid by the subsidiary

D   It includes dividends paid by the parent and the group share of dividends paid by the subsidiary

14.10 **Which THREE of the following statements are correct in relation to the 'equity attributable to the owners of the parent' year end figure in the consolidated statement of changes in equity?**

A   It should include profit from intragroup trading on items left in inventory at the year end

B   It should include the share capital and share premium of the parent and the year end consolidated reserves figure

C   It should come to the same number as equity before non-controlling interests in the year end consolidated statement of financial position

D   It can be calculated as the brought down equity attributable to the owners of the parent, plus total comprehensive income for the year attributable to the owners of the parent, less the parent's dividends paid plus any share issues by the parent in the year

E   It should include the share capital and share premium of the parent and its subsidiaries plus consolidated reserves at the year end

F   The non-controlling interests at the year end should be included in the 'equity attributable to the parent' year end figure

15 Consolidated statements of cash flows

15.1 RN Group: Consolidated statement of profit or loss for the year ended 31 December 20X5

	$
Profit before tax	500,000
Income tax expense	(150,000)
Profit for the year	50,000
Attributable to: Owners of the parent	295,000
Non-controlling interest	55,000
	350,000

RN Group: Consolidated statement of financial position as at 31 December

	20X5	20X4
	$	$
Non-controlling interest	550,000	525,000

During the year ended 31 December 20X5 RN acquired a 75% interest in the equity shares of PD when the net assets of PD were $400,000. It is group policy to measure non-controlling interests at the proportionate share of the subsidiary's net assets at acquisition.

What was the dividend paid to the non-controlling interest in the year ended 31 December 20X5?

A $130,000
B $180,000
C $30,000
D $20,000
E $330,000

15.2 AB Group: Consolidated statement of financial position (extract) as at 31 December:

	20X8	20X7
	$	$
Inventory	550,000	475,000
Trade receivables	943,000	800,000
Trade payables	620,000	530,000

AB Group: Consolidated statement of profit or loss (extract) for the year ended 31 December 20X8:

	$
Profit before tax	775,000

During the year AB acquired an 80% interest in the equity share capital of CD. Extracts from the statement of financial position of CD at acquisition are as follows:

	$
Inventory	80,000
Trade receivables	110,000
Trade payables	70,000

Assume there is no depreciation, investment income or interest expense.

What is the cash generated from operations figure to appear in the consolidated statement of cash flows of the AB Group for the year ended 31 December 20X8?

A $647,000
B $527,000
C $743,000
D $757,000
E $767,000

15.3 CONSOLIDATED STATEMENT OF PROFIT OR LOSS AND OTHER COMPREHENSIVE INCOME FOR THE YEAR ENDED 31 DECEMBER 20X2 (EXTRACT)

	$
Profit before interest and tax	50,000
Share of profit of associate	10,000
Profit before tax	60,000
Income tax expense	(25,000)
Profit for the year	35,000
Other comprehensive income	
Gain on property revaluation	20,000
Share of associate's other comprehensive income	5,000
Total comprehensive income for the year	60,000

CONSOLIDATED STATEMENT OF FINANCIAL POSITION (EXTRACT) AS AT 31 DECEMBER:

	20X2	20X1
	$	$
Investment in associate	116,600	107,900

What is the dividend received from the associate for inclusion in the consolidated statement of cash flows?

$ [   ]

15.4 **What is the correct treatment of dividends paid to non-controlling interests, in a group statement of cash flows?**

A   Include under the heading 'operating activities' or 'financing activities'.
B   Include under the heading 'operating activities' only.
C   Include under the heading 'financing activities' only.
D   Dividends do not need to be disclosed in a statement of cash flows.

15.5 BR acquired a 75% interest in the share capital of ED on 1 July 20X6. The property, plant and equipment of ED at that date was $500,000.

Extracts from the consolidated statement of financial position of BR as at 31 December are as follows:

	20X6	20X5
	$	$
Property, plant and equipment	4,100,000	3,700,000

Depreciation charged for the year ended 31 December 20X6 was $970,000.

What is the amount to be included in the consolidated statement of cash flows for additions to property, plant and equipment?

A $870,000
B $1,370,000
C $995,000
D $70,000

15.6 ST's extracts from the statement of financial position as at 31 December are as follows:

	20X4	20X3
	$m	$m
Property, plant and equipment (note 1)	192	175
Finance lease liabilities (note 2)		
– current	20	10
– non-current	51	45

Note 1: During 20X4, ST disposed of property, plant and equipment with a net book value of $10 million and charged depreciation of $42 million.

Note 2: All the finance leases relate to property, plant and equipment. Rentals paid during 20X4 amounted to $18 million. Interest charged to the statement of profit or loss amounted to $6 million.

What is the amount to be included in additions to property, plant and equipment in the 'investing activities' section of the statement of cash flows for the year ended 31 December 20X4?

A $41 million
B $35 million
C $69 million
D $53 million
E $51 million

15.7 CONSOLIDATED STATEMENT OF PROFIT OR LOSS AND OTHER COMPREHENSIVE INCOME FOR THE YEAR ENDED 31 DECEMBER 20X2 (EXTRACT):

	$
Group profit before tax	30,000
Tax	(10,000)
Profit for the year	20,000
Other comprehensive income	5,000
Total comprehensive income	25,000
Profit attributable to:	
Owners of the parent	14,000
Non-controlling interest	6,000
	20,000
Total comprehensive income attributable to:	
Owners of the parent	18,000
Non-controlling interest	7,000
	25,000

CONSOLIDATED STATEMENTS OF FINANCIAL POSITION (EXTRACTS) AS AT 31 DECEMBER:

	20X2	20X1
	$	$
Non-controlling interest	111,000	100,000

On 1 October 20X2, a new 75% subsidiary was acquired. It is group policy to measure non-controlling interest at fair value at acquisition which was $8,000 for the new subsidiary.

Calculate the dividends paid to the non-controlling interest for the year ended 31 December 20X2.

Dividends are $ [   ]

15.8 EF acquires 100% of the issued share capital of WG or $500,000 in consideration, comprising $150,000 in cash and 100,000 $1 ordinary shares with a market value of $3.50 each.

At the date of acquisition WG has an overdraft of $80,000.

What is/are the amount(s) to be disclosed in 'investing activities' in the consolidated statement of cash flows of EF in respect of the acquisition of WG?

A $230,000 outflow in one line
B $150,000 outflow and $80,000 outflow in two separate lines
C $70,000 outflow in one line
D $580,000 outflow in one line

15.9 SM has owned 75% of the ordinary shares in TR since 1 January 20X1. It sold the investment for $500,000 on 1 June 20X5. The net assets of TR on that date included the following:

	$
Cash and bank	15,000
Bank overdraft	(50,000)
Bank loan (repayable 20X9)	(300,000)

What will appear as the net cash inflow in respect of acquisitions and disposals in the consolidated statement of cash flows of SM for the year ended 31 December 20X5?

A $465,000
B $485,000
C $535,000
D $835,000

15.10 Which **FOUR** items from the list below would be included in the "cash flows from investing activities" section of the consolidated statement of cash flows?

A   Dividends paid to non-controlling interests

B   Profit on sale of property, plant and equipment

C   Cash paid to acquire an interest in an associate

D   Gain on sale of subsidiary

E   Acquisition of plant under finance leases

F   Acquisition of equipment for cash

G   Proceeds on sale of subsidiary (net of cash disposed of)

H   Dividends received from associate

16 Related parties (1114)

16.1 Under IAS 24 *Related party disclosures* transactions between the reporting entity and certain other types of entities are excluded from the disclosure requirements.

Which ONE of the following transactions would need to be disclosed under IAS 24?

(Assume all are material.)

A   A loan from Midwest Bank secured against machinery

B   A collective wages agreement with the main trade union employees belong to

C   Sponsorship for an industrial training programme agreed with the Mid Eastern Training and Enterprise Council

D   Arrangements entered into by the production director of the reporting entity to provide a review of the production facilities of a company controlled by his wife. The service will be provided at a full commercial price

16.2 IAS 24 *Related party disclosures* governs disclosures required for transactions between a company and parties deemed to be related to it.

Which THREE of the following will normally be held to be related parties of a company?

A   Its subsidiary companies

B   Its directors

C   Close family of the company's directors

D   Providers of finance to the company

E   A customer or supplier with whom the company has a significant volume of business

16.3 **Which TWO of the following aspects of a related party transaction should be disclosed under IAS 24 *Related party disclosures*?**

A   The names of the related parties involved in transactions.

B   The details of the transaction and a description of the relationships between the parties.

C   The amount involved.

D   The date the transaction occurred.

16.4 **Which TWO of the following would be related parties of Whither Co?**

A   A person with a controlling shareholding in the parent company of Whither Co.

B   An entity in which the wife of the finance director of Whither Co owns a controlling stake.

C   Boukir Co which has joint control with Whither Co over a joint venture.

D   Whither Co's major customer who accounts for 80% of Whither Co's revenue.

16.5 **Which of the following would find related party disclosures the most useful?**

A   Shareholders of a large listed entity

B   Group companies

C   Employees

16.6 **Which of the following items are related party transactions under IAS 24 *Related party disclosures*?**

Select ALL the options that are correct.

A   Purchase of inventory by a parent from an associate.

B   Sale of a company asset to the managing director of the reporting entity, at an externally agreed fair value.

C   Sale of an asset by Company A to an entity in which the wife of the managing director of Company A has a controlling interest.

D   Provision of venture capital by a venture capital company on the condition that the money will be repaid in 36 months.

E   Sale of goods at cost from one associate to another associate.

F   Purchases from a supplier which the entity uses for 75% of its purchases and receives a bulk discount.

16.7 **Which TWO of the following would be regarded as related parties of BS?**

A   TX, a major customer of BS.

B   The chief executive officer of the BS Board

C   EF, an entity with which BS shares control of a joint venture

D   CD, an entity in which the wife of the chief executive officer of the BS Board has a controlling shareholding

E   GH, BS's main banker

16.8 CB is an entity specialising in importing a wide range of non-food items and selling them to retailers. George is CB's chief executive officer and founder and owns 40% of CB's equity shares.

Which TWO of the following transactions should be disclosed in the financial statements of CB in accordance with IAS 24 *Related party disclosures*?

A   CB's largest customer, XC, accounts for 35% of CB's revenue. XC has just completed negotiations with CB for a special 5% discount on all sales.

B   During the accounting period, George purchased a property from CB for $500,000. CB had previously declared the property surplus to its requirements and had valued it at $750,000.

C   George's son, Arnold, is a director in a financial institution, FC. During the accounting period, FC advanced $2 million to CB as an unsecured loan at a favourable rate of interest.

D   FG and CB are associates within the same group. During the current year, the parent, HI required CB to sell goods to FG at cost.

16.9 XT owns 75% of R. XT also owns 40% of V, over which it exercises significant influence.

R owns 100% of P.

XT operates a defined benefit pension plan for all of its employees and sells 60% of its output to its main customer, G.

Which of the following would be considered related parties of XT, in accordance with international financial reporting standards?

A   R, V and G

B   R, G and the pension plan

C   R, V, P and G

D   R, V, P and the pension plan

16.10   AB has a subsidiary, CD and two associates, EF and GH. During the year ended 31 December 20X1, the following transactions took place:

- AB charged a management fee to each of CD, EF and GH.
- EF sold goods to GH at cost (EF's normal selling price is cost plus 20%).
- CD sold goods to AB at market value.

Which ONE of the following should be disclosed in the financial statements of EF?

A   The management fee payable by EF to AB.

B   The sale of goods by EF to GH.

C   The sale of goods by CD to AB.

D   The management fee payable by CD and GH to AB.

17 Earnings per share

17.1   **Which ONE of the following statements about the earnings per share ratio is correct?**

A   All entities must disclose earnings per share in their financial statements

B   Earnings per share represents the return on the investment for all capital providers

C   Earnings per share is calculated as profit after tax divided by the total number of ordinary shares at the year end

D   The denominator of the earnings per share ratio is the weighted average number of ordinary shares outstanding during the period

17.2   On 1 April 20X7 MK made a bonus issue of 1 for 2 from retained earnings.

MK reported basic earnings per share for the year ended 31 December 20X6 of 26.5c per share.

What is the comparative figure for basic earnings per share for the year ended 31 December 20X6 in the financial statements of MK for the year ended 31 December 20X7? (Give your answer to one decimal place.)

| | cents per share

17.3   The weighted average number of ordinary shares in issue for the year to 31 December 20X7 is 5,000,000.

Options to purchase 500,000 $1 ordinary shares at $2.80 per share were issued on 1 January 20X7. These options are exercisable between 1 January 20X9 and 31 December 20Y0. The average market value of each $1 ordinary share during the year ended 31 December 20X7 is $3.50.

The weighted average number of shares to be used in the calculation of diluted earnings per share for the year ended 31 December 20X7 is:

A   4.9 million

B   5.1 million

C   5.4 million

D   5.5 million

17.4   YZ had 80,000 shares in issue on 1 January 20X6 and made a 1 for 4 rights issue on 1 September 20X6 at $1.00 per share. The fair value before the rights issue was $1.50. Total earnings for 20X6 were $120,000.

What was the EPS for the year to 31 December 20X6 in $s (to 2 decimal places)?

$ [   ]

17.5   JKL is a listed entity preparing financial statements to 31 December. The figures correctly used in the basic earnings per share calculation for the year ended 31 December 20X4 were:

- Earnings after tax figure - $2,763,000
- Weighted average number of equity shares - 6,000,000 shares

On 1 January 20X4, JKL issued 5 year convertible loan notes of $2,000,000. The liability element of the loan notes on 1 January 20X4 was $1,836,000 and the effective interest is 7%. The terms of conversion (which are at the option of the stockholder) are as follows:

For each $100 of loan notes:

Conversion at 31 December 20X7: 105 shares

Conversion at 31 December 20X8: 103 shares

JKL is subject to an income tax rate of 30%.

What is the diluted earnings per share of JKL for the year ended 31 December 20X4?

A   35.2 cents
B   35.3 cents
C   35.4 cents
D   35.7 cents
E   46.1 cents
F   47.5 cents

17.6   NAT, a listed entity, had 10 million $1 ordinary shares in issue on 1 January 20X3.

On 1 October 20X3, NAT issued 2 million $1 ordinary shares at their full market price of $7.60 per share.

NAT's profit after tax for the year ended 31 December 20X3 was $8,200,000.

What is NAT's basic earnings per share of the year ended 31 December 20X3 in cents (rounded to 1 decimal place)?

[   ] cents

17.7   YZ had 80,000 shares in issue on 1 January 20X6 (and for all of 20X5). On 1 September 20X6 YZ made a 1 for 4 rights issue at $1 per share.

The fair value of a share before the rights issue was $1.50. Total earnings for 20X6 were $120,000.

What is the restated EPS for year ended 31 December 20X5 if the earning for that year were $100,000 (in $s, to two decimal places)?

$ [   ]

17.8   On 1 January 20X4, BG, a listed entity, had 1,000,000 $1 ordinary shares in issue. On 1 April 20X4 BG issued 300,000 $1 ordinary shares at their full market price. BG reported profit before tax of $180,000 and an income tax charge of $60,000 in the year to 31 December 20X4.

The basic earnings per share for the year to 31 December 20X4 is:

A   9.2 cents per share
B   9.8 cents per share
C   13.8 cents per share
D   14.7 cents per share

17.9 Throughout the year ended 31 December 20X9, CSA, a listed entity, had 3,000,000 $1 ordinary shares in issue.

The profit before tax of CSA for the year ended 31 December 20X9 was $1,040,000 and income tax for the year was $270,000.

On 1 January 20X9, CSA issued convertible loan stock. Assuming that the conversion was fully subscribed, there would be an increase of 2,400,000 ordinary shares in issues. The liability element of the loan stock is $4,000,000 and the effective interest is 7%.

CSA is subject to an income tax rate of 30%. What is the diluted earnings per share for the year ended 31 December 20X9 (in cents, to 1 decimal place)?

| | cents
| --- |

17.10 BNM is a listed entity preparing its financial statements for the year ended 31 December 20X1.

Throughout the year, BNM has 5,000,000 $1 shares in issue.

BNM generated profit after tax of $3.8 million for the year ended 31 December 20X1.

On 1 January 20X1, the ordinary shareholders of BNM held options to purchase 1,000,000 $1 ordinary shares at $3.10 per share. The options are exercisable between 31 December 20X2 and 31 December 20X4. No further options were issued in the year. The average market value of one $1 ordinary share of BNM during the year ended 31 December 20X1 was $4.00.

What is the diluted earnings per share for the year ended 31 December 20X1?

A   63.3 cents
B   75.8 cents
C   72.7 cents
D   76.0 cents

18 Ethics (1114)

18.1 RK is expanding and requires additional long term capital. The Board has approved the issue of redeemable preference shares. In discussions with the Finance Director, a CIMA member, the Chief Executive made it clear that he did not want the gearing ratio of RK to be adversely affected and that the preference shares should be classified as equity in the financial statements.

Which of the following statements about the redeemable preference shares is true?

A   As share certificates will be issued there is no ethical issue in classifying the shares as equity.

B   The Chief Executive has the ultimate responsibility for the financial statements and so the ethical burden would fall on him if there is any issue with the classification of the shares.

C   It is the responsibility of the directors to prepare the financial statements in an ethical manner and hence the shares should be classified as liabilities.

D   Preference shareholders are entitled to their dividend before ordinary shareholders and so the classification of the shares is irrelevant.

18.2 XY has recently begun to lease an expensive machine. The lease agreement effectively means that XY takes on substantially the risk and rewards associated with owning the asset.

The managing director has instructed XY's finance director to treat the lease as an operating lease in order to show a better financial position.

Which one of the following would be the most appropriate action for XY's finance director to take?

A   Account for the lease as an operating lease to ensure that he stays in favour with the managing director.

B   Explain to the managing director that under IAS 17 *Leases*, this lease should be treated as a finance lease.

C   Resign with immediate effect.

D   Call the CIMA Ethics Helpline.

18.3 The finance director of ZZ has set up a company, RR, through which ZZ conducts its investment activities. ZZ has paid $400 million to RR during the year and this has been included in dividends paid. The money was invested in a specified portfolio of investments. 95% of the profits and 100% of the losses in the specified portfolio of investments are transferred to ZZ. An investment manager has charge of the company's investments and owns all of the share capital of RR. An agreement between the investment manager and ZZ sets out the operating guidelines and prohibits the investment manager from obtaining access to the investments for the manager's benefit. An annual transfer of the profit/loss will occur on 31 December annually and the capital will be returned in four years' time. The only accounting entry made for the above agreement was to record the $400 million as dividends paid and no profit or loss has yet been transferred.

Which FOUR of the following statements are correct in relation to the above?

A   RR is not a subsidiary as ZZ does not own any of the share capital. Therefore, RR should not be consolidated in ZZ's group accounts.

B   The IFRS 10 definition of control has been met. Therefore, ZZ should consolidate RR in its group financial statements.

C   The $400 million has been incorrectly recognised as dividends paid. Instead it would be more accurate to record it as a loan.

D   There is an ethical risk that the finance director has deliberately set up RR to keep the investment activities of ZZ off balance sheet.

E   If the finance director does not consolidate RR, there is a risk that the finance director is associated with a report that omits or obscures information.

F   There is no ethical issue here. The finance director has accounted for RR in accordance with IFRSs and the *Conceptual Framework*.

18.4   JJ operates in the energy industry and undertakes complex natural gas trading arrangements, which involve exchanges in resources with other companies in the industry. JJ is entering into a long-term contract for the supply of gas and is raising a loan on the strength of this contract. The loan is to be repaid over four years. JJ wishes to report the proceeds as an operating cash flow because it is related to a long-term purchase contract. The directors of JJ receive extra income if the operating cash flow exceeds a pre-determined amount for the year.

Which THREE of the following statements are accurate in relation to the above proposal?

A   There is no ethical issue here as the directors' proposed accounting treatment is correct.

B   There is a self-interest threat here as if the proceeds of the loan are recorded as an operating cash flow the target needed for the directors to receive extra income is more likely to be met.

C   IAS 7 *Statement of cash flows* allows some flexibility in classification of cash flows but the proceeds from a loan should always be recorded as a financing cash flow.

D   If the proceeds of the loan are recorded as an operating cash flow, the directors of JJ will not be complying with IAS 7 and will be failing to comply with the CIMA Code of Ethics' principle of professional competence.

E   This proposed treatment would comply with IAS 7 *Statement of cash flows* as its overriding principle is to present the position as fairly as possible.

F   IAS 7 *Statement of cash flows* offers no flexibility in the classification of cash flows.

18.5   The BC group is suffering from liquidity problems. During the year, BC made a loan to one of its directors. The loan has no specific repayment date but is repayable on demand. The directors have included this loan in 'cash and cash equivalents' in the statement of financial position. They feel that there is no problem with this accounting entry as there is a choice within IFRSs.

Which ONE of the following statements is correct in relation to the above?

A   The directors' treatment of the loan is correct because it is repayable on demand.

B   It would be unethical just to treat the loan as 'cash and cash equivalents' purely to improve the perceived liquidity of the company.

C   The directors' treatment of the loan complies with the Conceptual Framework's qualitative characteristics.

D   The directors are acting in the best interests of the shareholders therefore there is no ethical issue

---

18.6   **Which TWO of the following would be a valid reason for an entity changing its revenue recognition policy?**

A   To reduce the entity's tax liability.

B   To align its accounting policies to the industry norm.

C   To provide information that is more relevant to the economic decision-making needs of the users of financial statements.

D   To improve the earnings per share figure.

18.7 **Complete the following sentences by writing in the correct narrative from the list provided.**

CIMA's Code of Ethics clearly states that a professional accountant should not be associated with reports believe that the information contains a materially false or [＿＿＿＿＿＿] statement; contains statements or information furnished [＿＿＿＿＿＿] ; or [＿＿＿＿＿＿] or obscures information.

Picklist for narratives

Misleading
Subjective
With bias
Recklessly
Hides
Omits

18.8 **Which ONE of the following is NOT one of the principles of CIMA *Code of Ethics*?**

A   Integrity

B   Objectivity

C   Confidentiality

D   Governance

18.9 The chief executive of PR has asked the finance director to classify a finance lease as an operating lease in the financial statements to ensure that a loan covenant based on the level of gearing is not breached.

Which would be the most appropriate course of action for the finance director to take?

A   Resign with immediate effect

B   Follow the accounting treatment proposed by the director

C   Report the chief executive immediately to the CIMA Ethics Helpline

D   Try to persuade the chief executive to change his mind and follow the required accounting treatment of IAS 17 Leases

18.10 IAS 27 *Separate financial statements* requires investments in subsidiaries, joint ventures or associates either at cost or in accordance with IAS 39 *Financial instruments: recognition and measurement* (i.e. at fair value).

The finance director of AA has decided to adapt his accounting policy to measure loss-making investments at cost and profit making investments in accordance with IAS 39.

Which ONE of the following statements is correct in respect of the finance director's decision?

A   As IAS 27 offers a choice of accounting treatment, the finance director's proposed treatment is correct.

B   The finance director is acting ethically in this decision as he is acting on the shareholders' behalf by trying to show the best possible financial performance.

C   IAS 27 requires the entity to apply the same accounting for each category of investments making this proposed policy unacceptable.

D   The finance director should call the CIMA Ethics Helpline immediately.

19 Analysis of financial performance and position I

19.1 What is the acid test ratio of Edward Co given the information in the table?

[handwritten: CA]

	$	*[handwritten: CL]*
[handwritten: ←] Receivables	158,000	
[handwritten: EXCLUDE ←] Inventories	20,000	
[handwritten: ←] Short term investments	18,000	
Trade payables	61,000 *[→]*	
Bank overdraft	64,000 *[→]*	
Corporate income tax payable	10,000 *[→]*	
Deposits received in advance	5,000 *[→]*	

- A 1.13:1
- B 1.26:1
- C 1.35:1
- D 1.40:1

[handwritten working:
$$CA - INV : CL$$
$$\frac{158+18}{61+64+10+5} \quad \frac{176}{140}$$
$$1.257 \cong 1.26$$
]

19.2 The table shows extracts from the financial statements of CD for the year ended 31 December 20X2.

Statement of financial position		Statement of profit or loss	
	$000		$000
Issued share capital	2,500	Profit before interest and tax	600
Retained earnings	1,050	Less loan interest	(120)
	3,550	Profit before tax	480
12% long term loan	1,000		
	4,550		

What is the return on capital employed?

- A 11%.
- B 13%.
- C 14%.
- D 17%.

[handwritten working:
$$\frac{PBIT}{TALCL} \quad \frac{600}{4550}$$
$$0.1318$$
]

19.3 PQ has an operating profit margin of 12% this year as compared to 11% last year. *[handwritten: no impact]*

Which ONE of the following choices would be a possible reason for the improvement?

[handwritten left margin: Rev X / Cos (X) / Exps (X) / Op Profit.]

- A PQ reclassified some expenses from administrative expenses to cost of sales in the current year.
- B PQ changed its financing structure during the year and as result had significant interest savings. *[handwritten: after O.P.]*
- C PQ increased sales during the year by offering better trade discounts to its customers. *[handwritten: X ⇒ lower GP.]*
- D *[handwritten ✓]* PQ moved to an out of town location where the rent and employment costs were less than in the previous year.

19.4 TH has a current ratio this year of 1.33:1 compared to 1.25:1 last year. *[handwritten: ⇒ better / more liquid.]*

Which TWO of the following would be possible explanations?

[handwritten left margin: Rec↑ / Inv↓ } profit / CA↓ / CL↓ / ↳ proport" greater.]

- A *[handwritten ✓]* TH made an unusually large sale immediately prior to the year end at a good profit margin.
- B *[handwritten ✓]* TH paid its payables earlier than usual out of a positive cash balance.
- C *[handwritten X]* TH made an usually large purchase of goods for cash immediately prior to the year end and these goods remain in inventory. *[handwritten: — reduce cash.]*
- D *[handwritten X]* TH paid its payables earlier than usual out of a bank overdraft. *[handwritten: — CL same]*
- E *[handwritten X]* TH purchased a machine shortly before the year end. *[handwritten: — if CA depends how pd for.]*
- F *[handwritten X]* TH reduced its customers' credit period in the current year. *[handwritten: cash in faster]*

[handwritten: but swapping rect Cash.]

[handwritten bottom: reduce CA if cash or increase CL if credit.]

BPP MEDIA

[Handwritten: No. of shares.]

19.5 BC, a listed entity, has 5,000,000 issued ordinary equity shares with a par value of 20 cents each. There were no movements of issued share capital during the year. BC had the following results for the year ended 30 April 20X3.

	$'000
Profit before tax	400
Income tax expense	100
Profit for the year	300 *[Handwritten: — Earnings.]*
Dividends paid	200
Retained profit for the year	100

The quoted price of BC shares on 30 April 20X3 was $1.50.

Calculate the P/E ratio of BC on this date. *[Handwritten: MV/EPS   150/0.06]*

| 25 |

[Handwritten: = 25]

19.6 X's asset turnover is very low compared with that of its main competitor. *[Handwritten: higher TALCL   Rev / TALCL.]*

Which ONE of the following could be the reason for this?

A   X carries its non-current assets at historic cost, while its competitor carries them at current value. *[Handwritten: lower TALCL. higher ROCE]*

B   X embarked on a major programme of capital investment towards the end of the previous year.

C   X has a smaller proportion of productive assets than its competitor. *[Handwritten: C should inc Rev in year.]*

D *[X]* X has recruited a number of additional production staff during the year.

19.7 SL's return on capital employed (measured as profit before interest and tax for the year as compared to capital employed at the end of the year) has deteriorated as compared to the previous year. *[Handwritten: PBIT / TALCL.]*

Which THREE of the following choices are possible reasons for this decline?

[Handwritten: higher TALCL] A ✓ In accordance with IAS 16 the company revalued its properties which resulted in a significant increase in the carrying value as compared to three years ago.

B ✓ Towards the end of the current year SL made major investments in plant and machinery financed by borrowing. *[Handwritten: Not had a chance to generate Rev yet.]*

C *[X]* SL converted $1million 10% loan notes into $1million share capital. *[Handwritten: no change TALCL?]*

D *[X]* SL issued $1million 10% loan notes to redeem $1 million redeemable preference shares at par.

E ✓ Asset turnover has reduced as compared to the previous year. *[Handwritten: PBIT = Margin x A T/O.]*

F *[X]* Asset turnover has increased as compared to the previous year.

19.8 As at 30 April 20X5 RS has a higher P/E ratio than its sector average. The last set of published accounts was for the year ended 31 December 20X4.

Which TWO of the following choices would be possible explanations for the high P/E ratio?

A *[X]* After many years of expansion in revenue and profits, problems have begun to emerge and profit warnings are expected.

B ✓ During the current year, a revolutionary product has been launched and sales have exceeded all expectations.

C ✓ During the previous year, RS discontinued one of its loss making activities which resulted in a significant drop in reported basic earnings per share, although the alternative earnings per share based on continuing operations showed above average growth.

D *[X]* Market expectations for the sector in which RS operates are low.

E *[X]* RS's competitors have recently invested in innovative technology which will result in production efficiencies.

19.9 An electrical store and a cake shop both have the same mark up on cost. However, the gross profit margin of the electrical store is significantly higher than that of the cake shop.

Volume does not impact on margin [handwritten]

Which ONE of the following is a possible reason for this?

A The electrical store takes advantage of trade discounts for bulk buying.
B The cake shop has a higher turnover of inventory than the electrical store.
C ✓ The cake shop has a higher level of wastage of inventory than the electrical store.
D The cake shop's revenue is increasing, while that of the electrical store is decreasing.

19.10 SP, a retailer of children's designer wear, makes a gross profit on sales of 25%, pays its suppliers one month after delivery, holds a cash balance equal to half a month's sales and inventory equivalent to one month's sales. There are no other current assets or liabilities.

If the inventory was increased to the equivalent of 1.5 month's sales, what would the immediate effect be?

Use Nos to illustrate [handwritten]

A The current ratio would increase, the quick ratio would increase
B The current ratio would increase, the quick ratio would decrease
C The current ratio would decrease, the quick ratio would increase
(D) The current ratio would decrease, the quick ratio would decrease

20 Analysis of financial performance and position II

20.1 AB wishes to increase its return on capital employed.

Which ONE of the following courses of action will help to achieve this in the short term?

A ✓ An increase in revenue. *— if profitable.* [handwritten]
B A decrease in the level of dividends paid to equity shareholders. *— ~~reduce~~ increase Retd + Cash.* [handwritten]
C The issue of ordinary equity shares. *— inc TALCL* [handwritten]
D An upward revaluation of land and buildings. *— inc TALCL* [handwritten]

20.2 DT's quick ratio has fallen from 0.9:1 to 0.6:1. *Excludes INV.* [handwritten]

Which ONE of the following actions might explain this decline?

*Rec } ¥ ↓
Cash }
OR
Liab. } ↑* [handwritten]

A Credit control has been poor.
B ✗ Inventory levels have fallen.
C The allowance for receivables has been reduced
D ✓ The entity has purchased a property for cash — *reduces cash.* [handwritten]

20.3 The finance director of QR is worried about its current ratio, which he has calculated to be 0.75. He is considering a number of actions that he hopes will improve QR's current ratio.

Which ONE of the following would increase QR's current ratio?

*Inv }
Rec } ↑
Cash ↓
Liab ↓.* [handwritten]

A Offer a settlement discount to customers *— rec ↓* [handwritten]
B Make a bonus issue of ordinary shares *— irrel free* [handwritten]
C ✓ Make a rights issue of ordinary shares *— ~~increase~~ cash* [handwritten]
D Sell current asset investments at the carrying value *—* [handwritten]
E All of the options

20.4 RS has ordinary shares with a nominal value of $1.00. The company has a price earnings ratio of 15 and the latest annual earnings per share figure was $0.36. The gross dividend yield is 3%.

What is RS's dividend cover ratio?

A 15 times
B 0.45 times
C 33.33 times
D 2.22 times

P/E = 15   E = 0.36   MV = 5.4
div = 0.162.
E = 36   DIV = 16.2   Cover
= 2.22.

20.5 AB wishes to forecast its financial performance and position for the forthcoming year. The forecast model used by the company incorporates the following relationships:

Revenue: total assets employed   2.5:1   *⟹ TA = 320.*
Current assets: current liabilities   1.8:1
Quick assets: current liabilities   1.2:1   *INV = 1/3 × CA*
Non-current assets: current assets   1.0:1   *⟹ NCA = 160   CA = 160.*

If revenue for the forthcoming year is expected to be $800,000, what is the forecast closing inventory figure?

A $53,333
B $71,111
C $85,926
D $96,000

INV = 53,333

20.6 An **upwards revaluation of property, plant and equipment** is likely to lead to which **THREE** of the following effects?

A ✓ Return on capital employed will decrease — *TALCL ↑   PBIT ↓*
B Gearing will increase ✗
C The current ratio will decrease ✗
D ✓ Net profit margin will decrease — *higher dep^n*
E ✓ Non-current asset turnover will decrease
F Interest cover will increase ✗

20.7 Which **ONE** of the following ratios would best assess the **efficiency of a manufacturing company**?

A P/E ratio
B Gearing
C Non-current asset turnover *⟶ how well assets are used to generate revenue.*
D Current ratio

20.8 FG holds several properties under operating leases. Many financial reporting experts believe that operating leases should be treated in exactly the same way as finance leases.

What would be the immediate effect of this change on the entity's key performance measures?

A Decrease in return on capital employed; decrease in gearing
B Decrease in return on capital employed; increase in gearing ✓
C Increase in return on capital employed; decrease in gearing
D Increase in return on capital employed; increase in gearing ✓

add asset
add liab..
dep^n ≈ lease rentals
+ fin costs.

20.9 The Northern Bank has provided a long term loan to Norwood, a small business.

Which of the following pairs of ratios is most likely to provide the bank with relevant information?

A Asset turnover and expenses to sales
B Gearing and interest cover *financial risk, ability to pay int..*
C Return on capital employed and gross profit margin
D Return on shareholders' equity and earnings per share

20.10 The accounting ratios of ABC are very similar to the average ratios for the industry in which it operates. ABC has an average operating profit margin of 24% and an average asset turnover of 0.9.

This entity is most likely to be:

A   An architect

B   A food retailer

C   An insurance broker

D   A manufacturer

21 Analysis of financial performance and position III

21.1   The following figures are taken from the accounts of WX:

	$
Inventories	400,000
Receivables	600,000
Cash	200,000
Payables	800,000
Loan notes redeemable in three years time	800,000

What is the quick ratio?

A   0.75

B   1.50

C   0.50

D   1.00

21.2   VW, a retailing company, earns a gross profit margin of 40% on its monthly sales of $60,000. The following changes are under consideration.

	Current	Proposed
Inventory turnover period	1.5 months	1.1 months
Trade payables payment period	1.0 months	1.5 months

By how much would VW's working capital be reduced if these changes were introduced?

A $3,600

B $14,400

C $32,400

D $54,000

21.3   Rickety Ltd has an acid test ratio of 0.4. It is planning two changes:

Proposal 1: Offering a 2% early settlement discount to credit customers

Proposal 2: Delaying payment to all trade payables by one extra month.

What effect would each of these proposals have on the acid test ratio?

A   *Proposal 1*   *Proposal 2*
     increase ratio   decrease ratio

B   *Proposal 1*   *Proposal 2*
     increase ratio   increase ratio

C   *Proposal 1*   *Proposal 2*
     decrease ratio   decrease ratio

D   *Proposal 1*   *Proposal 2*
     decrease ratio   increase ratio

21.4 Which **THREE** of the following are valid limitations of ratio analysis of published financial statements?

A ☒ Published financial statements are frequently unreliable as a result either of fraud or of error on the part of management

B ☑ Published financial statements contain estimates such as depreciation

C ☒ There are no prior year figures to compare to current year figures

D ☑ Accounting policies may vary between companies, making comparisons difficult

E ☑ The nature and character of a business may change over time, making strictly numerical comparisons misleading

F ☒ The nature of the industry may be volatile making intercompany comparison within the industry misleading.

21.5 Below are extracts from CD's statement of financial position at the end of 20X9:

	$
Current liabilities	50,000
Retained earnings	30,000
Revaluation reserve	20,000
Ordinary share capital	200,000
6% redeemable preference share capital	100,000
Non-current liabilities	475,000

What is CD's gearing ratio (calculated as [debt/(debt + equity)]) at the year end?

A 71.4%

B 75.8%

C 69.7%

D 74.2%

21.6 The following is an extract from the financial statements of RF for the year to 31 December 20X8:

Equity and liabilities	20X8	20X7
	$m	$m
Share capital	600	400
Share premium	360	40
Other reserves	16	-
Retained earnings	980	1,320
Total equity	1,956	1,760
Non current liabilities		
Long term borrowings	420	400

Which THREE of the following statements about the changes in the capital structure of RF could be realistically concluded from the extract provided above?

A Gearing of RF has decreased due to the increase in total equity.

B RF must have made a loss in the year as retained earnings have fallen.

C RF must have secured additional long-term borrowings of $20m.

D Shares were issued at a premium to nominal value.

E The only change in share capital has been a bonus issue on a 1 for 2 basis.

F RF may have paid a dividend to shareholders in 20X8.

21.7 An entity wishes to increase its return on capital employed (ROCE).

Which of the following courses of action will help to achieve this in the short term?

A Increase sales

B Restructure its long term finance exchanging debt for equity

C Issue ordinary shares

D Revalue land and buildings upwards

21.8 An analyst is comparing the non-current asset turnover ratios of two listed businesses engaged in similar activities. The non-current asset turnover ratio of one entity is almost 50% higher than that of the other entity, and she concludes that the entity with the higher non-current asset turnover ratio is utilizing its assets far more effectively.

Which THREE of the following suggest this conclusion might not be valid?

A   One entity revalues its properties and the other entity holds its assets under the historical cost model

B   One entity buys its assets for cash and the other entity buys the assets under finance leases

C   One entity has assets nearing the end of their useful life whilst the other entity has recently acquired new assets

D   One entity depreciates its assets over a much shorter useful life than the other entity

E   One entity pays a higher rate of interest on their borrowings than the other

F   One entity has significantly higher gearing than the other

21.9 An individual is considering acquiring a small shareholding in LP, an entity listed on the stock market. He has performed some limited analysis on the financial statements of LP but is concerned that its high gearing renders the entity a high risk investment.

Which THREE of the following options would be considered realistic next steps for the individual to take prior to investing?

A   Request copies of the board minutes for the month that new long term loan finance was secured.

B   Access the entities P/E ratio from the financial press and compare this with other entities in the sector to assess the market's view of the risk of LP.

C   Contact the Chief Financial Officer and clarify whether these funds were invested in the business and likely to bring future increased profits.

D   Review the narrative reports within the financial statements that give details of recent investment and related financing to assess if the business is undergoing expansion and likely to bring additional future returns.

E   Review the financial report to establish the dividend per share paid over the last few years and to identify whether increased gearing has negatively impacted on investor returns.

F   Request copies of forecasts to assess expected future performance.

21.10 LOP operates in the construction industry and prepares its financial statements in accordance with IFRS. It is listed on its local exchange. LOP is looking to expand its overseas operations by acquiring a new subsidiary. Two geographical areas have been targeted, Frontland and Sideland. Entity A operates in Frontland and entity B operates in Sideland. Both entities are listed on their local exchanges.

The financial highlights for entities A, B and LOP are provided below for the last trading period.

	A	B	LOP
Revenue	$160m	$300m	$500m
Gross profit margin	26%	17%	28%
Net profit	9%	11%	16%
Gearing	65%	30%	38%
P/E ratio	11.6	15.9	16.3

Which **THREE** of the following statements would be reasonable conclusions to draw regarding the **FINANCIAL PERFORMANCE** of the three entities?

A   Entity B is operating its core activities better than entity A but acquisition of either would cause LOP's gross margin to fall.

B   Entity B is controlling its overheads better than entity A but acquisition of either would cause LOP's net profit margin to fall.

C   The market confidence in the future of LOP is greater than in either of the two targets.

D   Entity A is the riskiest target because is has the highest gearing.

E   Acquisition of both entity A and entity B would cause LOP's gross and net margins to fall.

F   Entity B is almost double the size of entity A.

22 Analysis of financial performance and position IV

22.1   **Which ONE of the following is most likely to increase an entity's working capital?**

A   Delaying payment to trade payables
B   Reducing the credit period given to customers
C   Purchasing inventory on credit
D   Paying a supplier and taking an early settlement discount

22.2   **Which TWO of the following are valid reasons why the inventory days of a company might increase from year to year?**

A   A marketing decision to reduce selling prices
B   Increased inventory obsolescence
C   Slow down in trading
D   Seasonal fluctuations in sales orders
E   Changing a key supplier

22.3   TR has an operating profit margin of 8% in 20X9 compared with 5% in 20X8.

Which of the following might explain this increase?

A   TR increased its sales during the year, by offering better discounts to its customers.

B   TR moved to an out-of-town office location where rent and employment costs were lower than they were in 20X8.

C   Year end market research focused on public awareness of the company's product range indicates that the brands contained in closing inventory are more likely to sell this year than last.

D   TR restructured its long term finance during 20X9, managing to reduce its finance cost.

22.4   GH's current ratio was 1.4:1 in 20X9 compared with 1.2:1 in 20X8.

Which TWO of the following might explain the increase?

A   GH paid its payables earlier than usual by making use of its bank overdraft facility
B   GH bought a lot of goods for cash just before the year end, and these remained in inventory
C   GH made an unusually large sale just before the year end
D   GH paid its payables earlier than usual, because it had a positive cash balance

BPP
LEARNING MEDIA

22.5   SK's return on capital employed has worsened in 20X9 in comparison with 20X8.

The Finance Director has at various points espoused all of the following as possible explanations for this.

Which THREE of the following are valid?

A   Towards the end of 20X9, major investments were made in plant and machinery that were financed by borrowing.

B   SK converted $10m 10% loan notes into $10m share capital halfway through 20X9.

C   Asset turnover has increased in comparison with the prior year.

D   In line with IAS 16, SK revalued its properties, resulting in a significant increase in their carrying value.

E   SK issued $5m loan notes to redeem $5m redeemable preference shares (at par).

F   Asset turnover is down in comparison with 20X8.

22.6   LOP operates in the construction industry and prepares its financial statements in accordance with IFRS. It is listed on its local exchange. LOP is looking to expand its overseas operations by acquiring a new subsidiary. Two geographical areas have been targeted, Frontland and Sideland. Entity A operates in Frontland and entity B operates in Sideland. Both entities are listed on their local exchanges.

The financial highlights for entities A, B and LOP are provided below for the last trading period.

	A	B	LOP
Revenue	$160m	$300m	$500m
Gross profit margin	26%	17%	28%
Net profit	9%	11%	16%
Gearing	65%	30%	38%
P/E ratio	11.6	15.9	16.3

Complete the following sentence advising the management of LOP which of the targets would make the better investment by writing in the correct narrative from the list provided. (Do not use each word more than once).

Entity [   ] would make the better investment as it has the [   ] net profit margin, is [   ] risky and the market has greater confidence in its [   ].

Picklist of narratives

A
B
better
worse
more
less
future
past

22.7   LOP operates in the construction industry and prepares its financial statements in accordance with IFRS. It is listed on its local exchange. LOP is looking to expand its overseas operations by acquiring a new subsidiary. Two geographical areas have been targeted, Frontland and Sideland. Entity A operates in Frontland and entity B operates in Sideland. Both entities are listed on their local exchanges.

The financial highlights for entities A, B and LOP are provided below for the last trading period.

	A	B	LOP
Revenue	$160m	$300m	$500m
Gross profit margin	26%	17%	28%
Net profit	9%	11%	16%
Gearing	65%	30%	38%
P/E ratio	11.6	15.9	16.3

Which **THREE** of the following would qualify as potential limitations in using this type of analysis to decide on a potential takeover target?

A   Entity A and B may have different accounting policies causing lack of comparability between their ratios.

B   The indicators only cover profitability and gearing. There are no measures of efficiency or liquidity, both of which are very important for an entity's survival.

C   All of the indicators relate to past performance yet future prospects should also be considered.

D   Entity A and B operate in different geographical areas which will impact tax rates, interest rates and share prices and cause lack of comparability.

E   LOP is a potential investor yet no investor ratios have been calculated.

F   All three entities operate in different business sectors.

22.8   The following information is available for 2 potential acquisition targets. The entities have similar capital structures and both operate in the retail sector.

	AB	*CD*
Revenue	$220m	$240m
Gross profit margin	12%	21%
Profit for the year/revenue margin	6%	7%

Which of the following statements is a realistic conclusion that can be drawn from the above information?

A   CD operates at the luxury end of the market and is able to charge a higher price for its goods sold compared to AB.

B   CD's management exercises greater control of the entity's overheads than AB's management.

C   AB has a supplier that grants a significant discount on the goods purchased for resale.

D   CD has access to cheaper interest rates on its borrowings than AB.

22.9   **Which ONE of the following ratios would be the LEAST appropriate to calculate for a supermarket?**

A   Gross margin
B   Receivable days
C   Payable days
D   Return on capital employed

22.10 Statement of financial position (extract):

	$m
Property, plant and equipment	10 ← low
Inventories and work in progress	120 ← high
Trade receivables	35
Cash	2
	167
Trade payables	(30)
Borrowings	(50)
Net assets	87

The above statement of financial statement is likely to relate to an entity operating in which one of the following industries?

A   Insurance broker
B   Retail store
C   Investment in properties for rental
D   Construction

23 Analysis of financial performance and position V

23.1 LM is a listed company whose 5 million issued ordinary shares each have a par value of 20c. Its share capital did not change during the year, and its results for the year were as follows:

	$000
Profit before tax	500
Tax	(100)
Profit for the year	400
Dividends paid	(150)
Retained profit	250

LM's shares are quoted at $1.50 at the year end.

What was LM's year end P/E ratio?

A   15

B   19

C   30

D   50

23.2 The following is an extract from the statement of cash flows of QW for the year ended 31 December 20X1:

	$m
Cash flows from operating activities	600
Cash flows from investing activities	(800)
Cash flows from financing activities	(200)
Net decrease in cash and cash equivalents	(400)
Cash and cash equivalents at the beginning of the period	100
Cash and cash equivalents at the end of the period	(300)

Based on the information provided, which ONE of the following independent statements would be a realistic conclusion about the financial adaptability of QW for the year ended 31 December 20X1?

A   The failure of QW to raise long term finance to fund its investing activities has resulted in a deterioration of QW's financial adaptability and liquidity.

B   QW must be in decline as there is a negative cash flow relating to investing activities.

C   The management of QW has shown competent stewardship of the entity's resources by relying on an overdraft to fund the excess outflow on investing activities not covered by the inflow from operating activities.

D   The working capital management of QW has deteriorated year on year.

23.3 **Complete the formulae used to calculate return on capital employed and operating profit margin, by writing in the correct narratives from the list provided.**

Return on capital employed   *Operating profit margin*

┌──────────────┐   ┌──────────────┐
│   │   │   │
└──────────────┘   └──────────────┘
┌──────────────┐   ┌──────────────┐
│   │   │   │
└──────────────┘   └──────────────┘

Picklist for narratives

Profit before interest and tax

Equity

Cost of sales

Profit for the year

Revenue

Profit before tax

Equity + Debt − Investments

Equity + Debt

23.4 BC has a current ratio of 1.5:1. It decides to use surplus cash balances to settle 30% of its total current liabilities.

The current ratio will...

A   Decrease by more than 30%
B   Decrease by less than 30%
C   Increase by more than 30%
D   Increase by less than 30%

23.5 Information from the statement of financial position of MNO has been expressed as percentages of total assets less current liabilities:

	%
Land and property	78
Other non-current assets	19
Inventories and work in progress	–
Trade receivables	459
Cash/short term investments	89
	645
Bank overdraft	(5)
Trade payables	(540)
Total assets less current liabilities	100

In which of the following industries could MNO be operating?

A   Housebuilding
B   Insurance broking
C   Manufacturing
D   Retailing

23.6 The following information relates to GF for the year ended 31 December 20X2:

Earnings per share	32 cents
Share price	$3.90
Dividends	£10 million
Number of ordinary 50 cent shares	100 million

DIV YIELD = DIV / MV.
0.10 / 3.90
= 0.0256.

Calculate the dividend yield to 1 decimal place.

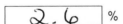 2.6   %

23.7 The following is an extract from the statement of financial position of WR:

Equity	$m
Share capital ($1 shares)	30
Share premium	10
Revaluation reserve	20
Retained earnings	160
	220
Non-controlling interest	24
Total equity	244
Non-current liabilities	
Long term borrowings	100
Redeemable preference shares	40
Deferred tax	16
Total non-current liabilities	156

Giving your answer to one decimal place, the gearing ratio (calculated as debt/equity) for WR is:

23.8 An extract from KER's statement of financial position is shown below:

	$m
Current assets	
Inventories	145
Receivables	247
Cash and cash equivalents	50
Non-current liabilities	
Loans	400
Current liabilities	
Payables	99
Overdraft	37

What are KER's current and quick ratios?

	Current ratio	*Quick ratio*
A	3.25	2.88
B	4.46	3.96
C	0.82	0.73
D	2.88	3.25

23.9 **Which ratio does the following statement relate to?**

'This ratio is a measure of the market's confidence in the future of an entity.'

A   Dividend yield
B   Earnings per share
C   Return on capital employed
D   P/E ratio

23.10 XX has the following working capital ratios:

	20X9	20X8
Current ratio	1.2	1.5
Receivables days	75 days	50 days
Payables days	30 days	45 days
Inventory days	42 days	35 days

Which ONE of the following statements is correct?

A   XX's liquidity and working capital has improved in 20X9.
B   XX is receiving cash more quickly from customers in 20X9 than in 20X8.
C   XX is suffering from a worsening liquidity situation in 20X9.
D   XX is taking longer to pay suppliers in 20X9 than in 20X8.

24 Analysis of financial performance and position VI

24.1   BC has 400 million $1 ordinary shares in issue. BC paid an ordinary dividend of $80 million in respect of the year ended 31 December 20X3 and reported earnings per share (EPS) of 24 cents per share. The share price of BC was $2.62 on 31 December 20X3.

Calculate the price/earnings (P/E) ratio for BC at December 20X3.

Give your answer to one decimal place. [   ]

24.2   ST, UV and WX are listed entities operating in the same business sector. At 31 October 20X6, their P/E ratios were reported as follows:

ST 16.2

UV 12.7

WX 8.4

Which ONE of the following statements about these P/E ratios is correct?

The P/E ratios suggest that:

A   ST is regarded by the market as the riskiest of the three entities.

B   ST has the highest earnings per share of the three entities.

C   UV represents the safest investment because its P/E lies approximately midway between the other two.

D   WX's share price may be relatively lower than that of ST and UV because of an adverse effect such as a profit warning.

24.3   **What would be the immediate effect on an entity's P/E ratio and dividend yield of an announcement which caused a substantial rise in the share price?**

A   *P/E ratio*   *Dividend yield*
        Decrease   Decrease

B   *P/E ratio*   *Dividend yield*
        Decrease   Increase

C   *P/E ratio*   *Dividend yield*
        Increase   Decrease

D   *P/E ratio*   *Dividend yield*
        Increase   Increase

24.4   The Return of Capital Employed (ROCE) for JT has reduced from 22.6% to 14.4% in the year to 31 December 20X3.

Which THREE of the following independent options would be a valid reason for this reduction?

A X Increase in the average interest rate payable on existing borrowings
B ✓ Increase in payroll costs due to staff bonuses — reduce PBIT
C ✓ Major investment in property, plant and equipment shortly before the year end. — inc TALCL
D X A large tax bill accrued in the year end accounts
E ✓ A revaluation of property in the year resulting in a significant uplift in value — inc TALCL.
F X Repayment of a long term bond during the year.

ROCE ↓   PBIT ↓ or TALCL ↑.

24.5   Z Co's extract financial statements for the year ended 31 December 20X3 are as follows:

Extract statement of profit or loss of Z for the year ended 31 Dec 20X3	$m
Gross profit	320
Operating expenses	(184)
	136
Finance costs	(42)
Profit before tax	94

Extract statement of financial position of Z as at 31 Dec 20X3	$m
Non-current liabilities:	
Borrowings	310
Deferred tax	30
	340

The interest cover (to two decimal places) for Z for the year to 31 December 20X3 is:

$$\boxed{3.24} \qquad 136/42 = 3.238$$

24.6   **Which ONE of the following statements is true?**

A   The interpretation of an entity's financial statements using ratios is only useful for potential investors.

B   Ratios based on historical data always predict the future performance of an entity.

C   The analysis of financial statements using ratios provides useful information when compared with previous performance or industry averages.

D   An entity's management will not assess an entity's performance using financial ratios.

24.7   The following are extracts from GH's financial statements:

	$'000
Profit before interest and tax	10,200
Finance costs	(1,600)
Income tax expense	(3,300)
Profit for the year	5,300
Share capital	20,000
Reserves	15,600
	35,600
Loan liability	6,900
	42,500

What is GH's return on capital employed (to the nearest %)?

$\rule{3cm}{0.4pt}$ %

24.8   AB prepares its financial statements in accordance with international financial reporting standards and is listed on its local stock exchange. AB is considering the acquisition of overseas operations. Two geographical areas have been targeted, S-land and Y-land. Entity S operates in S-land and entity Y operates in Y-land. Each entity is listed on its local stock exchange and uses its local accounting standards.

The most recent financial statements of entities S and Y have been converted into AB's currency for ease of comparison. The financial indicators from these financial statements and those of AB are provided below.

	AB	S	Y
Revenue	$500m	$220m	$380
Gross profit margin	27%	33%	17%
Profit for year/revenue × 100	15%	11%	12%
Gearing	29%	60%	30%
Average rate of interest available to each entity in the last 12 months	7%	4%	9%
P/E ratio	15.9	9.3	14.5

Which ONE of the following statements is a realistic conclusion that could be drawn from the above information?

A   Y's management is less efficient at controlling administrative expenses than S's management. *– cannot tell*

B   Y's management appears to have secured better supplier discounts than either of the other two entities. *– higher GP.*

C✓   S is less likely to be benefiting from economies of scale. *– lowest Rev..*

D   S-land has a lower tax rate than Y-land. *– cannot tell.*

24.9   AB prepares its financial statements in accordance with international financial reporting standards and is listed on its local stock exchange. AB is considering the acquisition of overseas operations. Two geographical areas have been targeted, S-land and Y-land. Entity S operates in S-land and entity Y operates in Y-land. Each entity is listed on its local stock exchange and uses its local accounting standards.

The most recent financial statements of entities S and Y have been converted into AB's currency for ease of comparison. The financial indicators from these financial statements and those of AB are provided below.

	AB	S	Y
Revenue	$500m	$220m	$380m
Gross profit margin	27%	33%	17%
Profit for year/revenue × 100	15%	11%	12%
Gearing	29%	60%	30%
Average rate of interest available to each entity in the last 12 months	7%	4%	9%
P/E ratio	15.9	9.3	14.5

Which THREE of the following statements are true, based on just the information provided?

A   Y would be the riskier investment for AB because it has a higher P/E ratio. ✗

B   S's high gearing is likely to be a deliberate strategy to take advantage of low borrowing rates. ?

C   S would be the riskier investment for AB because it has high gearing. ✓

D   The market is more confident about the future performance of S than of Y. ✗

E   AB's P/E ratio would definitely fall if it acquired either S or Y. ✗ *– relative weightings.*

F   Y would give AB greater benefit in terms of additional borrowing capacity. ✓

24.10   AB prepares its financial statements in accordance with international financial reporting standards and is listed on its local stock exchange. AB is considering the acquisition of overseas operations. Two geographical areas have been targeted, S-land and Y-land. Entity S operates in S-land and entity Y operates in Y-land. Each entity is listed on its local stock exchange and uses it local accounting standards.

The most recent financial statements of entities S and Y have been converted into AB's currency for ease of comparison. The financial indicators from these financial statements and those of AB are provided below.

	AB	S	Y
Revenue	$500m	$220m	$380m
Gross profit margin	27%	33%	17%
Profit for year/revenue × 100	15%	11%	12%
Gearing	29%	60%	30%
Average rate of interest available to each entity in the last 12 months	7%	4%	9%
P/E ratio	15.9	9.3	14.5

Which ONE of the following statements concerning the use of ratio analysis to make a decision about investing in S or Y is false?

A   S and Y are listed on different stock exchanges which reduces comparability of their P/E ratios.

B   S and Y may be subject to different tax rates which would reduce the comparability of their operating profit margins.

C   S and Y incur different levels of finance costs which reduces comparability of their P/E ratios.

D   S and Y apply different accounting standards in the preparation of their financial statements which reduces the comparability of their gearing ratios.

25 Mixed Bank 1

25.1   **Which THREE of the following are characteristics of non-cumulative preference shares?**

      A   They rank before ordinary shares in the event of liquidation.
      B   They carry limited voting rights where dividends are in arrears.
      C   If the entity makes higher profits than expected, the dividend will not rise.
      D   Arrears have to be paid before ordinary dividends can be paid.
      E   The entity cannot claim tax relief on the dividends paid.

25.2   UH issued a $4 million 6% convertible bond on 1 January 20X4 at its nominal value. In 5 years' time the bond is redeemable at par or can be converted into equity shares. The prevailing market rate at 1 January 20X4 for a similar bond without conversion rights is 9% per annum. Its has been established that the present value of the principal and interest cash flows associated with the bond is $3,689,000 using 9% as a discount rate.

      The value that will be credited to equity on the issue of this instrument (to the nearest $) is:

      $ [   ]

25.3   V rents a building under a non cancellable operating lease, but vacates the building shortly before the year end. The building can not be sub let, the annual rental is $12,000 and the remaining term on the lease is 5 years.

      Which THREE of the following statements are correct?

      A   V has a present obligation.

      B   V must disclose a contingent liability.

      C   The annual rents will be recorded in the statement of profit or loss over the next five years at $12,000 per year.

      D   A provision for $60,000 should be created.

      E   V should do nothing.

      F   It is not likely that payments will need to be made in the future.

      G   V will incur an expense of $60,000 in the profit or loss for the current year.

25.4 TY grants 150 share appreciation rights to a director on 1 January 20X6 provided they continue to work for TY until 31 December 20X8. The fair value of the rights are as follows:

31 Dec 20X6 $4.50
31 Dec 20X7 $4.20
31 Dec 20X8 $5.10

How much should be included in the statement of profit or loss for the year ended 31 December 20X8?

A $225
B $420
C $345
D $765

25.5 Jennifer holds an 80% interest in the share capital of Juniper.

During the year Juniper sold goods to Jennifer for $30,000, including a mark-up of 25%. Half the goods remain in inventory at the year end.

Extracts from the companies' statements of profit or loss are as follows:

	Jennifer	Juniper
	$	$
Revenue	250,000	180,000

What is the amount to be included in the consolidated statement of profit or loss for revenue?

A $400,000
B $415,000
C $406,000
D $418,000

25.6 TG disposed of 70% of the equity shares of one of its wholly owned subsidiaries, DR, on 1 November 20X8.

Which THREE of the following statements are true in respect of the preparation of the group financial statements of TG for the year to 31 December 20X8?

A   The consolidated statement of financial position will no longer include 100% of the asset and liabilities of DR.

B   The consolidated profit or loss will include its share of the associate, DR, from 1 November 20X8.

C   Goodwill arising on the acquisition of DR will remain in the consolidated statement of financial position as TG continues to have influence over DR.

D   The consolidated profit or loss will include non-controlling interest of 30% for the first 10 months of the year.

E   A gain or loss on the deemed disposal of DR will be included in consolidated profit for the year.

F   There will be a deemed disposal of DR and a gain or loss on the disposal will be included in other comprehensive income.

25.7 CXP owns 75% of the ordinary share capital of its subsidiary, DYQ. The shares were acquired on 1 November 20X5 when DYQ's reserves stood at $152,000. DYQ acquired a 65% investment in its subsidiary, EZR, on 1 May 20X5. EZR's reserves were $190,000 on 1 May 20X5, and $202,000 on 1 November 20X5.

Reserves for the three entities at 31 October 20X6, the entities' year end, were as follows:

CXP $266,000

DYQ $178,000

EZR $214,000

There had been no impairment of goodwill in respect of either investment since acquisition.

What is the balance of consolidated reserves for inclusion in the consolidated statement of financial position of the CXP group at 31 October 20X6?

A $301,100
B $297,200
C $291,350
D $293,300

25.8   ST acquired 80% of the 250,000 $1 ordinary shares of UV on 1 May 20X1.

On 1 October 20X4 ST disposed of 20,000 $1 ordinary shares of UV for $115,000. The non-controlling interests on 1 October 20X4 prior to the disposal amounted to $180,000.

Complete the working for the disposal of the shares in UV in the consolidated statement of changes in equity for the ST Group for the year ended 31 December 20X4, by writing in the correct numbers (to the nearest thousand) or use 'BLANK' as appropriate.

Extract from the consolidated statement of changes in equity for ST Group for the year ended 31 December 20X4

	Attributable to owners of the parent	Non-controlling interest
	$000	$000
Balance at the start of the year	X	X
Total comprehensive income for the year	X	X
Dividends paid	(X)	(X)
Adjustment to NCI for sale of shares in UV		
Adjustment to parent's equity for sale of UV shares		
Balance at the end of the year	X	X

25.9   **Which THREE of the following would not normally be treated as a related party of HJ in accordance with IAS 24 *Related party disclosures*?**

A   KL – an entity in which the controlling shareholder of HJ has a 30% shareholding and significant influence

B   MN – both HJ and MN are associates of the same parent company

C   Mr Smith – the domestic partner of Ms Wilson who is a director of HJ

D   WX - the defined benefit pension plan for the employees of HJ

E   Ms Green - the secretary to the chief executive officer at HJ

F   The trade union to which the majority of HJ's employees belong

---

25.10   Analysis of the statement of financial position of CD for the year ended 20X9 reveals the following relationships:

Current ratio	2:1
Revenue: current assets	5:1
Acid-test ratio	1:5:1

If revenue for the year was $30 million, what is the value of inventory that will appear in the statement of financial position?

A $1.5m
B $3.0m
C $4.5m
D $10.5m

26 Mixed Bank 2

26.1 **Which TWO of the following are most likely to be associated with a share issue that is required in order to finance an investment a long-term construction project?**

    A   Underwriters are paid a fee for guaranteeing that the shares will be purchased.

    B   Lower gearing.

    C   Finance can be raised more quickly than an equivalent bank loan.

    D   Higher interest cover.

26.2 On 1 January 20X3, an entity issued a debt instrument with a coupon rate of 3.5% at a par value of $6,000,000. The directly attributable costs of issue were $120,000. The debt instrument is repayable on 31 December 20X9 at a premium of $1,100,000. The effective interest rate is 6%.

The entity accounted for the proceeds and issue costs correctly on 1 January 20X3 and recorded the interest paid in profit or loss on 31 December 20X3.

What is the accounting entry to correct the amount recognised as a finance cost in profit or loss in relation to this debt for the year ended 31 December 20X3?

    A   Dr Finance costs $150,000
            Cr Financial liability $150,000

    B   Dr Finance costs $352,800
            Cr Bank $352,800

    C   Dr Bank $210,000
            Cr Finance costs $210,000

    D   Dr Finance costs $142,800
            Cr Financial liability $142,800

26.3 **Which THREE of the following statements about IAS 37 *Provisions, contingent liabilities and contingent assets* are correct?**

    A   Provisions should be made for constructive obligations (those arising from a company's pattern of past practice) as well as for obligations enforceable by law.

    B   Discounting may be used when estimating the amount of a provision if the effect is material.

    C   A restructuring provision must include the estimated costs of retraining or relocating continuing staff.

    D   A restructuring provision may only be made when a company has a detailed plan for the reconstruction and a firm intention to carry it out.

    E   For onerous contracts, a provision should be made at the higher of the cost of fulfilling the contract and penalties from failure to fulfill the contract.

    F   Contingent assets should be recognised in the statement of financial position when an inflow of economic benefits is probable.

26.4 YY provides its employees with 10 share options on 1 January 20X5, but the options do not vest until 31 December 20X6. The employees must remain employed by YY to be entitled to the options.

The fair value of the options on the grant date is $18 and there are 1,200 employees of YY at 1 January 20X5. All of the employees are still employed at the end of December 20X5, but only 90% are still employed at 31 December 20X6.

What is the journal to record the share based payment in the year ended 31 December 20X6?

A Dr Staff costs $194,400
  Cr Other components of equity $194,400

B Dr Staff costs $86,400
  Cr Other components of equity $86,400

C Dr Staff costs $108,000
  Cr Other components of equity $108,000

D Dr Staff costs $194,400
  Cr Liability $194,400

26.5 On 31 May 20X8, DNT purchased 175,000 of BL's 250,000 $1 ordinary shares for $700,000. At 1 September 20X7, BL's retained earnings were $650,000 (there were no other reserves). During the year ended 31 August 20X8, BL made a profit for the year of $40,000. It can be assumed that BL's revenue and expenses accrue evenly throughout the year.

It is the group policy to value non-controlling interests at fair value at the date of acquisition. The fair value of the non-controlling interest at 31 May 20X8 was $262,500.

Calculate the amount of the non-controlling interest for inclusion in DNT's group statement of financial position at 31 August 20X8.

$ [   ]

26.6 AMY, an entity with a 30 September year end, holds several investments in subsidiaries. On 1 April 20X6, it disposed of 10,000 of its 40,000 $1 shares in its subsidiary BNZ for $95,000. AMY had acquired the shares, which represented 80% of BNZ's ordinary share capital, on 1 April 20X4 for $250,000, when BNZ's reserves totaled $186,000. BNZ's net assets at the date of disposal were $275,000. It is group policy to measure non-controlling interests at acquisition at the proportionate share of the net assets. Since acquisition, there has been no impairment of goodwill.

Which of the following correctly describes the accounting treatment for the investment in BNZ in the consolidated financial statements of AMY for the year ended 30 September 20X6?

	Consolidated statement of profit or loss and other comprehensive income	**Consolidated statement of financial position**
A	Consolidate for 6 months; equity account for 6 months Record a profit on disposal of $40,000	Equity account
B	Consolidate for a full year and pro-rate non-controlling interests	Consolidate assets and liabilities Reduce non-controlling interests by $55,000 Record an adjustment to equity of $40,000 in consolidated retained earnings
C	Consolidate for a full year and pro-rate non-controlling interests Record a profit on disposal of $24,700	Consolidated assets and liabilities
D	Consolidate for 6 months Record a profit on disposal of $40,000	Exclude from consolidation

26.7 The following transactions have occurred in the XC group:

Shares purchased by	Shares purchased in	No of shares purchased	Date of purchase	Consideration paid
XC	F	60,000 out of 100,000	31 July 20X5	750,000
XC	G	24,000 out of 150,000	31 Sept 20X7	25,000
F	G	90,000 out of 150,000	31 Sept 20X7	450,000

Which THREE of the following statements correctly describes the group?

A XC is the parent
B The NCI in G is 48%
C XC has control of both F and G
D F is the sub-subsidiary
E The NCI in F is 36%
F XC has control of F but not of G

26.8 BC acquired 90% of DE's 100,000 $1 shares on 1 January 20X4 when DE's reserves were $90,000. It is group policy to measure non-controlling interests at fair value at acquisition. The fair value of one share in DE on 1 January 20X4 was $2.20.

DE's total comprehensive income for the year ended 31 December 20X4 of the year was $25,000. DE paid dividends of $5,000 during the year.

Write in the figures required to complete the non-controlling interests column in the consolidated statement of changes in equity for the BC group for the year ended 31 December 20X4.

EXTRACT FROM THE CONSOLIDATED STATEMENT OF CHANGES IN EQUITY OF THE BC GROUP FOR THE YEAR ENDED 31 DECEMBER 20X4

	Non-controlling interests $
Balance at 1 January 20X4	
Total comprehensive income for the year	
Dividends paid	
Balance at 31 December 20X4	

26.9 **Which one of the following would be regarded as a related party transaction of the entity NV?**

A A close family member of the Chief Executive of NV purchased an asset from NV.
B XYZ Bank lent NV $100,000 on commercial loan terms.
C The government of Country X awarded NV a grant of $25,000 to help fund a new production facility.
D YU supplied 60% of NV's raw materials.

26.10 EP has the following balances under current assets and current liabilities.

Current assets
Inventory $50,000
Trade receivables $70,000
Cash $10,000

Current liabilities
Trade payables $88,000
Interest payable $7,000

What is EP's quick ratio?

A   0.80:1
B   0.84:1
C   0.91:1
D.   1.37:1

27 Mixed Bank 3

27.1   **Complete the following statement by writing in the correct narratives from the list provided:**

A bond will normally be issued at the [_____] and redeemed at the [_____]. Bonds are normally [_____] and the interest payments will often be [_____] an equivalent bank loan because of their marketability.

Picklist for narratives

redeemable
irredeemable
convertible
more than
less than
the same as
market price
nominal value

27.2   PS issued 1,000,000 $1 cumulative, redeemable preferred shares on 1 April 20X8. The shares were issued at a premium of 25% and pay a dividend of 4% per year.

The issue costs incurred were $60,000. The shares are redeemable for cash of $1.50 on 31 March 20Y8. The effective interest rate is 5.18%. Ignore all tax implications.

The management accountant of PS has extracted the following amounts from the preferred shares ledger account, for the year ended 31 March 20X9:

Account Preferred shares	$
Net amount received on issue	1,190,000
Finance cost @5.18%	61,642
Less dividend paid	40,000
Balance at 31 March 20X9	1,211,642

Complete the pro forma below by writing in the correct amounts and headings (or use 'BLANK' as relevant) to be recorded in the financial statements of PS for the year ended 31 March 20X9 in related to these preferred shares.

	Statement of financial position	Statement of profit or loss and other comprehensive income	Statement of changes in equity
Heading	[ ]	[ ]	[ ]
Amount (in$)	[ ]	[ ]	[ ]

27.3 DH has the following two legal claims outstanding:

- A legal action against DH claiming compensation of $700,000, filed in February 20X7. DH has been advised that it is probable that the liability will materialise.

- A legal action taken by DH against another entity, claiming damages of $300,000, started in March 20X4. DH has been advised that it is probable that it will win the case.

How should DH report these legal actions in its financial statements for the year ended 30 April 20X7?

A   *Legal action against DH*   *Legal action taken by DH*
          Disclose by a note to the accounts   No disclosure

B   *Legal action against DH*   *Legal action taken by DH*
          Make a provision   No disclosure

C   *Legal action against DH*   *Legal action taken by DH*
          Make a provision   Disclose as a note

D   *Legal action against DH*   *Legal action taken by DH*
          Make a provision   Accrue the income

27.4 On 1 January 20X8 PP grants 120 share appreciation rights to each of its 900 staff when the fair value of the rights were $9.50. The employees must remain in PP's employment for a further three years. The rights had a fair value of $9.90 at 31 December 20X8, $10.30 at 31 December 20X9 and $11.00 at 31 December 20Y0.

The journal to reflect the transaction in 20X8 will be:

Complete the table by writing in the correct account references and amounts.

	Account reference	$
Dr		
Cr		

27.5 On 31 May 20X8, DNT purchased 175,000 of BL's 250,000 $1 ordinary shares for $700,000. At 1 September 20X7, BL's retained earnings were $650,000 (there were no other reserves). During the year ended 31 August 20X8, BL made a profit for the year of $40,000. It can be assumed that BL's revenue and expenses accrue evenly throughout the year.

It is the group policy to value non-controlling interests at fair value at the date of acquisition. The fair value of the non-controlling interest at 31 May 20X8 was $262,500.

Calculate the goodwill that arose on the acquisition.

$ [   ]

27.6 KK acquired an 18% investment in GG on 1 January 20X7 for $150,000. The fair value of this investment at 1 July 20X8 is $340,000.

On 1 July 20X8 KK acquired an additional 60% of the 500,000 $1 shares of GG for $670,000. The retained earnings of GG were $280,000 on 1 January 20X8 and the profits for the year to 31 December 20X8 were $95,000. The group policy is to measure non controlling interests at the proportionate share of net assets.

How much is the profit on de-recognition of the original 18% investment recorded in the consolidated statement of profit or loss and other comprehensive income 31 December 20X8?

A $88,800
B $190,000
C $228,000
D $330,000

27.7 PH acquired 75,000 of the 100,000 $1 ordinary shares JG for $480,000 on 1 January 20X4. JG acquired 64,000 of the 80,000 $1 ordinary shares in TR for $320,000 on 1 January 20X5.

Extracts from the statements of profit or loss for PH, JG and TR for the year ended 31 December 20X8 are:

	PH	JG	TR
	$'000	$'000	$'000
Profit for the year	650	725	450

PH elected to measure the non-controlling interest in JG and TR at acquisition at fair value.

During 20X8 PH impaired the goodwill in JG by $25,000.

The non controlling interest in the consolidated statement of profit or loss for the year ended 31 December 20X8 is:

$ _____

27.8 P acquired 80% of S on 1 January 20X4 for $20 million when its retained earnings were $12.3 million.

P acquired 30% of A on 1 January 20X6 for $1.9 million when its retained earnings were $3 million.

During the year ended 31 December 20X7, S sold goods to P which cost $1,000,000 for $1,400,000. Three quarters of these goods had been sold to third parties by the year end.

Equity at 31 December 20X7 of the three entities comprises:

	P	S	A
	$'000	$'000	$'000
Share capital	2,900	1,500	1,000
Retained earnings	78,200	38,500	16,000
	81,100	40,000	17,000

What is the equity attributable to the owners of the parent as at 31 December 20X7 for inclusion in the consolidated statement of changes in equity of the P group?

A $102,980,000
B $105,240,000
C $105,860,000
D $105,880,000
E $108,380,000

27.9 Key figures from a company's statement of profit or loss for the year ended 31 December 20X2 include:

	$
Profit before tax	1,000,000
Tax	200,000
Non-controlling interests	100,000
Preference dividend	20,000
Ordinary dividend	55,000

The weighted average number of shares were 1,278,376.

What is the EPS for the year ended 31 December 20X2?

A 62.5c
B 54.8c
C 53.2c
D 48.9c

27.10 The table below shows some extracts from the financial statements of CD for the year ended 31 October 20X9.

Statement of financial position		Statement of profit and loss and other comprehensive income	
	$'000		$'000
Issued share capital	2,200	Profit before tax	450
Retained earnings	1,850	Finance Cost	(80)
	4,050	Net Profit	370
9% Long term loan	800		
	4,850		

What is CD's return on capital employed?

A   7.6%

B   9.1%

C   9.3%

D   11.0%

28 Mixed Bank 4

28.1 **Complete the following sentence below by writing in the correct narrative from the list provided:**

Investors in preference shares require a [   ] level of return than ordinary shareholders because they face less [   ] over the level of their return, and therefore face [   ] risk.

Picklist for narratives

less
more
higher
lower
certainty
uncertainty

28.2 A acquired 10% of B by purchasing 40,000 ordinary shares on 1 January 20X2 for $2.12 per share. Transaction costs of 3% were paid to a broker on the acquisition date. The investment was classified as available for sale on recognition. At the year end (31 March 20X2) the shares were trading at $2.43.

What amounts should be included in the statement of profit or loss and other comprehensive income for the year ended 31 March 20X2?

A   Expense to profit or loss $2,544, Gain to OCI $9,856.

B   Gain to OCI $9,856.

C   Expense to profit or loss $2,544, Gain to OCI $12,400.

D   Gain to profit or loss $9,856.

28.3 **In which of the following circumstances would a provision be recognised under IAS 37 *Provisions, contingent liabilities and contingent assets* in the financial statements for the year ending 31 March 20X6?**

I   A board decision was made on 15 March to close down a division with potential costs of $100,000. At 31 March the decision had not been communicated to managers, employees or customers.

II There are anticipated costs from returns of a defective product in the next few months of $60,000. In the past all returns of defective products have always been refunded to customers.

III It is anticipated that a major refurbishment of the company Head Office will take place from June onwards costing $85,000.

A   I and II only
B   II and III only
C   II only
D   III only

28.4 **Which of the following is the correct formulae for calculating the year end balance in equity for an equity settled transaction?**

A	Estimated no. of employees entitled to benefits	×	No. of instruments per employee	×	FV per instrument at year end	×	Proportion of vesting period elapsed at year end
B	Estimated no. of employees entitled to benefits	×	No. of instruments per employee	×	FV per instrument at grant date	×	Proportion of vesting period elapsed at year end
C	Estimated no. of employees entitled to benefits	×	No. of instruments per employee	×	FV per instrument at grant date	×	Proportion of exercise period elapsed at year end
D	Estimated no. of employees entitled to benefits	×	No. of instruments per employee	×	FV per instrument at year end	×	Proportion of exercise period elapsed at year end

---

28.5 On 1 March 20X5, PB, a listed entity, acquired 80% of 3,000,000 issued ordinary shares of SV. The consideration for each share acquired comprised a cash payment of $1.20, plus two ordinary shares in PB. The market value of a $1 ordinary share in PB on 1 March 20X5 was $1.50, rising to $1.60 by the entity's year end on 31 March 20X5. Professional fees paid to PB's external accountants and legal advisers in respect of the acquisition were $400,000.

What is the fair value of consideration in respect of this acquisition, for inclusion in PB's financial statements for the year ended 31 March 20X5?

A $10,080,000.
B $10,480,000.
C $10,560,000.
D $10,960,000.

28.6 PJ acquired 70% of the 1,000,000 $1 ordinary shares of DF on 1 January 20X3 for $1,800,000 when DF's retained earnings were $500,000. The group policy is to measure non-controlling interests at proportionate share of net assets. The fair value of non-controlling interests at 1 January 20X3 was $600,000. There has been no impairment of goodwill since the date of acquisition.

PJ acquired a further 10% of DF's share capital on 1 October 20X5 for $120,000.

The retained earnings reported in the financial statements of PJ and DF as at 31 December 20X4 were $3,500,000 and $950,000 respectively.

Profits of both entities can be assumed to accrue evenly throughout the year. The profits for the year of PJ and DF respectively were $690,000 and $120,000. There was no other comprehensive income in either entity. Neither entity paid any dividends in the year.

Calculate the non-controlling interest in the consolidated statement of profit or loss and other comprehensive income for the year ended 31 December 20X5.

$ [   ]

28.7 PH acquired 75,000 of the 100,000 $1 ordinary shares JG for $480,000 on 1 January 20X4. JG acquired 64,000 of the 80,000 $1 ordinary shares in TR for $320,000 on 1 January 20X5.

The retained earnings of PH, JG and TR were:

	31 Dec 20X5	1 Jan 20X5	1 Jan 20X4
	$'000	$'000	$'000
PH	1,200	980	820
JG	360	400	480
TR	500	360	450

PH elected to measure the non-controlling interest in JG and TR at acquisition at fair value. The fair value of the non-controlling interest in JG at 1 January 20X4 was $150,000. The fair value of one equity share in TR at 1 January 20X5 was $1.10.

Consolidated retained earnings at 31 December 20X5 are:

A $1,140,000
B $1,194,000
C $1,216,500
D $1,222,000

28.8 **Which TWO of the following would result in an increase in non-controlling interests (NCI) in the year in the consolidated statement of changes in equity?**

A Increasing the shareholding in a subsidiary from 80% to 90%
B Decreasing the shareholding in a subsidiary from 75% to 60%
C Dividends paid by a subsidiary
D Total comprehensive income for the year of a subsidiary (multiplied by the NCI share)
E A share issue by the parent

28.9 You are the Finance Director of RS, and the Managing Director wants to check his understanding of EPS.

Which TWO of the following assertion are correct?

A A bonus issue of shares may increase the EPS
B A bonus issue will have no effect on RS's capacity to generate earnings in the future
C A rights issue will have no effect on EPS
D A rights issue is a combination of an issue of shares at full market price with a bonus element

28.10 SD has 3% convertible bonds in issue and they are due to be converted or redeemed within the next two months. Assume no further debt is issued by AD in the year.

Which of the following statements are TRUE if all of the holders choose to convert to ordinary shares in AD?

Select ALL that apply.

A   Interest cover will fall and earnings per share will increase if all of these instruments are converted.

B   Earnings per share and the P/E ratio of AD will both decrease following the conversion.

C   Interest cover will increase and the P/E ratio of AD will decrease following the conversion.

D   The P/E ratio will move according to how the market reacts to the majority of the holders converting to ordinary shares.

E   Gearing will decrease and profit available for distribution will be allocated over a greater number of ordinary shares.

F   Interest costs will decrease and gearing will increase following the conversion.

29 Mixed Bank 5

29.1 Xenon Co has $300 million of 6% bonds in issue. This debt was originally issued at its par value of $100 and is now trading at 95% of this value. Xenon pays corporate income tax at 25%.

Calculate Xenon's post tax cost of debt:

| | % to two decimal places.

29.2 A company leases some plant on 1 January 20X4. The cash price is $9,000, and the company is to pay four annual installments of $3,000, beginning on 1 January 20X4.

The company uses the sum-of-the-digits method to allocate interest.

What is the interest charge for the year ended 31 December 20X5?

A $750
B $500
C $900
D $1,000

29.3 The following information relates to an entity.

- At 1 January 20X8, there were taxable temporary differences of $850,000 relating to property, plant and equipment.

- For the year ended 31 December 20X8, the entity claimed depreciation for tax purposes of $500,000 and charged depreciation of $450,000 in the financial statements.

- During the year ended 31 December 20X8, the entity revalued a freehold property. The revaluation surplus was $250,000. The entity has no plans to sell the property and realise the gain in the foreseeable future.

- Assume a tax rate of 25%.

Calculate the deferred tax liability in respect of property, plant and equipment required by IAS 12 _Income taxes_ as at 31 December 20X8.

$ | |

29.4 CF, a contract cleaning entity, signed a contract to provide 12 months' cleaning of an office block. The contract for $12,000 commenced on 1 June 20X2. The terms of the contract provided for payment six monthly in advance on 1 June and 1 December 20X2. CF received $6,000 and started work on 1 June 20X2.

How should CF account for the contract in its financial statements for the year ended 30 June 20X2?

A   Debit cash $6,000 and credit revenue $6,000

B   Debit cash $6,000, credit revenue $1,000 and credit deferred income $5,000

C   Debit cash $6,000, debit receivables $6,000 and credit revenue $12,000

D   Debit cash $6,000 and credit deferred income $6,000

29.5 On 1 January 20X2 A purchased 40% of the equity share capital of B for $60,000. At this date the reserves of B stood at $30,000. During the year ended 31 December 20X4 A, sold goods to B for $10,000 and these goods were still in inventory at the year end. A makes a gross profit margin of 25% on intragroup sales.

The statement of financial position sheet of B at 31 December 20X4 showed the following:

	$'000
Net assets	320
Share capital	100
Reserves	220
	320

At what amount should A's interest in B be stated in its consolidated statement of financial position at 31 December 20X4 (rounded to the nearest $'000)?

$'000 [   ]

29.6 PJ acquired 70% of the 1,000,000 $1 ordinary shares of DF on 1 January 20X3 for $1,800,000 when DF's retained earnings were $500,000. The group policy is to measure non-controlling interests at proportionate share of net assets. The fair value of non-controlling interests at 1 January 20X3 was $600,000. There has been no impairment of goodwill since the date of acquisition.

PJ acquired a further 10% of DF's share capital on 1 October 20X5 for $120,000.

The retained earnings reported in the financial statements of PJ and DF as at 31 December 20X4 were $3,500,000 and $950,000 respectively.

Profits of both entities can be assumed to accrue evenly throughout the year. The profits for the year of PJ and DF respectively were $690,000 and $120,000. There was no other comprehensive income in either entity. Neither entity paid any dividends in the year.

Calculate the non controlling interest in the consolidated statement of financial position as at 31 December 20X5.

$ [   ]

29.7 RR presents its consolidated financial statements in A$. RR has one subsidiary NN which uses B$ as its functional currency. NN was acquired on 1 January 20X1 and goodwill arising on the acquisition was initially measured at B$510,000. There has been no impairment of this goodwill. Relevant exchange rates are:

1 January 20X1	A$/B$2.10
31 December 20X2	A$/B$2.50
Average rate for the year ended 31 December 20X2	A$/B$2.40

The value of goodwill that will be presented in RR's consolidated financial statements at 31 December 20X2 to the nearest whole number is:

$[   ]

29.8 The sentence below describes the accounting treatment for a disposal of a subsidiary in the consolidated statement of cash flows.

Complete the sentences by writing in the correct narrative from the list provided:

On disposal of a subsidiary, the proceeds from the sale of the [   ] are recorded as a cash [   ] in the [   ] section of the statement of cash flows. The cash balance of the subsidiary at the disposal date is [   ] the sales proceeds (or for an overdraft, [   ]) and the [   ] figure is shown in the statement of cash flows.

Picklist for narratives:

net assets
shares
deducted from
added to
outflow
inflow
operating
investing
financing
net
gross

29.9 On 1 January 20X3, WB has 500,000 $1 ordinary shares. On 1 March 20X3, WB made a 1 for 5 rights issue at $5 a share. The market price of one ordinary share immediately before the exercise on 1 March 20X3 was $11.

During the year ended 31 December 20X3, WB made a profit for the year of $320,000. Dividends of $20,000 on irredeemable preference shares were paid on 31 December 20X3.

The basic earnings per share figure for WB for the year ended 31 December 20X3 is:

A   50.7c.
B   54.1c.
C   50.0c.
D   51.1c.

29.10 GH has a P/E ratio of 10.7 at 31 December 20X8. At that date one its main competitors, KL, reported a P/E ratio of 13.1.

Complete the following sentences by writing in the correct narrative from the list provided.

The market has [   ] confidence in the [   ] performance of KL and it is likely that KL has been established for a longer time and has proven track record for success. Investing in GH is likely to be [   ] than investing in KL.

Picklist for narratives

greater
less
future
past
more risky
less risky

30 Mixed Bank 6

30.1 A company has issued 10% bonds that are redeemable at par in three years' time. Interest is paid annually, and the interest payment for the most recent year has just been paid. The current market price of the bonds is 103.2 cents. The rate of tax is 25%. The net present value of the cash flows relating to these bonds has been calculated as follows:

NPV at 5% = +3.21

NPV at 10% = −9.51

Using this information calculate the cost of these bonds to the nearest one decimal place.

To the nearest one decimal place, the cost of the bonds is:

[   ] %

30.2 HP entered into an operating lease for a machine on 1 May 20X7 with the following terms:

- Five years non-cancellable lease
- 12 months rent free period from commencement
- Rent of $12,000 per annum payable at $1,000 a month from month 13 onwards
- Machine useful life 15 years

Calculate the amount that should be charged to profit or loss in HP's financial statements in respect of the lease, for the year ended 30 April 20X8.

$ [   ]

30.3 Current liabilities include accrued expenses with a carrying amount of $1,500. The related expense will be deducted for tax purposes on a cash basis.

Interest receivable has a carrying amount of $700. The interest revenue will be taxed on a cash basis.

What are the tax bases of these items?

A   Accrued expenses nil, interest receivable nil.
B   Accrued expenses $1,500, interest receivable nil.
C   Accrued expenses nil, interest receivable $700.
D   Accrued expenses $1,500, interest receivable $700.

30.4 LP received an order to supply 10,000 units of product A every month for 2 years. The customer had negotiated a low price of $200 per 1,000 units and agreed to pay $12,000 in advance every 6 months.

The customer made the first payment on 1 July 20X2 and LP supplied the goods each month from 1 July 20X2.

LP's year end is 30 September.

In addition to recording the cash received, how should LP record this order, in its financial statements for the year ended 30 September 20X2, in accordance with IAS 18 *Revenue*?

A   Include $6,000 in revenue for the year and create a trade receivable for $36,000
B   Include $6,000 in revenue for the year and create a current liability for $6,000
C   Include $12,000 in revenue for the year and create a trade receivable for $36,000
D   Include $12,000 in revenue for the year but do not create a trade receivable or current liability

---

30.5 LR owns 35% of the equity share capital of GH. During the year to 31 December 20X3, LR purchased goods with a sales value of $500,000 from GH. One quarter of these goods remained in LR's inventories at the year ended 31 December 20X3. GH includes a mark-up of 25% on all sales.

Which one of the following accounting adjustments would LR process in the preparation of its consolidated financial statements in relation to these goods?

A   Dr Share of profit of associate $25,000 Cr Inventories $25,000
B   Dr Cost of sales $25,000 Cr Inventories $25,000
C   Dr Investment in associate $8,750 Cr Cost of sales $8,750
D   Dr Share of profit of associate $8,750 Cr Inventories $8,750

30.6 H disposes of its entire 80% holding in Q on 1 November 20X6. The year end is 31 December 20X6.

Complete the following sentences by writing in the correct narrative from the list provided:

When the shares in Q are disposed of, its resources cease to be [   ] by the group on 1 November 20X6. The consolidated statement of profit or loss will include the income and expenses for the [   ] to 1 November 20X6, the non controlling interest of 20% will be calculated on the profits for the same period and the group profit or loss on disposal of the shares should be included in the results. The profit or loss is calculated as the fair value of the [   ] received less the net assets and goodwill on 1 November 20X6 plus the non controlling interest on 1 November 20X6.

Picklist for narratives

consideration
controlled
year
owned
10 months
investment

30.7 HM acquired 80% of the ordinary share capital of a foreign entity, OS, on 1 January 20X1 for Crowns 13,984,000. At the date of acquisition the net assets of OS had a fair value of Crowns 15,800,000.

The group policy is to value non-controlling interest at fair value at the date of acquisition. The fair value of the non-controlling interest at the date of acquisition was Crowns 3,496,000. The fair value adjustments related to non-depreciable land.

Goodwill on acquisition of OS was Crowns 1,680,000 and was impaired by 20% during 20X1. Impairment is translated at the average rate and is charged to group other expenses.

The condensed statements of profit or loss for HM and OS for the year ended 31 December 20X1 are shown below.

	HM	OS
	$'000	Crowns'000
Revenue	5,200	4,500
Cost of sales	(3,200)	(3,000)
Gross profit	2,000	1,500
Other expenses	(1,420)	(1,050)
Profit for the year	580	450

Exchange rates:
1 January 20X1	$1=Crowns	1.61
31 December 20X1	$1=Crowns	1.52
Average rate for 20X1	$1=Crowns	1.58

Cost of sales (to the nearest thousand) in the consolidated statement of profit or loss and other comprehensive income for the year ended 31 December 20X1 is:

- A $5,063,000
- B $5,099,000
- C $5,174,000
- D $6,200,000

30.8   The following information appears in the consolidated statement of financial position of the Queen group at 31 December 20X8:

	20X8	20X7
	$'000	$'000
Property, plant and equipment	720	515
Revaluation surplus	50	–

The depreciation charge for the year was $60,000. On 1 July 20X8 Queen acquired a subsidiary which had property, plant and equipment of $90,000. There were no disposals of property, plant and equipment during the year.

What was cash paid to acquire property, plant and equipment during the year ended 31 December 20X8?

- A $65,000
- B $125,000
- C $175,000
- D $215,000

30.9   YY has announced that it wishes to sell one of its subsidiaries, D, because of its poor liquidity position.

On 31 December 20X3 (the last day of D's financial year end), the directors of YY purchased inventory from D at a price of $3 million and paid in full. This inventory had originally cost D $1.8 million. The directors of YY intend to reverse this sale in January 20X4.

Which of the following statements in respect of this transaction is true?

- A   It is a deliberate attempt to mislead potential acquirers who might rely on D's financial statements and as a result the directors are acting unethically.

- B   It results in a transfer of cash and therefore represents a valid accounting transaction between two entities, in accordance with international financial reporting standards.

- C   It will be eliminated in the consolidated financial statements and so it does not cause an ethical issue.

- D   The transaction will be reversed so it does not create an ethical issue within the financial statements of D for the year ended 31 December 20X3.

30.10   GH has changed its accounting policy in the year and now revalues all of its property and depreciable plant.

Which THREE of the following ratios would be directly affected by this change in policy resulting in a lack of comparability of this year's ratio to that calculated last year?

- A   Gearing
- B   Return on capital employed
- C   Receivable days
- D   Dividend per share
- E   Interest cover
- F   Quick ratio

31 Mixed Bank 7

31.1 A company has issued 6% irredeemable preference shares of $1 each. The current market value of the preference shares is $0.75 each. The rate of tax is 30%.

What is the cost of the preference shares?

A   6%
B   4.2%
C   8%
D   5.6%

31.2 On 1 January 20X1, a lessee leases a non-current asset on a non-cancellable lease contract of five years, the details of which are:

- The asset has a useful life of six years.
- The rental is $21,000 per annum payable at the end of each year.
- The lessee also has to pay all insurance and maintenance costs.
- The fair value of the asset was $88,300.

The lessee uses the sum of digits method to calculate finance charges on the lease.

The current lease liability for the year ended 31 December 20X1 to the nearest $ is: $ [　　　　　]

The depreciation charge for the year ended 31 December 20X1 to the nearest $ is: $ [　　　　　]

31.3 **Which of the following will NOT give rise to a deferred tax liability?**

A   Receipt of a non-taxable government grant.
B   Capitalised development costs which attract tax relief when paid.
C   Prepaid expenses where tax relief is granted when expenses are paid.
D   Depreciation in excess of tax allowances on an asset.

31.4 AE has a three year contract which commenced on 1 April 20X4. At 31 March 20X5, AE had the following balances in its ledger relating to the contract:

	$'000	$'000
Total contract value		60,000
Cost incurred up to 31 March 20X5:		
Attributable to work completed	21,000	
Inventory purchased for use in year ended 31 March 20X6	3,000	
		24,000
Progress payments received	25,000	
Other information:		
Expected further costs to completion		19,000

At 31 March 20X5, the contract was certified as 50% complete.

What is the amount that should be recorded in cost of sales in relation to this contract in AE's statement of profit or loss for the year ended 31 March 20X5?

A $18,500
B $20,000
C $21,000
D $21,500

31.5 T has a 25% share in UV, which is a joint operation.

How should T account for their interest in UV in their individual financial statements?

A   Nothing should be included in the individual statements, it is only included on consolidation.

B   At the cost of the investment in UV as an investment in non current assets.

C   Include 25% of the assets and liabilities of UV and 25% of the revenue and expenses generated by UV.

D   As an available for sale financial asset at fair value

31.6 KK acquired an 18% investment in GG on 1 January 20X7 for $150,000 on 1 January 20X4. The fair value of this investment at 31 December 20X8 is $340,000.

On 1 July 20X8 KK acquired an additional 60% of the 500,000 $1 shares of GG for $670,000. The retained earnings of GG were $280,000 on 1 January 20X8 and the profits for the year to 31 December 20X8 were $95,000. The group policy is to measure non controlling interests at the proportionate share of net assets.

Following the acquisition of the additional shares in GG the investment was impaired by $15,000.

How much is the goodwill that is included in the consolidated statement of financial position for the KK group as at 31 December 20X8?

A $nil
B $364,500
C $401,600
D $513,500

31.7 HM acquired 80% of the ordinary share capital of a foreign entity, OS, on 1 January 20X1 for Crowns 13,984,000. At the date of acquisition the net assets of OS had a fair value of Crowns 15,800,000.

The group policy is to value non-controlling interest at fair value at the date of acquisition. The fair value of the non-controlling interest at the date of acquisition was Crowns 3,496,000. The fair value adjustments related to non-depreciable land.

Goodwill on acquisition of OS was Crowns 1,680,000 and was impaired by 20% during 20X1. Impairment is translated at the average rate and is charged to group other expenses.

The condensed statements of profit or loss for HM and OS for the year ended 31 December 20X1 are shown below.

	HM	OS
	$'000	Crowns'000
Revenue	5,200	4,500
Cost of sales	(3,200)	(3,000)
Gross profit	2,000	1,500
Other expenses	(1,420)	(1,050)
Profit for the year	580	450

Exchange rates:		
1 January 20X1	$1=Crowns	1.61
31 December 20X1	$1=Crowns	1.52
Average rate for 20X1	$1=Crowns	1.58

The calculation of exchange differences charged to other comprehensive income in the year ended 31 December 20X1 is:

Complete the workings in the table below.

	$'000
On translation of net assets	
Closing net assets at closing rate	
Opening net assets at opening rate	
	X
Less profit	
	X
Translation differences on goodwill	54
	X

31.8 HJ's consolidated statement of financial position shows non-controlling interest (NCI) of $4,875,000 at 31 December 20X8 and $4,550,000 at 31 December 20X7.

In 20X8 HJ acquired 75% of the equity shares of VB when the fair value of VB's net assets was $1,100,000. The NCI in VB is to be measured at its proportionate share of net assets.

The profit for the year that was attributable to the NCI and reported in the consolidated profit or loss of HJ was $425,000 for the year ended 31 December 20X8.

Assuming no other transactions affected NCI in the year, the dividend paid to NCI to be included in HJ's consolidated cash flow statement is:

A $50,000
B $100,000
C $375,000
D $425,000

31.9 WB's directors are concerned about the results for the year in the statement of profit or loss and other comprehensive income and the subsequent effect on the statement of cash flows. They have suggested that the proceeds of the sale of property, plant and equipment and the sale of investments should be included in 'cash generated from operations'. The directors are afraid of an adverse market reaction to their results and of the importance of meeting targets to ensure job security, and feel that the adjustments for the proceeds would enhance the 'cash health' of the business.

Which THREE of the following statements are correct?

A   This treatment would maximise the share price and benefit the shareholders, making the directors proposed treatment ethically acceptable.

B   This proposed treatment results in non-compliance with IAS 7 *Statement of cash flows* which requires these proceeds to be treated as 'investing' rather than 'operating'.

C   As these cash flows are one-off rather than recurring, it would be misleading to the users of financial statements to classify them as 'operating'.

D   There is a self-interest threat here as the motivation for this accounting treatment is the job security of the directors.

E   As IAS 7 *Statement of cash flows* allows some flexibility in classification of cash flows, the directors would be demonstrating the CIMA Code of Ethics' principle of professional competence by pursuing this accounting treatment.

31.10 The following is an extract from the statement of cash flows for LM for the year ended 31 December 20X9:

	$m
Cash flows from operating activities	2,150
Cash flows from investing activities	(4,100)
Cash flows from financing activities	2,000
Net cash flow in the year	(50)

Based on the information provided, which one of the following independent statements would be a reasonable conclusion about the financial adaptability of LM for the year to 31 December 20X9?

A   The management of LM has failed to exercise competent stewardship of the entities resources since there is a net cash outflow despite generating cash inflow from operating activities.

B   LM must be in decline as there is a negative cash flow relating to investment activities.

C   LM's management has shown competent stewardship of the entity's resources by increasing long term finance to partly fund investing activities.

D   LM must be insolvent at 31 December 20X9 because it has a net cash outflow for the year.

32 Mixed Bank 8

32.1   CRC has 40m shares in issue with a nominal value of $1 which are trading at a share price of $2.40 cum div. CRC has paid a constant dividend of 20 cents per share in recent years which represents 50% of its post tax profits.

CRC has $20m of 5% irredeemable debentures with a nominal value of $100m, and these are trading at 94% of their nominal value.

CRC pays corporate income tax at a rate of 25%.

Which of the following shows the correct cost of debt and equity to be used in the calculation of CRC's WACC?

A   Cost of debt = 3.75%
     Cost of equity = 8.3%

B   Cost of debt = 5.0%
     Cost of equity = 18.2%

C   Cost of debt = 3.75%
     Cost of equity = 9.1%

D   Cost of debt = 4.0%
     Cost of equity = 9.1%

32.2   BB enters into a lease for a piece of machinery which had a fair value of $80,000 on inception of the lease. The lease required ten annual payments of $10,500 made in arrears. BB is responsible for the maintenance of the machine which has a useful life of eleven years.

The present value of the lease payments is $74,000.

The journal entry to initially record the lease is:

	Account reference	$
Dr		
Cr		

32.3 QW prepares it financial statements to 31 December each year. On 31 December 20X6 QW had unused tax losses. At that time it was budgeted that QW would not generate sufficient taxable profits in the future against which all of these losses could be recovered.

At 31 December 20X7, the unused tax losses create a deferred tax:

A liability which will be provided for in full to ensure that liabilities are complete in the statement of financial position.

B asset which as long as it can be measured reliably will be included in the financial statements at a value equal to the unused tax losses multiplied by the tax rate.

C liability which will be treated as contingent liability because not all of the losses are recoverable.

D asset which will be included in the statement of financial position at the amount that is expected to be able to be recovered from future expected profits.

32.4 On 1 January 20X5, MN entered into a contract with a customer to bore a river tunnel at a fixed price of $100 million. At 31 December 20X5, the work is believed to be approximately 25% complete. However, as this is the first river tunnel that MN has built, it is not possible to reliably estimate future costs or a completion date. The costs to date are $20 million. MN has invoiced the customer for $23 million, all of which had been received by 31 December 20X5.

How much revenue should MN recognise in respect of this contract for the year ended 31 December 20X5?

A Nil
B $20 million
C $23 million.
D $25 million.

32.5 **Which FOUR of the following are required by IFRS 12 *Disclosure of interests in other entities* to be disclosed in the consolidated financial statements?**

A The fair value of each class of financial assets and financial liabilities

B The significant judgments and assumptions made in determining whether the entity has control, joint control or significant influence of the other entities, and in determining the type of joint arrangement

C Information to understand the composition of the group and the interest that non controlling interests have in the group's activities and cash flows

D Entries made to remove the effects of any intragroup transactions

E The nature, extent and financial effects of interests in joint arrangements and associates, including the nature and effects of the entity's contractual relationship with other investors

F The nature and extent of interests in unconsolidated structured entities

32.6 U holds a 15% investment in the ordinary shares of V. The shares were purchased for $85,000 in 20X2 and are measured as an available for sale financial asset in the accounts of the U group.

In 20X8 U purchases a further 80% of the shares in V for $1,200,000 on which date the original 15% investment has a fair value of $210,000.

Which THREE of the following statements regarding the original 15% investment are correct in the consolidated financial statements for the year ended 31 December 20X8?

A   The investment is revalued to its fair value at the date control is obtained and continues to be recognised in the consolidated financial statements at its fair value

B   In substance the 15% investment has been sold

C   A profit or loss on de-recognition of the 15% shares is calculated as the proportion of the cost of the new shares (i.e. 15%/80% × $1,200,000) less the original cost

D   The investment is disposed of with gains and losses recognised in other comprehensive income

E   A profit or loss on de-recognition of the 15% shares is calculated as the fair value of the 15% at the date control is achieved less original cost

F   Previous revaluation gains on the available for sale investment are reclassified out of other comprehensive income

32.7 HM acquired 80% of the ordinary share capital of a foreign entity, OS, on 1 January 20X1 for Crowns 13,984,000. At the date of acquisition the net assets of OS had a fair value of Crowns 15,800,000.

The group policy is to value non-controlling interest at fair value at the date of acquisition. The fair value of the non-controlling interest at the date of acquisition was Crowns 3,496,000. The fair value adjustments related to non-depreciable land.

Goodwill on acquisition of OS was Crowns 1,680,000 and was impaired by 20% during 20X1. Impairment is translated at the average rate and is charged to group other expenses.

The condensed statements of profit or loss for HM and OS for the year ended 31 December 20X1 are shown below.

	HM	OS
	$'000	Crowns'000
Revenue	5,200	4,500
Cost of sales	(3,200)	(3,000)
Gross profit	2,000	1,500
Other expenses	(1,420)	(1,050)
Profit for the year	580	450

Exchange rates:		
1 January 20X1	$1=Crowns	1.61
31 December 20X1	$1=Crowns	1.52
Average rate for 20X1	$1=Crowns	1.58

The exchange gains charged to other comprehensive income in the consolidated statement of profit or loss and other comprehensive income for the year ended 31 December 20X1 were $646,000.

The total comprehensive income attributable to the owners of HM is:

A $143,000
B $985,000
C $1,155,000
D $1,039,000

32.8 GPX's financial statements included an investment in associate at $6,600,000 in its consolidated statement of financial position at 30 September 20X5. At 30 September 20X6, the investment in associate had increased to $6,750,000. GPX has a 30% holding in the associate. The associate had a profit for the year of $700,000 and other comprehensive income of $200,000.

There were no impairments to the investment in associate, or acquisitions or disposals of shares during the financial year.

What is the amount of the cash flow related to this investment for inclusion in the consolidated cash flow statement for the year ended 30 September 20X6?

$ _____

32.9 **Which threat under the CIMA Code of Ethics is defined as where 'an accountant may act inappropriately due to actual or perceived pressure over them'?**

A   Self-interest
B   Self-review
C   Advocacy
D   Familiarity
E   Intimidation

32.10 **Complete the formulae used to calculate dividend cover and dividend yield by writing in the correct narrative from the list provided.**

Dividend cover   *Dividend yield*

Pickist for narratives

Earnings per share
Share price
Dividend per share
Profit available for distribution to ordinary shareholders
Number of ordinary shares issued
Profit for the year

Answers to objective test questions

1 Sources of long-term finance

1.1   A,D,E   The correct answers are:

- Bonds and shares are both securities which can be traded in the capital markets.
- The ability to sell bonds on the capital markets enhances their attractiveness to bond holders.
- Bond holders will normally be paid a fixed return known as the coupon rate.

It is <u>not correct</u> to say that either bond holders or shareholders have a right to cash payment. Shareholders receive a dividend only if the company decides to pay a dividend - there is no automatic right to a dividend payment.

It is also incorrect to say that bonds and shares will normally be redeemable at any point in time - most bonds are redeemable and the redemption date is *fixed* and is not changeable at the company's discretion.

1.2   The correct answer is:

- Ordinary shares carry voting rights and **entitlement** to any declared dividend. They are a **flexible** form of finance from the company's perspective.

There is no entitlement to a dividend but if a dividend is declared then ordinary shareholders <u>do</u> have an entitlement to receive their share in this dividend. A key attraction of equity finance is that a dividend does not have to be paid - this is risky to the shareholder but is flexible from the <u>company's perspective</u>.

1.3   D   A negative loan covenant.

This limits the borrower's behaviour.

A positive covenant normally involves achieving something e.g. maintaining a key ratio at a certain level. Charges secure a loan against a specific asset (fixed) or the assets in general (floating).

1.4   B   All else being equal the value of the business is likely to be unaffected.

Increased regulation and transparency reduce the actual and perceived risk from the point of view of shareholders, making the shares more attractive and hence more valuable.

In addition listed company shares are naturally more liquid than an equivalent unlisted company, again adding to their value. The process of listing <u>is therefore likely to create value</u>.

1.5   A,B,C   The correct answers are:

- Underwriters are paid a fee for guaranteeing that the bonds will be purchased

- The company issuing the bonds reduces its reliance on bank lending

- Interest costs are often lower than an equivalent bank loan because the bonds can be sold by investors

The process of producing a prospectus and organising underwriting for a bond issue takes time – a bank loan is quicker to arrange.

Underwriters do not guarantee to the investors that the company can pay the interest on the bond, they simply guarantee to the company that the bonds will be purchased.

1.6   D   A rights issue allows shareholders the right to ensure that their existing shareholding is not diluted.

A rights issue is normally at a discount to the existing market price to encourage shareholders to participate in it. Any entity, whether listed or not, can initiate a rights issue and it is open to any shareholders whether institutional or not.

1.7   B   The obligation to convert into shares at the expiry of the bond.

There is no obligation to convert into shares - it is the choice of the convertible bond holder whether to convert or not - if they prefer, they are entitled (but not forced) to redeem the bond at its par value.

1.8   A   I, II, III, IV

In the event of liquidation, the creditor hierarchy dictates the priority of claims. Debt finance is paid off before equity. This makes debt a safer investment than equity. This is why debt investors demand a lower rate of return than equity investors.

Loans with charges are secured on assets and are therefore less risky than trade payables that are unsecured.

1.9   B   A higher issue price.

A placing involves selling to institutional shareholders who will negotiate a lower price at which they will buy the share.

A placing has lower admin costs because they will be no underwriting or advertising.

Both a placing and an offer for sale will dilute the ownership, and therefore control, of existing shareholders.

1.10   C   II, III, I, IV.

Bonds are riskiest from the company's view because interest has to be paid, regardless of a company's cash flow position. Convertible bonds carry the extra risk that the company's share price is high at the point at which bondholders convert - which will result in bondholders enjoying a capital gain at the expense of ordinary shareholders.

Ordinary shareholders carry no rights to a dividend so they are less risky than preference shares which do have rights to a fixed dividend.

2 Cost of capital

2.1   The correct answer is:

The post-tax cost of debt for a convertible bond is the **internal rate of return** of the relevant cash flows associated with it. The relevant cash flows are the market value of **the bond** now, the annual interest payments **after** tax and the higher of the redemption value of the bond in the future or the anticipated share price if conversion occurs.

2.2   C   The correct answer is: 8%.

The cost of equity = $d_1 / P_0 + g$

Therefore cost of equity = $20 \times 1.04 / 530 + 0.04 = 0.079 = \textbf{7.9\%}$

2.3   B   The correct answer is: 14.9%.

Cost of bonds = 11% (1 − 0.40) / 100 = 6.6%

V_e = 80m × \$1 = \$80m   (Value of shares)

V_d = \$3m   (11% bonds)

WACC = 18 × 80/110 + 6.6 × 30/110 = **14.9%**

2.4   A,C   The correct answers are:

- 2 × (1-0.25)
- 128.8

The expected share price in 5 years is $4 \times 1.1^5 = \$6.44$ so 20 shares will be worth \$128.8. So conversion is likely to happen.

The cost to the company will be an IRR calculation using the cost of the interest payments post tax and the likely cost of redemption which is 128.8.

2.5   The correct answer is: 2.4%.

An undated bond is irredeemable so the correct approach to use is:

$$K_d = \frac{i(1-T)}{P_0}$$

$i = 4$

$(1-t) = 0.75$

$P_0 = 125$

$K_d = 4 \times 0.75 / 125 = 0.024$ or **2.4%**

2.6   The correct answer is: 15.5%

Using $K = d_1 / P_0 + g$

$g = 0.1$

$P_0 = 4.20 - 0.20 = 4.00$ ex div

$d_1 = 0.2 \times 1.1 = 0.22$

$K = 0.22 / 4 + 0.1 = 0.155$ or **15.5%**

2.7 A 2.33%.

The implicit dividend growth rate can be calculated using the Dividend Growth Model.

$K = d_1 / P_0 + g$

$0.1 = (3 \times (1 + g)) / 40 + g$

$0.1 = (3 + 3g) / 40 + g$

$0.1 = 0.075 + 0.075 g + g$

$0.1 = 0.075 + 1.075g$

$0.1 - 0.075 = 1.075g$

$0.025 = 1.075g$

$0.025 / 1.075 = 0.0233$ or **2.33%**

2.8 D 7.6%.

Cost of debt $= I (1-t) / P_0$

Cost of debt $= 6(1 - 0.25)/105$

                 $= 4.286\%$

MV of equity (V_e) $= 400$ m shares $(100 / 25c) \times \$5 = \$2,000m$

MV of debt (V_d) $= 800 \times 1.05 = \$840$ million

WACC $= K_e (V_e / (V_e + V_d)) + K_d (1-t) (V_d / (V_e + V_d))$

          $= 9 (2000 / 2840) + 5.7 \times 0.75 \times (840 / 2840) = \textbf{7.6\%}$

2.9 A,C The correct answers are:

- Lower interest repayments
- The possibility of lower cash repayments at the end of the term of the debt.

Convertible debt normally pays a low rate of interest because investors can sometimes make a capital gain if they decide to switch their bonds into shares. If they do then there are no cash repayments at the end of the debt.

However, this cannot be forced onto bond holders by the company - it is the <u>investors decision</u> whether or not to switch their bonds into shares.

Tax relief on interest payments will be a feature of <u>both</u> convertible debt and a bank loan.

2.10   D   5.0%.

the cost of debt is calculated using $K_d = I(1-t) / P_0$

$I = 6$

$(1-t) = 0.75$

$P_0 = 90\%$ of $100 = 90$

So $K_d = 6 \times 0.75 / 90 = 0.05$ or **5%**

---

3 Financial instruments

3.1   D   All of the options would result in an impairment as the present value of the principle and interest payments will be lower than the carrying amount in all circumstances. The payments being made are either at a later date (lower present value when discounted) or smaller.

3.2   D   These assets are restated to fair value and gains and losses are recognised in profit or loss.

Financial assets that are loans and receivables, or held to maturity are measured at amortised cost.

Available for sale financial assets are measured at fair value with gains and losses recognised in other comprehensive income.

3.3   D   The dividend payable will be included in Z's finance cost as a period expense.

Financial instruments are recognised according to their substance, not their legal form. These redeemable preference shares have an obligation to pay cash, thus they must be classified as a liability, irrespective of the fact they are named shares and may have share certificates attached to them.

The dividend or cost attached to the share should be treated in the same way as the share itself. If the share is classified as a liability the dividends will be treated as finance costs in the SLPOCI not as a deduction from retained earnings.

3.4   The correct answer is: $20,073,690.

	$
Fair value of net proceeds [(290,000 × $66) – 22,200]	19,117,800
Interest at 5%	955,890
	20,073,690

3.5   The correct answer is: $27,450.

This instrument is convertible debt, containing elements of debt (obligations to pay interest and repay the principal) and equity (the right to a share).

Therefore, the proceeds need to be split into the component parts. The debt component is calculated as the present value of future cash flows (interest and principal) discounted at the market rate of non-convertible debt. The equity component is calculated as the residual (i.e. the proceeds less the debt component).

	$	$
Proceeds (1,500 bonds × $500 par value)		750,000
Financial liability component:		
Present value of interest ($750,000 × 5% × 1.808)	67,800	
Present value of principal ($750,000 × 0.873)	654,750	
		(722,550)
Equity component		27,450

3.6 D Available for sale; fair value with gains or losses in other comprehensive income.

The fact that PZG intends to hold this investment for the long term means that it is not held for trading and therefore will not be classified as 'at fair value through profit or loss'. It is an investment in equity shares (which have no maturity date) so cannot be classified as held to maturity. It is clearly not a loan or receivable. Therefore, by default, it falls in the 'available for sale' category which under IAS 39 must be measured at fair value, with gains or losses in other comprehensive income.

3.7 A Held for trading; fair value through profit or loss.

The fact that GZP intends to realise the investment within a few months means that it will be classified as held for trading. Gains or losses on held for trading financial assets are recognised in profit or loss.

3.8 The correct answer is:

Liability	$
Opening balance	**3,800,000**
Plus: finance cost	**319,200**
Less: interest paid	(X)
Closing balance	X

Transaction costs are deducted from the initial nominal value of a debt instrument (4,000,000 – 200,000).

The finance costs are calculated at the effective interest rate on the opening balance (3,800,000 × 8.4%).

3.9 D $22,842.

Convertible debt must be split into its liability and equity component parts. The liability element is calculated as the present value of future cash flows (interest and capital), discounted at the market rate of non-convertible debt. The equity component is the residual (i.e. the proceeds less the liability component).

	$	$
Proceeds (3,000 bonds × $100 par value)		300,000
Liability component:		
Present value of interest ($300,000 × 6% × 2.531)	45,558	
Present value of principal ($300,000 × 0.772)	231,600	
		(277,158)
Equity component (residual)		22,842

3.10 C DR Investment $2,020,000

CR Bank $2,020,000

The instrument is recorded initially at its nominal value and transaction costs are added to the asset, not expensed.

4 Leases

4.1 B $237,000.

IAS 17 requires capitalisation at the lower of the fair value and the present value of the minimum lease payments.

4.2 B $32,400.

The incentive is spread over the whole period of the lease.

	$
Total cost for 5 years (3,000 × 60)	180,000
Less 6 months (3,000 × 6)	(18,000)
	162,000
Cost for one year (162,000/5)	32,400

4.3 The correct answer is: $1,440.

		$
1 Jan 20X7	Asset	18,000
	Deposit	(6,000)
		12,000
	Interest (12,000 × 12%)	1,440
	Payment	(7,080)
31 Dec 20X7	Liability c/d	6,360

4.4 A $7,000.

		$
Deposit		30,000
Instalments	(8 × $20,000)	160,000
		190,000
Fair value		154,000
Finance charge		36,000

$$\text{Sum of digits} = \frac{n(n+1)}{2}$$

$$\text{Sum of digits} = \frac{8 \times 9}{2} = 36$$

(n = 8 as payments in arrears so all instalments interest-bearing)

6 month to	June × 1	8/36 × $36,000	
	Dec × 1	7/36 × $36,000	
	June × 2	6/36 × $36,000	
	Dec × 2	5/36 × $36,000	
	June × 3	4/36 × $36,000	= £4,000
	Dec × 3	3/36 × $36,000	= $3,000
			= $7,000

4.5 B,C The correct answers are:

- DR Asset (with the fair value of the leased asset).
- CR Lease liability (with the present value of the minimum lease payments).

IAS 17 requires the asset and liability to be recorded at the lower of the fair value of the asset and the present value of the minimum lease payments. Finance charges are spread over the primary leasing period according to IAS 17, using either the actuarial or sum of digits method.

4.6 A $453.

Operating lease hire charges are expensed on a straight-line basis.

Thus, the expense per annum is calculated as ($130 +(4 × $420))/4years = $453.

4.7　A　　$900.

$$\text{Sum of digits} = \frac{n(n+1)}{2}$$

Where n = number of interest bearing instalments. Here as payments are in arrears, all instalments include interest and n = 4.

$$\text{Sum of digits} = \frac{4 \times 5}{2}$$

$$= 10$$

The year ended 31 December 20X5 is the second year of the lease so the interest charge for the year is $3/10 \times \$3,000 = \$900$ (the first year of the lease would be calculated as $4/10 \times \$3,000$)

4.8　　　The correct answer is: $35,697

		$
Cost	1.1.X4	80,000
Interest	7.93%	6,344
Instalment		(20,000)
Balance	31.12.X4	66,344
Interest	7.93%	5,261
Instalment		(20,000)
Balance	31.12.X5	51,605
Interest	7.93%	4,092
Instalment		(20,000)
Balance	31.12.X6	35,697
Current liability	(51,605 – 35,697) =	15,908
Non-current liability		**35,697**
Total balance at 31.12.X5		51,605

4.9　B,D,E　The correct answers are:

- The minimum lease payments are likely to cover the fair value of the plant at the inception of the lease.

- The plant would need to be modified to be used by another entity.

- There is an option to purchase the plant at significantly less than fair value in 5 years' time.

The fact that the lease term is not for the whole of the assets useful life could lead you think this was an operating lease, not a finance lease. A lease for substantially all of an assets useful life would be an indicator that the lease was a finance lease.

The intention of the company to not keep the asset past the lease term could also indicate the lease is an operating not a finance lease.

4.10　D

Rental in the profit or loss	Deferred income in the statement of financial position
$37,500	$25,000

Dr Profit or loss $37,500 Cr Deferred income $37,500

In 20X7:

Dr Profit or loss	$37,500
Dr Deferred income	$12,500
Cr Cash	$50,000

Resulting in deferred income of 25,000 at the end of 20X7.

5 Provisions, contingent liabilities and contingent assets

5.1   C   CDE was ordered by its local authority in October 20X1 to carry out an environmental cleanup in 20X2, following pollution from one of its factories.

The entity has a legal obligation to carry out the work at 31 December 20X1, imposed by the local authority, therefore it is acceptable to create a provision.

XYZ: The contract was for a feasibility study - there is no commitment to the reorganisation. Provisions should only be recognised when a legal/constructive obligation to transfer economic benefits as a result of past events exists. There is as yet no detailed plan for the reorganisation.

ABC: The commitment was entered into after the year end therefore no provision should be established at 31 December 20X1.

FG: Provisions for future operating losses must not be set up at acquisition.

5.2   A   nil.

Under IAS 37, a provision should only be recognised when it is **probable** that an outflow embodying economic benefits will be required to settle the obligation. An outflow is only regarded as probable if the event is **more likely than not** to occur i.e. **more than a 50%** chance of occurring. Here, as the percentage is less than 50%, the outflow is not probable so no provision should be made.

5.3   A $360,000.

	$'000
Minor repairs (3m × 5%)	150
Major repairs (7m × 3%)	210
	360

5.4   A,D   The correct answers are:

- An entity should not recognise a contingent liability in the statement of financial position.

- If discounting is used the compounding back of the liability over time should be recognised as an interest expense

A provision must be recognised when an entity has a present obligation (ie a legal or constructive obligation) as a result of a past event, it is probable that a transfer of economic benefits will be required to settle the obligation and a reliable estimate can be made of the amount of the obligation. Note: A constructive obligation is where the event (which may be an action of the entity) creates valid expectations in other parties that the entity will discharge the obligation.

An entity should NOT recognise a contingent asset. Note: reimbursements should be recognised only when they are virtually certain.

An entity MUST discount a provision where it is material.

Entities are never allowed to 'build up' provisions. Either an obligatory event exists and the provision is recognised in full, or no obligating event exists, when no provision can be recognised.

5.5   D   A provision of $1 million and only disclosure of the contingent asset.

IAS 37 states that a provision can be recognised if there is an obligation based on a past event, a probable outflow which can be reliably estimated, which is the case for the $1 million damages.

The contingent asset regarding the counter claim should not be recognised in the financial statements unless the claim is virtually certain. This would not seem the case as D does not yet appear to even have started proceedings against C. This should be disclosed in the notes to the financial statements as a contingent asset.

5.6   B   Announces the main features of the restructuring plan to those who will be affected by it.

By announcing its plan to the affected parties, the entity has raised a valid expectation and an obligation is said to exist.

5.7   C   A company has moved its offices out of London but is tied into the lease of the London building for another 6 months and is not permitted to sub-let to another tenant.

This is an onerous lease as the costs of meeting the obligations under the contract exceed the economic benefits expected to be received under it.

The company is not obliged to incur the restructuring costs because it has not yet communicated the closure decision to those affected by it.

No provision should be made for the cost of installing the safety guards because no obligating event has yet occurred i.e. the installation of safety guards. Furthermore, the company could avoid installing the safety guards by selling the machinery.

No provision can be made for the damages as the amount cannot be estimated reliably.

5.8   A $3.6 million.

A provision should definitely be made as there is a probable outflow i.e. it is more likely that not that Cactus will have to pay the claim (greater than a 50% chance).

Where there is a single outcome, as in this scenario, IAS 37 requires a provision to be made for the individual most likely outcome. Expected values are only used where the provision being measured involves a large population of items which is not the case here.

The answer of $2.7 million is reached by incorrectly multiplying the most likely outcome of $3.6 million by 75%. The answer of $0.9 million is reached by incorrectly multiplying $3.6 million by 25%.

5.9   C   There is a probable outflow of economic benefit but the timing and amount is uncertain and so a contingent liability be included in ER's financial statements at 31 December 20X3.

At the year end an assessment should be made regarding whether the company has any obligations. If these obligations are probable and can be reliably estimated a provision is calculated, if they are probable but can not be reliably estimated a contingent liability is disclosed.

5.10   The correct answers are:

Account reference	$
Dr **Machinery**	**272,400**
Cr **Provision**	**272,400**

As the costs will be incurred in 5 years' time, the time value of money is material and the provision must therefore be discounted: $400,000 \times 0.681 = \$272,400$.

Instead of debiting expenses, the provision should be added to the asset which will then be depreciated through profit or loss ensuring that the costs match the revenue generated through use of the asset.

6 Deferred taxation

6.1   The correct answers are:

	$
Property	500,000
Deferred tax liability	**60,000**
Revaluation surplus	**140,000**

The deferred tax liability is calculated as follows:

	$
Temporary difference (= revaluation gain) ($500,000 − $300,000)	200,000
Deferred tax liability (30% × $200,000)	60,000

The double entry to record this deferred tax is:

	$
Dr Other comprehensive income (and revaluation surplus)	60,000
Cr Deferred tax liability	60,000

Therefore the balance on the revaluation surplus at the year end is calculated as follows:

	$
Revaluation gain ($500,000 − $300,000)	200,000
Less: Deferred tax on revaluation gain	(60,000)
Balance on revaluation surplus at 31 December 20X8	140,000

6.2   The correct answer is: $42,750.

This is calculated by comparing the carrying amount to the tax base as at 30 September 20X4 to find the temporary difference. This temporary difference is then multiplied by the tax rate of 30% to calculate the deferred tax liability.

The carrying amount is calculated as follows:

	$
Cost	600,000
Less: Accumulated deprecation (X3, X4) [2/10 × 600,000]	(120,000)
Carrying amount at 30 September 20X4	480,000

The tax base is calculated as follows:

	$
Cost 1 October 20X2	600,000
Tax allowance (25% × 600,000)	(150,000)
Tax written down value 30 September 20X3	450,000
Tax allowance (25% × 450,000)	(112,500)
Tax written down value 30 September 20X4	337,500

Therefore, the temporary difference is $480,000 − $337,500 = $142,500.

The deferred tax liability is 30% × $142,500 = $42,750.

6.3   The correct answer is:

Items	Yes	No
Differences between accounting depreciation and tax allowances for capital expenditure	X	
Expenses charged in the statement of profit or loss and other comprehensive income but disallowed for tax		X
Revaluation of a non-current asset	X	
Unrelieved tax losses	X	

A temporary difference arises when an item is recognised in both the accounts and by the tax authorities but in different periods.

With the accounting depreciation and the tax allowances for capital expenditure, the full asset will have been recognised in both the accounts and the tax computation by the end of the asset's life but at different rates making it a temporary difference.

The revaluation is recognised in the accounts at the date of revaluation but not by the tax authorities until the asset is sold or the carrying amount of the asset is recovered through use generating taxable income in excess of tax allowance. Therefore this is also a temporary difference.

Unrelieved losses arise in the account immediately but no tax relief is granted by the tax authorities until sufficient future taxable profits arise, again making this a temporary difference.

However, where expenses are charged in the accounts but disallowed for tax purposes, this is a permanent rather than a temporary difference.

6.4   A,C,D   The correct answers are:

- Accrued expenses that will never be deductible for tax purposes

- Accrued expenses that have already been deducted in determining the current tax liability for current or earlier periods

- Accrued income that will never be taxable

Where accrued expenses will never be deductible for tax purposes, this is a permanent difference so the tax base is made the same as the carrying amount of the liability so that the temporary difference comes to zero. The same applies to accrued income that will never be taxable.

With accrued expenses that have already been deducting in determining the current tax liability for current or earlier periods, the treatment in the accounts and by the tax authorities is effectively the same i.e. the item is recognised in the accounts and granted tax relief on an accruals basis. Therefore, the carrying amount and the tax base are the same.

For the following, the carrying amount and tax base differ giving rise to a temporary difference:

- Accrued income that will be taxed on a receipts basis - the carrying amount is the accrued income and the tax base is zero as the income has not yet been recognised by the tax authorities

- An allowance for doubtful debts where tax relief is granted when the debt goes bad - the carrying amount is the allowance and the tax base is zero as the tax relief will not be granted until the debt goes bad.

- An intangible asset relating to development costs which are granted tax relief when paid - the carrying amount is an intangible asset for the unamortised development costs whereas the tax base is zero as tax relief has already been granted on the full amount.

6.5   The correct answers are:

	Account reference	Amount in $
Debit	**Deferred tax liability**	**630**
Credit	**Deferred tax expense (P/L)**	**630**

Workings

1   *Temporary difference*

	Carrying Amount $	Tax base $
Cost	60,000	60,000
Depreciation/Tax-depreciation	(12,000)	30,000
Balance at 31.3.X7	48,000	30,000
Depreciation/Tax-depreciation	(9,600)	(7,500)
Balance at 31.3.X7	38,400	22,500

2   *Deferred/Tax-depreciation*

	$
At 31.3.X7 [(48,000 – 30,000) × 30%]	5,400
Movement (to P/L)	(630)
At 31.3.X8 [38,400 – 22,500) × 30%]	4,770

Note: As there is a reduction to the deferred tax liability, it must be debited. The other side of the double entry is to credit the deferred tax expense in profit or loss.

6.6   A   A deferred tax liability would still be necessary on the revaluation gain as the property will generate taxable income in excess of the depreciation allowed for tax purposes.

Under IAS 12 deferred tax must be recognised for all temporary differences between the tax base of assets and the amount at which they are carried in the statement of financial position. This is true even if there is no intention to sell the asset.

6.7   The correct answer is: -$4,000 (income).

Look at the deferred tax account over the years:

	Year 1	Year 2	Year 3	Year 4	Year 5
	$'000	$'000	$'000	$'000	$'000
Carrying amount	180	160	140	120	100
Tax base	150	100	50	0	0
Taxable temporary difference	30	60	90	120	100
Opening deferred tax liability	0	6	12	18	24
Deferred tax expense	6	6	6	6	(4)
Closing deferred tax liability @ 20%	6	12	18	24	20

6.8   C   Sale of a non-current asset.

Tax losses can be set against earlier or later periods, tax-allowable depreciation will be recognised in different periods from accounting depreciation, interest capitalised will only be recognised as an expense in the accounts as it is amortised, whereas it is deductible for tax purposes as soon as it is paid.

However, profit on sale of a non-current asset is recognised at the moment of sale for both tax and accounting purposes.

6.9   The correct answer is:

As F is expected to make **profits** in the future, a deferred tax **asset** of **$1.12** million can be recorded in the financial statements for the year ended 31 December 20X7.

A deferred tax asset is created as the tax payable in the future will be reduced by the losses that F can carry forward. The deferred tax asset is calculated as the losses carried forward that can be used multiplied by the tax rate of 28%.

6.10   The correct answers are:

	Account reference	$
Dr	**Deferred tax liability**	270,000
Cr	**Tax expense**	270,000

The deferred tax liability at 31 December 20X7 is calculated as:

	$
Carrying value	1.9m
Less Tax base	(1.3m)
Temporary difference	0.6m

Temporary difference 0.6m × 30% = $180,000

The opening liability is $450,000, therefore the journal needs to be posted to reduce the liability from $450,000 to £180,000, by $270,000.

7 Share-based payments

7.1   B $437,167.

Expense for the year ended 31 December 20X5:

= (610 employees × 500 SARs × $4.30 FV at year end × 1/3 vested) = $437,167

Note: The number of employees should be adjusted to remove the **year end estimate** of total leavers over the entire vesting period. The leavers are removed as they will never be entitled to the share-appreciation rights. For cash-settled share-based payments, the fair value **at the year end** is used to give the **best estimate** of the amount payable to employees. The **expense** should be **spread over the vesting period** (here - 3 years) to match the revenue generated by employees working for the entity.

7.2   A   Dr Expense $24,000, Cr Equity $24,000.

This is an equity-settled share-based payment which should be recorded as a credit to equity (rather than as a liability). The debit side of the double entry should be recorded as a remuneration expense and should be spread over the two year vesting period to match to revenue generated by the directors over this period. For equity-settled share-based payments, the fair value at the grant date (rather than at the year end) should be used. Here as all 8 directors are expected to remain in employment for the 2 year vesting period, no directors need to be removed in the calculation.

The amount is calculated as:

500 options × 8 directors × $12 fair value at grant date × 1/2 vested = $24,000.

7.3   The correct answer is:

Account reference	$
Debit Profit or loss	**393,750**
Credit **Other components of equity**	**393,750**

The amount which should be recognised in respect of the share options is calculated as follows:

1000 × (400–25–60) × 5 × ¼ = 393,750

The transaction is equity settled, so the other side of the double entry goes to equity.

7.4   The correct answer is:

Any changes in estimates of expected number of employees being entitled to receive sharebased payment is treated as a change in accounting **estimate** and recognised in the period of the change.

Changes in the expected number of employees is a change in estimate and is treated prospectively.

7.5   B

	$
Dr Liability	177,300
Dr Staff costs	224,860
Cr Cash	402,160

The liability is built up as follows:

20X8	Yr end liab	80 × (600-12-7) × 12.90 × 1/2 =	299,796	Dr Staff costs Cr Liability
	Exercised	80 × 457 × 11.00 =	(402,160)	Dr Liability Cr Cash
		Bal fig	224,860	Dr Staff costs Cr Liability
20X9	Yr end liab	80 × (600-12-15-457) × 13.20 × 2/2 =	122,496	

7.6   B $185,500.

This is an equity-settled share-based payment so should be measured at the fair value at the grant date ie. $1.40. Leavers over the whole vesting period must be removed and the expense should be spread over the two year vesting period.

It is calculated as:

(300 employees − [20 + 15 leavers] × 1,000 options × $1.40 fair value at grant date × ½ vested = $185,500

7.7   B   Dr Expense $288,750, Cr Liability $288,750.

As this is a cash-settled payment, a liability rather than equity should be recorded as a credit balance (credits increase liabilities). Cash should not be credited as no money will be paid to employees until the SARs are exercised. Since the payment relates to employees' service, it is a remuneration expense, not an asset. Expenses are debit balances.

Cash-settled share based payments should be measured at the year end fair value as the best estimate of the amount the employees will be paid. The intrinsic value will only relevant when the SARs are actually exercised and the cash paid to employees. The total cost should be spread over the 3 year vesting period to which the employees' service relates.

The amount is calculated as:

3,500 employees × 25 SARs × 55% remaining in employment for whole vesting period × $18 year end fair value × 1/3 vested = $288,750

7.8   D   DEBIT the statement of profit or loss   CREDIT equity

These are equity-settled share-based payments. A remuneration expense should be recorded in profit or loss with a corresponding credit to equity as these instruments will potentially become shares (on exercise of the options).

7.9   A,D,E   The correct answers are:

- Vesting conditions must be satisfied for the other party to become entitled to receive the share based payment

- The share based payment expense is spread over the vesting period to reflect the value of the goods or services consumed over that period

- A minimum period of service for an employee is an example of a vesting condition

The grant date is the date on which the parties agree to the share based payment arrangement. Once the vesting conditions have been fulfilled the options can be exercised.

7.10   A,E   The correct answers are:

- When measuring a cash settled share based payment, the fair value used in the calculation is adjusted at each period end

- The fair value of the option at the grant date is used to calculate the cost of equity settled transactions

The number of leavers in a employees scheme are adjusted at each period end to reflect the expectations.

The expense is never spread over the exercise period, it is spread over the vesting period.

The company will create a liability for the expected costs of fulfilling a cash settled scheme.

8 Revenue and construction contracts

8.1   B   Recognise the revenue associated with the development of the software and recognise the revenue from the support services evenly over the 24-month support period.

IAS 18 *Revenue* requires fees from the development of customised software to be recognised as revenue by reference to the stage of completion of the development, including completion of services provided for post - delivery service support.

Here we can assume that as the customer has been invoiced for the development, that phase has been completed and revenue for the development should be recognised immediately. Revenue from the post-delivery support should then be spread over the 24 months' support period

8.2   D   Dr Cash $90,000; Cr Deferred income $90,000

Under IAS 18 *Revenue*, the sale of goods is not recorded until the entity has transferred the significant risks and rewards of ownership. This is usually on despatch of the goods. However, here the goods have not yet been dispatched as at the 31 March 20X7 year end so no revenue should be recorded. Instead the $90,000 cash received should be recorded as a deferred income liability in the statement of financial position. In the year ended 31 March 20X8, once the goods have been delivered, the amount will be transferred from deferred income in the statement of financial position to revenue in the statement of profit or loss.

8.3   C   The correct answer is:

SPLOCI: Revenue $540,000; Cost of sales $840,000
SOFP: Gross amounts due from customers $20,000

SPLOCI:

	$
Revenue (60% × 900)	540,000
Cost of sales: contract expenses(60% × [720 + 480])	(720,000)
expected loss (balancing figure)	(120,000)
Loss (900 – 720 – 480)	(300,000)

SOFP:	
Costs incurred	720,000
Recognised loss	(300,000)
Progress billings	(400,000)
Due from customer	20,000

Note: Revenue and expenses on a contract are normally recognised by stage of completion. However, when there is an expected loss on the contract, the full loss must be recognised immediately. The SOFP amount should be recorded as 'gross amounts due from customers' if it is a positive balance (a debit) and 'gross amounts due to customers' if it is a negative balance (a credit). Trade receivables represents the different between amounts invoiced and amounts received from customers – in this scenario, the balance is nil.

8.4   The correct answers are:

Revenue = $ 18 m
Profit   = $ 2.7 m

First you need to work out whether the contract is profit or loss making:

	$m
Total revenue	40
Total expected costs (16 + 18)	(34)
Overall profit	6

Then you need to apply the % complete to the total revenue and total profit:

Revenue	= 45% × $40m	= $18m
Profit	= 45% × $6m	= $2.7m

8.5   B,D   The correct answers are:

- Dr trade receivables, Cr amounts due from customers.
- Dr amounts due from customers, Cr revenue.

When invoices are issued to customers in the year, a trade receivable is recorded but instead of crediting revenue, the interim SOFP account 'amounts due from customers' is credited.

At the year end, revenue is recognised based on stage of completion. The amount is transferred out of the SOFP interim account 'amounts due from customers' and is transferred to revenue in the statement of profit or loss.

8.6   C   Dr Cash $150,000; Cr Deferred income $100,000, Cr Revenue $50,000

Per IAS 18, revenue from sale of goods should be recognised when the entity has transferred to the buyer the significant risks and rewards of ownership of the goods. Here, this will be on delivery of the magazines. By the year end of 31 October 20X7, two of the six months' worth of magazines have been delivered and so 2/6 × $150,000 = $50,000 revenue should be recognised. The remaining $100,000 received ($150,000 - $50,000) should be treated as deferred income in the statement of financial position as the risks and benefits have not yet been transferred.

8.7   B $3,000.

IAS 18 *Revenue* requires revenue from services to be recognised on a stage of completion basis. As at the year end, 6 months' work has been completed meaning that 6 × $500 = $3,000 should be recognised as revenue in profit or loss. The remaining $3,000 not yet earned should be treated as deferred income in the statement of financial position.

The incorrect answers include recognising a full year's revenue ($6,000), including only 3 months instead of 6 months ($1,500), including 1 month instead of 3 months ($500) and recognising no revenue even though work has been completed.

8.8   The correct answer is: $60,000

As the outcome of the contract cannot be reliably measured the revenue should be recognised to the extent that costs are expected to be recovered.

8.9   D   Revenue: $165m; Profit: $16.5m

Workings

1   Overall profit

	$'000
Total revenue	300
Total expected costs (170 + 100)	(270)
Overall profit	30

Note: the expected costs figure should be the best estimate at the current year end (here: 31 March 20X9) which is why $270m rather than the original estimate of $240m has been used.

2   Stage of completion of contract (on work completed basis)

= 165/300 × 100% = 55%

3   Amounts recognised in SPLOCI for the year ended 31 March 20X9

	$'000
Revenue (300 × 55%)	165.0
Profit (30 × 55%)	16.5

8.10	A

Gross amounts due from customers (asset): $56.5m

Stage of completion of contract (on work completed basis) = 165/300 × 100% = 55%

Amount to be recorded in the SOFP:

	$'000
Costs incurred	170.0
Profit recognised (300 – 170 – 100) × 55%)	16.5
	186.5
Less progress billings	(130.0)
Amount recognised as an asset/(liability)	56.5

Recognise an asset in statement of financial position under current assets:
Gross amount due from customers — $56,500

9 Basic groups

9.1 B $3,137,000.

	$
Cash	1,200,000
Deferred consideration (500,000 × 1/1.072)	437,000
Shares in MN	1,500,000
	3,137,000

9.2 C $44,000.

	$
TCI	238,000
FV deprecation	(8,000)
Goodwill impairment	(10,000)
	220,000
NCI share (20%)	**44,000**

9.3 A,C,E,G The correct answers are:

- Revenue will need to be reduced by $1,000,000 to reflect the intra-group trading.

- Cost of sales will need to be reduced by $1,000,000 to eliminate the intra-group purchase.

- Cost of sales will need to be increased by $100,000 to remove the unrealised profit from closing inventory.

- Non-controlling interest will need to be adjusted to reflect the unrealised profit in closing inventory.

The intra-group sales price of $1,000,000 must be eliminated from revenue and cost of sales so that only third party revenue and cost of sales are shown in the group accounts. Cost of sales will also need to be increased to remove the unrealised profit from closing inventory. A common mistake is to deduct unrealised profit from cost of sales but this would have the unwanted effect of increasing rather than decreasing profit.

As S charges a mark-up of 25% on sales, cost of sales is 100% and sales 125%. Unrealised profit is therefore calculated as:

$1,000,000 × 1/2 in inventory × 25/125 mark up = $100,000.

If it had been incorrectly calculated using a 25% margin, the incorrect answer of $125,000 would have been reached ($1,000,000 × 1/2 × 25/100 margin).

As the subsidiary is the seller, the unrealised profit must be deducted from the subsidiary's profit and total comprehensive income in the non-controlling interests working.

9.4 B The existence of contingent liabilities in the books of the subsidiary at the acquisition date.

The normal rule of IAS 37 *Provisions, Contingent Liabilities and Contingent Assets* of disclosing rather than recognising a contingent liability does not apply on acquisition of a subsidiary. Where there is a present obligation arising from past events and the fair value can be measured reliably, IFRS 3 *Business Combinations* requires a contingent liability to be recognised.

The purpose of fair value adjustments is to record true goodwill at the acquisition date. Therefore post acquisition changes in net assets are not relevant. Nor should a provision be recognised for post-acquisition reorganisation costs or anticipated losses as no obligation exist at the acquisition date.

9.5 The correct answer is: $180,000.

	$	$
Consideration transferred		450,000
Fair value of non-controlling interest (3.75 × 20,000)		75,000
Fair value of net assets:		
Share capital	100,000	
Retained earnings	165,000	
Fair value adjustment	80,000	
		(345,000)
Goodwill		180,000

9.6 The correct answer is: $18,060

	$'000
ZA NBV	16,000
PJ NBV	1,750
FV uplift (2,200 – 1,890)	310
	18,060

9.7 B $660,000

		$
Consideration transferred		3,700,000
Non controlling interest acquired		1,140,000
Fair value of net assets acquired		
Share capital	2,000,000	
Retained earnings	1,770,000	
FV of PPE	310,000	
		(4,080,000)
		760,000
Less: impairment losses on goodwill to date		(100,000)
		660,000

9.8 A $397,500.

	$
Per question	2,400,000
Pre-acquisition retained earnings	(1,770,000)
	630,000
Group share of HJ's post acquisition reserves: (630,000 × 75%)	472,500
Less impairment loss on goodwill: (100,000 × 75%)	(75,000)
	397,500

9.9 B,C,D The correct answers are:

- It will be included at its fair value on acquisition plus share of post-acquisition earnings of AB.
- It will be included as a separate component of equity.
- 25% of the impairment in the goodwill arising on acquisition will be debited to it.

Post acquisition earnings will be credited to non-controlling interest, not debited. Non-controlling interest is included in the equity of the ZA Group, not non-current liabilities.

9.10   The correct answer is: **$15 million**

	$m
Consideration transferred	50
Non-controlling interests (at fair value)	30
Less: Fair value of net assets at acquisition	(65)
	15

The provision for reorganisation costs cannot be included in the goodwill calculation because it reflects the acquirer's intentions, rather than an actual liability of E at the date of acquisition (IFRS 3 and IAS 37).

10 Associates and joint arrangements

10.1   The correct answer is: $407,030.

With an associate, the group share of the unrealised profit needs to be removed at the year end:

Unrealised profit = $10,000 × 3/4 in inventory × 20/100 margin × 30% = $450.

The adjustment should be made in the parent's column (even though the associate is the seller) to avoid multiplying the unrealised profit by the group share twice.

The consolidated retained earnings working is as follows:

	EF Group $	SR $
Per question	390,000	90,000
Provision for unrealised profit	(450)	
Pre-acquisition		(22,000)
		68,000
Group share of SR's post acquisition retained earnings (68,000 × 30%)	20,400	
Less: Impairment of investment in associate	(2,920)	
	407,030	

10.2   The correct answer is: $126,900.

	$
Cost of associate	75,000
Share of post-acquisition reserves [($270,000 – $50,000) × 30%]	66,000
	141,000
Impairment (10% × $141,000)	(14,100)
	126,900

10.3 A,D   The correct answers are:

- A joint venture is always structured through a separate vehicle.
- A joint venture must have a contractual arrangement.

A **joint operation** is a joint arrangement whereby the parties that have joint control have **rights to the assets and obligations for the liabilities** relating to the arrangement.

A **joint venture** is a joint arrangement whereby the parties that have joint control have **rights to the net assets** of the arrangement.

A joint venture must be structured through a separate vehicle. However, an arrangement that is structured through a separate vehicle may also be a joint operation, depending on the terms and the circumstances (i.e. whether the parties have rights to the assets and obligations for the liabilities OR rights to the net assets).

Both joint ventures and joint operations need to have a contractual arrangement and joint control. This is what distinguishes them from associates.

10.4 A,D The correct answers are:

- Joint ventures must be equity accounted.

- Joint operations are accounted for by including the investor's share of assets, liabilities, income and expenses as per the contractual arrangement.

10.5 A Disclose information that enables users to evaluate the nature of and risks associated with interest in other entities and the effect of those on financial position, performance and cash flows.

This is the objective direct from IFRS 12.

The other options are incorrect for the following reasons:

As well as covering associates and subsidiaries, IFRS 12 applies to joint arrangements and unconsolidated structured entities. Investments which are treated under IAS 39 in the group accounts are outside the scope of IFRS 12. Consolidation of subsidiaries and elimination of intragroup transactions are requirements of IFRS 10 not IFRS 12. Equity accounting for associates and joint ventures is required by IAS 28 not IFRS 12.

10.6 B $570,000.

	$'000
Cost of investment	650
Share of post-acquisition retained earnings (1,600 – 720) × 25%	220
Impairment	(300)
	570

10.7 C $222,270.

	$
Group share of profit for the year (721,000 × 35%)	252,350
PUP (240,000 × 40% × 30%) × 35%	(10,080)
Impairment loss	(20,000)
	222,270

10.8 A,D The correct answers are:

- The parties with joint control have rights to the assets and obligations for the liabilities of the joint venture.

- The arrangement is contractual.

If the parties with joint control have rights to the net assets of the arrangement, then the arrangement is a joint venture.

A joint operation may, in certain cases be structured through a separate entity.

10.9 B,D,E The correct answers are:

- Spice will be treated as a joint venture in this case, but only because of the requirement that key policy decisions require the consent of at least five of the directors.

- Sugar should equity account for Spice in its consolidated financial statements

- In Sugar's own financial statements, the investment in Spice should either be held at cost or in accordance with IAS 39

To be a joint arrangement, joint control is required so simply owning one third of the shares each is not enough. Unanimous consent is required and as all three investors' votes are needed here, there is joint control.

Spice is a joint venture rather than a joint operation as Sugar has rights to the net assets of Spice. The correct accounting treatment in the individual financial statements for a joint venture is to record the investment at cost or per IAS 39 (at fair value with gains/losses in OCI). The correct accounting treatment in the consolidated financial statements is to equity account.

Accounting for Sugar's share of Spice's assets, liabilities, expenses and revenue is incorrect because this would be the accounting treatment for a joint operation.

11 Changes in group structures

11.1 D $2,950,000.

	$'000	$'000
Consideration transferred		10,350
Non-controlling interests (at full FV)		5,400
Fair value of acquirer's previously- held equity interest		2,000
Less: Fair value of identifiable net assets at acquisition		
Share capital	10,000	
Retained earnings	4,800	
		(14,800)
		2,950

11.2 A $76,000,000.

	$'000
Funny	30,000
Peculiar	32,000
Strange (28,000 × 6/12)	14,000
	76,000

Funny owned a 75% stake in Strange (6m/8m shares) prior to the disposal of the shares in Strange on 30 June 20X7, making Strange a subsidiary for the first 6 months of the year.

Then on 30 June 20X7, Funny sold a 35% stake in Strange(2.8m/8m shares), retaining a 40% stake (3.2m/8m shares), making Strange an associate for the last 6 months of the year.

Therefore, Funny only needs to consolidate Strange for the first 6 months of the year (for the second 6 months, equity accounting would apply i.e. share of profit/OCI of associate × 6/12).

This is why only 6/12 of Strange's revenue has been included above.

11.3 C $620,000 adjustment to parent's equity.

		$'000	$'000
Fair value of consideration received			4,400
Increase in NCI at date of disposal:	Share capital	10,000	
	Retained earnings	8,900	
		18,900	
× 20%			(3,780)
			620

Goodwill is not included in the 'increase in NCI at date of disposal' figure because **NCI** was measured **at the proportionate share of net assets** at acquisition (i.e. the partial goodwill method) which means that no goodwill has been recognised in respect of the NCI.

Before the disposal, JL held an 80% stake in DP (8m/10m shares), making DP a subsidiary. JL then sold 25% of their 8m shares in DP i.e. 2m shares which represents a 20% holding in DP (2m of the total 10m shares), retaining 6m shares i.e. a 60% stake (6m/10m shares), meaning that DP was still a subsidiary.

Therefore this is a **subsidiary to subsidiary disposal** i.e. the parent retains control and therefore the control boundary has not been crossed. In substance, this is a transaction between group shareholders rather than a disposal i.e. the parent sells a 20% stake to NCI. This is why an **adjustment to equity** rather than a profit on disposal is required.

11.4   **B** $365,000 profit.

	$	$
Fair value of consideration received		4,000
Fair value of 40% investment retained (1m × 40% × $10.10)		4,040
Less: Share of consolidated carrying value when control lost		
Net assets (8,500 + (800 × 6/12))	8,900	
Goodwill	1,000	
Non-controlling interests	(2,250)	
		(7,670)
Profit on disposal		365

This part disposal leaves SP with an investment that will be treated as an associate so control has been lost. This means that a profit or loss must be recognised in the statement of profit or loss, and the remaining holding in MN must be remeasured to its fair value as at the date of the disposal. Goodwill is written off in full at the point where control is lost. In this example, the disposal occurs part way through the year so the net assets at the date of the disposal need to be calculated by taking the opening figure plus a portion of the subsidiary's current year profit.

11.5   **D,E,F**   The correct answers are:

- The remaining 30% shareholding is revalued to fair value

- CV is consolidated into the statement of profit or loss for the first three months of the year

- CV appears as an investment in an associate in the statement of financial position at the year end

An adjustment to equity is only required when there is no change in substance, i.e. the disposal still results in a subsidiary. There is no non controlling interest (as it is a 100% subsidiary) and on disposal it becomes an associate.

11.6   **A** $68,500 debit.

	$
Fair value of consideration paid	(135,000)
Decrease in NCI in net assets on acquisition	
(20/40 × 133,000*)	66,500
Adjustment to parent's equity	(68,500)
*NCI at 28.2.X7	$
NCI b/fwd 1.9.X6	127,000
Profit attributable to NCI to 28.2.X7	
30,000 × 6/12 × 40%)	6,000
NCI at 28.2.X7 133,000	

The complete journal to reflect the transaction would be:

DR Non-controlling interests	$66,500	
DR Parent's equity	$68,500	
CR Cash		$135,000

11.7   **A** $650,000 profit.

First, NCI at disposal must be calculated as it is needed for the group profit on disposal calculation:

	$
NCI at acquisition (at fair value)	150,000
NCI share of post acquisition reserves [20% × [710,000 - 460,000]]	50,000
NCI at disposal	200,000

Then the group profit on disposal can be calculated

	$	$
Consideration received		750,000
Fair value of 40% investment retained		700,000
Less: Share of consolidated carrying value when control lost		
Net assets (100,000 share capital + 710,000 reserves)	810,000	
Goodwill	190,000	
Non-controlling interests (see above)	(200,000)	
		(800,000)
Group profit on disposal		650,000

Note: ST was an 80% subsidiary prior to disposal. Then PQ sold half of its 80% shareholding in ST i.e. a 40% stake, leaving a 40% associate. Therefore, the control boundary has been crossed. In substance, PQ has sold an 80% subsidiary and acquired a 40% associate. This is why a profit on disposal is required and the remaining 40% shareholding must be revalued to fair value.

11.8 C $4,800,000.

	$'000
Cost of associate (fair value at date control lost)	4,500
Share of post acquisition reserves (2,000 × 6/12 × 30%)	300
	4,800

Prior to the disposal, Rose was a 60% subsidiary. Geranium sold half of its shareholding in Rose i.e. a 30% stake, retaining a 30% holding, making Rose an associate. Therefore, the correct treatment in the consolidated statement of financial position is to equity account for Rose.

The cost of the associate is the fair value at the date control is lost (i.e. 1 July 20X9) because in substance at that date Geranium sold a subsidiary and acquired an associate.

11.9 B,D,E The correct answers are:

- The non-controlling interest will be initially recognised on 31 December 20X9.

- Goodwill is initially calculated at 31 December 20X9 and will include the fair value of the original 10% holding in Y.

- Goodwill and non-controlling interests are recognised only when S controls Y.

Goodwill is not calculated on the initial purchase of 10% as it is only calculated when the parent obtains control.

The goodwill is calculated on the entire holding once the parent gains control, ie on the 10% plus the additional 60%.

11.10 B X s|b C

Dr NCI	$2,800
Dr Group retained earnings	$200
Cr Bank	$3,000

The NCI is decreased by the share of net assets they have sold at the acquisition date: ($14,000 × 20%) = $2,800

Cash is reduced by the $3,000 paid to acquire the shares.

The balance goes to group retained earnings.

12 Indirect control of subsidiaries

12.1   The correct answer is: $'000 179.

	Sassoon		Thomas	
	$'000	$'000	$'000	$'000
Consideration transferred		400		
(90% × 100)				90
Non-controlling interest (atFV)		44		75
Less: Net assests at acquisition				
Share capital	100		50	
Retained earnings (1.1.X5)	200		80	
		(300)		(130)
		144		35

Total goodwill = $144,000 + $35,000 = $179,000

Note: Goodwill is calculated at the date the parent gains control of the entity. Owen does not gain control of Thomas until Owen acquires Sassoon on 1 January 20X5. Therefore, the retained earnings used in the calculation of goodwill in Thomas are as at 1 January 20X5 (not 1 January 20X4). Also, remember that as the investment in the sub-subsidiary (Thomas) is in the subsidiary's (Sassoon's) books, we need to multiply it by the parent's share in the subsidiary i.e. 90%.

12.2 D $7.68 million.

Effective interest in F   = 80% × 60%
                       = 48%

Post acquisition profits in F = 48% × (30 − 14)
                                = $7.68m

The acquisition date of the sub-subsidiary F is 1 January 20X2, the date when D gained control of E. This is because at that date, E already had control of F and prior to that date, D had no interest in either entity. Therefore the pre-acquisition reserves are as at 1 January 20X2.

12.3 D $7,600.

NCI in P:

Effective interest in P = 60% × 80% =	48%
Therefore NCI in P =	52%
	100%

NCI in G (40% × 6,000) + NCI in P (52% × 10,000) = $7,600.

12.4 C   36%

This is calculated as 60% × 60% = 36%. As AB controls CD directly and EF indirectly (via CD), EF would be treated as a sub-subsidiary of AB and consolidated in the group accounts of AB.

12.5 A $19,500.

	$
NCI at acquisition	45,000
NCI share of post acquisition reserves (30% × (180,000 − 80,000))	30,000
Share of impairment losses (30% × 25,000)	(7,500)
NCI share of investment in K (30% × 160,000)	(48,000)
	19,500

12.6 B,C,D The correct answers are:

- 100% of the trade receivables balances of both B and G will be included in the statement of financial position.

- The consolidated profit or loss will include 100% of the revenue of G earned in the seven months to 31 December 20X4.

- P controls both B and G and both will be consolidated as subsidiaries as at 31 December 20X4.

P has direct control over B by virtue of the 60% share holding, and indirect control over G, by virtue of having control of B who in turn has control of G through the 70% share holding. On consolidation 100% of the assets and liabilities of B and G will be included as P has control over each. When calculating equity P will include the effective interest in G, of 60% × 70% = 42%, and will attribute 58% to the non-controlling interest.

12.7 A $3,560,000.

HI and JK did not become part of the FG group until 31 December 20X1. Therefore we need the post acquisition profits from that date using the effective interest in JK of 60% (80% × 75%).

	$
HI (12,200,000 − 10,000,000) × 80%	1,760,000
JK (10,600,000 − 7,600,000) × 60%	1,800,000
	3,560,000

12.8 D $553,000.

Current assets = 230,000 + 180,000 + 160,000 − 5,000 + 6,000 − 6,000 − 12,000 = 553,000

PUP = 60,000 × 20/120 × ½ = 5,000

The PUP must be eliminated from inventory which sits within current assets.

The adjustment for cash in transit is to reduce the receivables by $6,000 and to increase cash by $6,000 in D's books. This results in a nil net effect on current assets. After this adjustment, the intragroup receivable is D's books is $12,000 ($18,000 - $6,000) which agrees with the intragroup payable in F's books. The intragroup receivable is D's books. The intragroup receivable and payable of $12,000 are then eliminated from current assets and current liabilities respectively.

12.9 The correct answer is: $12,000.

	$'000
Consideration transferred (75% × 320,000)	240
Non controlling interest (300,000 × 40% × $1.10)	132
Net assets acquired	(360)
	12

The effective interest in JM is 75% × 80% = 60%, making NCI 40%. The investment is in the subsidiary's (YH's) books and so must be multiplied by the parent's share in the subsidiary (YH) i.e. 75%. The NCI share (25%) of the investment is cancelled in the subsidiary's (YH's) NCI working.

12.10 The correct answer is:

In order to calculate the consolidated retained earnings of the YH group **60.5%** of the post acquisition reserves of LP are consolidated. To calculate the non controlling interest on the statement of financial position for YH an NCI percentage of **39.5%** is used.

The percentages used for the sub-subsidiary are the effective rates (70% × 75% + 8%) = 60.5% and thus the NCI is 39.5%.

13 Foreign subsidiaries

13.1 B   A $62,250 loss.

The exchange loss is arrived at by comparing the increase in net assets to the retained profit for the year. The increase in net assets is calculated as the closing net assets at closing rate less the opening net assets at the opening rate. The retained profit is the profit at the average rate less the dividend at the actual rate.

	A$	A$
Closing net assets at closing rate (B$6,510,000/1.6)		4,068,750
Opening net assets at opening rate (B$4,557,000/1.4)		(3,255,000)
		813,750
Profit for the year (B$1,674,000/1.5)	1,116,000	
Dividend (B$372,00/1.55)	(240,000)	
		(876,000)
		(62,250)

Note that other comprehensive income should include 100% of this loss (whereas consolidated reserves would include the group share of the loss).

The incorrect answers result from taking the group share of the exchange loss in error (A$49,800), translating the dividend at the average rather than the actual rate (A$54,250) and ignoring the dividend (A$302,250).

13.2 B $7,027,000.

	€000
Consideration transferred	20,000
Non-controlling interest	4,200
	24,200
Fair value of net assets	(19,000)
Goodwill	5,200
Translated at closing rate 0.74 Euro to $1	$7,027,000

13.3 A $70,720.

The total effect of the acquisition on group reserves includes:

- The group share of the subsidiary's post acquisition reserves
- The group share of exchange differences on net assets and profit

The subsidiary was acquired part-way through the current period. Therefore the post-acquisition reserves are going to comprise the profit for the 9 months in the year the subsidiary was owned (1 April 20X7 – 31 December 20X7). This figure is given in the question as 97,920 Crowns and should be divided by the average rate for the period of 1.7 giving post acquisition profits of $57,600 (97,920 Crowns/1.7).

The group share of exchange differences on net assets and profit is calculated as follows:

	$
Closing net assets at closing rate (489,600 Crowns/1.6)	306,000
Opening net assets at opening rate (391,680 Crowns/1.8)	(217,600)
	88,400
Less: retained profit translated at average rate (97,920 Crowns/1.7)	(57,600)
Exchange gain	30,800

The total amount to be recognised in group reserves is calculated as follows:

	$
Group share of post acquisition reserves (57,600 × 80%)	46,080
Group share of exchange differences (30,800 × 80%)	24,640
Total amount to be recognised in group reserves in relation to EF	70,720

13.4 B,D The correct answers are:

- It is the currency of the year end financial statements.
- The entity may choose which presentation currency to use.

The currency of the primary economic environment is the definition of the functional currency of an entity. The currency that mainly influences the entity's sales price is one of the factors IAS 21 requires to be considered when determining the functional currency.

The currency of the year end financial statements and the currency the entity may choose both relate to the presentation currency which is defined as the currency in which the financial statements are presented. IAS 21 allows the entity to choose its own presentation currency.

13.5 The correct answers are:

When a foreign subsidiary has a different functional currency to the presentation currency of the group financial statements, **all** assets and liabilities of the subsidiary must be translated at the **closing rate**, income and expenses at the **average rate** and exchange differences should be reported in **other comprehensive income**.

13.6 A $17,980.

Consolidated revenue is calculated as follows:

	$
ST	12,000
WX (28,050 Blops/3.75)	7,480
Less: Intra-group revenue (5,700 Blops/3.8)	(1,500)
Group revenue	17,980

WX's revenue is translated at the average rate of 3.75 as an approximation of the actual rate. However, the actual date of the intra-group revenue is known i.e. 12 September 20X5 so the actual exchange rate on that date of 3.8 is used to translate it. Another reason for using the actual rate for the intra-group revenue is that the intra-group cost of sales would have been recorded in ST's (the parent's) financial statements at the spot rate at the transaction date and the same amount must be cancelled out of revenue and cost of sales.

13.7 B I and III.

IAS 21 defines the functional currency as the currency of the primary economic environment in which the entity operates. One of the indicators that a subsidiary's functional currency is its own local currency is that its activities are carried out with a significant degree of autonomy.

Both I and III operate largely autonomously therefore their functional currencies will be their own local currency. However, II's activities are carried out as an extension of its parent. Therefore its primary economic environment is that of the parent, and its functional currency is the parent's currency (rather than its own local currency).

13.8 The correct answer is: $1,902,000.

Translation of Mole's SOFP:

	Unit'000	Rate	$'000
Other assets	1,260	2.5	504
Share capital	500	2.0	250
Pre-acquisition reserves	220	2.0	110
Post-acquisition reserves (460 – 220)	240	Bal.	24
			384
Liabilities	300	2.5	120
			504

Consolidated reserves:

	Rat $'000	Mole Unit'000
Per question/translation working (110 + 24)	1,900	134
Less: pre-acquisition		(110)
		24
Share of Mole's post acquisition reserves (24 × 75%)	18	
Exchange losses arising on goodwill (given)	(16)	
	1,902	

Note: 100% of the exchange losses on goodwill have been deducted as it is the partial goodwill method (NCI is measured at the proportionate share of net assets) meaning that all of the goodwill and all of the associated exchange differences belong to the group.

13.9   B,D   The correct answers are:

- The functional currency of OP will be determined by the currency that dominates the primary economic environment in which OP operates.

- OP operates autonomously and raises its own finance which indicates that its functional currency should be Ludd.

Functional currency is determined by the primary economic environment within which it operates. Companies within the same group can have different functional currency, the functional currency of a subsidiary is not determined by the functional currency of the parent. Presentational currency can be any currency that an entity chooses to use.

13.10   The correct answer is: $'000 425.

	Sh'000	Sh'000	Rate	$'000
Consideration transferred		3,000		
Non-controlling interest		1,200		
Less: FV of identifiable NA:				
Share capital	1,000			
Pre-acq'n reserves	1,500			
		(2,500)		
		1,700	5	340
Exchange gain/(loss) – 20X8 *				85
		1,700	4	425

* The exchange gain did not need to be calculated here but is included for future reference.

14 Consolidated statement of changes in equity

14.1   B $1,100,000.

The dividends to include in the consolidated statement of changes in equity are:

	$
Attributable to the owners of the parent (SP's dividend)	1,000,000
Non-controlling interests (AX's dividend × NCI%) [400,000 × 25%]	100,000
Total	1,100,000

Note that the group share of the associate's dividend i.e. 30% × $200,000 = $60,000 is excluded as it cancels on consolidation. Instead the group share of the associate's profit and other comprehensive income would be included in the consolidated statement of profit or loss and other comprehensive income when equity accounting for the associate.

14.2   The correct answers are:

	Attributable to equity holders of the parent $000	Non-controlling interest $000
Balance at the start of the year	3,350	650
Comprehensive income for the year	1,280	150
Dividends paid	(200)	(30)
Adjustment to NCI for additional purchase of GH shares	**BLANK**	**(506)**
Adjustment to parent's equity for additional purchase of GH shares	**(14)**	**BLANK**

(handwritten: } 770.)

(handwritten: ?Given in Q.)

Fair value of consideration paid	(520)
Decrease in NCI on acquisition (759 × 20%/30%)	506
Adjustment to parent's equity	(14)

(759 is circled)

Double entry:

Dr NCI	506
Dr Parent's retained earnings	14
Cr Cash	520

14.3   D

TCI for owners of parent	TCI for non-controlling interests
$278,400	$19,600

	$
Consolidated total comprehensive income	298,000
($200,000 + $100,000 − [PUP: $15,000 × 2/3 in inventories × 20/100 margin])	
Total comprehensive income attributable to:	
Owners of the parent (balancing figure)	278,400
Non-controlling interests ([$100,000 − PUP $2,000] × 20%)	19,600
	298,000

14.4   C,E,F   The correct answers are:

- Issue of share capital
- Total comprehensive income for the year
- Dividends

A gain on revaluation of a property form part of the total comprehensive income for the year figure so would not require separate line disclosure. Total comprehensive income for the year comprises both profit for the year and other comprehensive income, therefore, they do not need separate disclosure in their own right.

14.5 C As an increase to the 'equity attributable to the owners of the parent' of $1,000,000.

The equity attributable to the owners of the parent includes the parent's share capital and premium and consolidated reserves. Therefore, both the increase to share capital (500,000 × 50 cents = $250,000) and the increase to share premium (500,000 × $1.50 = $750,000) should both be recorded as an increase to the 'equity attributable to the owners of the parent'.

This is not an intragroup transaction as the shareholders of the parent are outside the group.

There is no non-controlling interests impact as the shares have been issued by the parent rather than the subsidiary.

14.6 The correct answers are:

	Attributable to the owners of the parent $'000	Non-controlling interest $'000
Balance at 1 September X6	449,600	127,000
Total comprehensive income	119,970	9,000
Adjustment to NCI for additional purchase of CMU shares	**BLANK**	**(66,500)**
Adjustment to parent's equity for additional purchase of CMU shares	**(13,500)**	**BLANK**

Adjustment to equity:

	$
Consideration transferred	(80,000)
Decrease in NCI (133,000 × 20%/40%)	66,500
	13,500

NCI on 28 February 20X7:

	$
NCI at 1 September 20X6	127,000
NCI share of profit up to 28 February 20X7 (30,000 × 6/12 × 40%)	6,000
	133,000

14.7 B,C,D,E The correct answers are:

- It is a primary statement required by IAS 1 *Presentation of Financial Statements*

- The total comprehensive income for the year line comes from the ownership reconciliation in the consolidated statement of profit or loss and other comprehensive income

- It reconciles equity from the prior year's consolidated statement of financial position to equity from the current year's consolidated statement of financial position

- Movements in equity in the year include consolidated total comprehensive income, share issues and dividends paid

Adjustments to equity arising from subsidiary to subsidiary step acquisitions or disposals result in a movement in equity and therefore must be included in the 'equity attributable to the owners of the parent' with a corresponding decrease or increase in non-controlling interest in the 'non-controlling interests column.

The group share of the subsidiary is included in the 'equity attributable to the owners of the parent' column. The NCI share of the subsidiary is included in the 'non-controlling interests' column.

Whilst associates are included in the consolidated statement of changes in equity (the group share of post acquisition reserves), they will be included in the 'equity attributable to the owners of the parent' column rather than a separate column in their own right.

14.8   The correct answer is: $5,812,500

Consolidated reserves at 1 January 20X5:

	LK	SW
	$	$
Reserves at 1 January 20X5 per question	4,500,000	500,000
Less: Pre-acquisition reserves		(350,000)
		150,000
Share of SW post-acquisition (150,000 × 75%)	112,500	
	4,612,500	

Equity attributable to the owners of the parent comprises:

	$
Parent's share capital	1,000,000
Parent's share premium	200,000
Consolidated reserves	4,612,500
	5,812,500

14.9   B   It includes dividends paid by the parent and dividends paid by the subsidiary to its external shareholders.

The 'equity attributable to the owners' of the parent column includes the parent's dividends and the 'non-controlling interests' column includes dividends paid by the subsidiary to the NCI.

Dividends paid by the parent to the subsidiary are cancelled on consolidation as they are an intragroup item.

Dividend income from subsidiaries and associates will be included in the parent's total comprehensive income figure. As they are intragroup items, they must be cancelled as a consolidation adjustment before entering the total comprehensive income line into the consolidated changes in equity.

14.10 B,C,D   The correct answers are:

- It should include the share capital and share premium of the parent and the year end consolidated reserves figure

- It should come to the same number as equity before non-controlling interests in the year end consolidated statement of financial position

- It can be calculated as the brought down equity attributable to the owners of the parent, plus total comprehensive income for the year attributable to the owners of the parent, less the parent's dividends paid plus any share issues by the parent in the year

The other answers are incorrect because unrealised profit on intragroup trading is cancelled on consolidation, the share capital and share premium of the subsidiary are excluded from the consolidated statement of financial position and the non-controlling interests relate to the subsidiary not the owners of the parent.

15 Consolidated statements of cash flows

15.1 A $130,000.

You need to draw up a non-controlling interests working to find the dividends paid to NCI as a balancing figure:

	$
B/d (from 20X4 SOFP)	525,000
TCI attributable to NCI	55,000
NCI in subsidiary acquired	
(400,000 × 25%)	100,000
	680,000
Dividends paid to NCI	
(balancing figure)	(130,000)
C/d (from 20X5 SOFP)	550,000

The incorrect answers would have been arrived at by mixing up the b/d and c/d balances ($180,000), excluding NCI in the subsidiary acquired ($30,000), deducting NCI in profit instead of adding it ($20,000) and taking the group share of the subsidiary acquired rather than the NCI share ($330,000).

15.2 E $767,000.

Cash generated from operations is calculated as follows:

	$
Profit before taxation	775,000
Decrease in inventories (W1)	5,000
Increase in receivables (W1)	(33,000)
Increase in payables (W1)	20,000
Cash generated from operations	767,000

Workings

1 Movement in working capital

	Inventories $	Receivables $	Payables $
B/D	475,000	800,000	530,000
Acquisition of subsidiary	80,000	110,000	70,000
	555,000	910,000	600,000
Increase/(decrease) [bal. figure]	(5,000)	33,000	20,000
C/d	550,000	943,000	620,000

Be careful with the signs when posting the movements to the statement of cash flows. If inventory has decreased, we've sold some so it's a cash inflow.

If receivables have increased, that means more credit sales which is bad for our cash flow so should be negative. But if payables have increased, it is good for our cash flow as we're not having to pay for cash purchases so it should be postive in the cash flow.

The incorrect answers would have arisen from ignoring the acquisition ($647,000), deducting rather than adding the acquisition ($527,000), adjusting for the group share rather than 100% of the acquisition ($743,000) or treating the decrease in inventory as an increase ($757,000).

15.3 The correct answer is: $6,300.

You need to complete an investment in associate working to find the dividends received as a balancing figure:

	$
B/ d	107,900
Share of profit	10,000
Share of other comprehensive income	5,000
	122,900
Dividends received (balancing figure)	**(6,300)**
C/ d	116,600

15.4 A Dividends can be shown under either operating activities or financing activities.

15.5 A $870,000.

You need to complete a property, plant and equipment working to find additions as a balancing figure:

	$
B/ d	3,700,000
Acquisition of subsidiary	500,000
Depreciation	(970,000)
	3,230,000
Additions (balancing figure)	870,000
C/ d	4,100,000

Don't forget to include 100% of the PPE of the subsidiary acquired because this subsidiary will be consolidated for the first time this year and when we consolidate, we add across 100% of the assets and liabilities of subsidiary (rather than the group share).

15.6 A $41 million.

First, you need to do a finance lease liability working to find additions to property, plant and equipment under finance leases:

Finance lease liability:	$m
B/d (10 + 45)	55
Rentals paid	(18)
Interest	6
	43
Additions under finance leases (balancing figure)	28
C/d	71

Then you need to do a property, plant and equipment working to find cash additions to property, plant and equipment:

Property, plant and equipment:	$m
B/d	175
Disposals	(10)
Depreciation	(42)
Additions under finance leases (see finance lease working above)	28
	151
Additions for cash (balancing figure)	**41**
C/d	192

Note that the cash flow in relation to finance leases is the rental paid of $18 million and this would be split into its interest and capital components. The interest of $6 million would be posted to 'operating activities' and the capital of $12 million to 'financing activities'.

15.7 The correct answer is: $4,000

You need to prepare a non-controlling interests working to find the dividends paid as a balancing figure:

	$
B/d	100,000
NCI in	TCI 7,000
NCI in subsidiary acquired	8,000
	115,000
Dividends paid (balancing figure)	**(4,000)**
C/d	111,000

Note: The consolidated SPLOCI figure that you should use for the NCI working should be the NCI in total comprehensive income (not profit) as you need to include everything that makes NCI go up in the year (i.e. their share of profit and OCI).

15.8 A $230,000 outflow in one line.

You only need to include the cash element of the consideration paid to buy the subsidiary which is $150,000 (the share element is non-cash). This is a cash outflow. You also need to add to this the subsidiary's overdraft of $80,000 which will be consolidated for the first time on acqisition of the subsidiary - this will cause group cash to fall so is also an outflow. IAS 7 requires these two cash flows to be aggregated resulting in a total cash outflow of $230,000 (i.e. $150,000 + $80,000).

15.9 C $535,000.

	$
Sales proceeds	500,000
Cash balance deconsolidated	(15,000)
Overdraft deconsolidated	50,000
	535,000

The bank loan is not included as it does not fall within the definition of cash and cash equivalents.

15.10 C,F,G,H The correct answers are:

- Cash paid to acquire an interest in an associate
- Acquisition of equipment for cash
- Proceeds on sale of subsidiary (net of cash disposed of)
- Dividends received from associate

Dividends paid to non-controlling interest and acquisition of plant under finance lease are financing cash flows.

Profit on sale of property, plant and equipment and gain on sale of subsidiary are adjusted out of the 'operating activities' section of the statement of cash flows, as they do not represent cash flows.

16 Related parties

16.1   D   Arrangements entered into by the production director of the reporting entity to provide a review of the production facilities of a company controlled by his wife. The service will be provided at a full commercial price.

The director is a related party because he is considered to be key management personnel. The IAS 24 definition of a related party also extends to the close family of key management personnel. Close family includes children, spouse, domestic partner and dependents. Therefore, the director's wife is a related party. Under IAS 24, entities controlled by a related party also qualify as a related party. Therefore the company controlled by the director's wife is a related party. This is why the transaction requires disclosure.

The fact that a full price has been charged is irrelevant, all material related party transactions must be disclosed.

Trade unions in the normal course of their activities are not related parties (unless they have the capacity to control the entity).

Providers of finance and government departments and agencies are also deemed not to be related parties.

16.2   A,B,C   The correct answers are:

- Its subsidiary companies
- Its directors
- Close family of the company's directors

Under IAS 24, members of the same group are related parties (parent and subsidiaries) as are key management personnel (including directors) and close family of key management personnel.

However, providers of finance are not considered to be a related party by virtue of their normal dealings with the entity; nor are customers and suppliers with whom the company has a significant volume of business.

16.3   B, C   The correct answers are:

- The details of the transaction and a description of the relationships between the parties.
- The amount involved.

IAS 24 requires the disclosure of the details of the related party transactions including a description of the relationships between the related parties and the amount involved. However, there is no specific requirement disclose either the name of the parties involved nor the date of the transaction. The only requirement regarding names is to disclose the controlling party and the ultimate controlling party.

16.4   A,B   The correct answers are:

- A person with a controlling shareholding in the parent company of Whither Co.
- An entity in which the wife of the finance director of Whither Co owns a controlling stake.

A person who has control over the entity meets the definition of a related party (IAS 24 para 9(a)(i)).

The finance director of Whither Co would qualify as a related party as he is key management personnel (IAS 24 para 9(a)(iii)) and so would his wife as she is close family (IAS 24 para (a)(i)). The entity in which the finance director's wife has a controlling stake would also be a related party of Whither Co (IAS 24 para 9(b)(vii)).

According to IAS 24 para 11, the following are not related parties:

- Two joint venturers simply because they share joint control over a joint venture
- A customer with whom the entity transacts a significant volume of business.

16.5 A Shareholders of a large listed entity.

Generally shareholders are not involved in the day to day running of a large listed entity. Therefore they need to be informed of any related party transactions.

However as directors and employees are responsible for the day to day running of the company, they should already be aware of related party transactions. Members of the same group qualify as related parties so will be aware of transactions amongst themselves.

16.6 A,B,C The correct answers are:

- Purchase of inventory by a parent from an associate.

- Sale of a company asset to the managing director of the reporting entity, at an externally agreed fair value.

- Sale of an asset by Company A to an entity in which the wife of the managing director of Company A has a controlling interest.

An associate, key management personnel, close family of key management and entities in which a related party has controlling interest are all related parties under IAS 24. Transactions must still be disclosed even if they are all related parties under IAS 24. Transactions must be disclosed even if they are at market value.

The other answers are incorrect because two associates, providers of finance (eg venture capital company) and suppliers with whom the entity transacts a large volume of business do **NOT** qualify as related parties under IAS 24.

16.7 B,D The correct answers are:

- The chief executive officer of the BS Board

- CD, an entity in which the wife of the chief executive officer of the BS Board has a controlling shareholding

The CEO of the BS Board is a related party as he is considered to be key management personnel. CD is a related party because it is an entity which a close family member of key management personnel controls.

TX is not a related party as IAS 24 states that a customer with whom an entity transacts a significant volume of business is not a related party simply by virtue of the resulting economic dependence. EF is not a related party because IAS 24 states that two joint venturers are not related simply because they share joint control of a joint venture. GH is not related as providers of finance are not considered to be related parties by virtue of their normal dealings with the entity.

16.8 B,C The correct answers are:

- During the accounting period, George purchased a property from CB for $500,000. CB had previously declared the property surplus to its requirements and had valued it at $750,000.

- George's son, Arnold, is a director in a financial institution, FC. During the accounting period, FC advanced $2 million to CB as an unsecured loan at a favourable rate of interest.

A customer with whom the entity transacts a significant volume of business is not a related party simply by virtue of the resulting economic dependence.

As the chief executive officer, George is considered to be key management personnel and therefore a related party of CB, meaning that the sale of the property by CB to George needs to be disclosed.

Close family of a person who is a related party is considered to also qualify as a related party. The definition of close family includes children therefore, as George is a related party, his son Arnold is also a related party of CB. Normally a provider of finance is not considered to be a related party but as a related party (Arnold) has a controlling interest in FC, FC is also considered to be a related party and therefore the loan should be disclosed.

Associates within the same group are not considered to be related parties as common significant influence is insufficient. Therefore, the sale of goods from CB to FG does not require disclosure.

16.9 D R, V, P and the pension plan.

Significant customers are not deemed to be related parties just by virtue of the large volume of sales.

16.10 A The management fee payable by EF to AB.

EF is a related party of AB as it is an associate of AB. Therefore, the management fee charged by AB should be disclosed.

However, two associates are not considered to be related parties under IAS 24. Therefore even though the sales by EF to GH are at cost, they are not required to be disclosed.

The question specifically asked about disclosure in EF's financial statements. Therefore, transactions between other group entities (i.e. sale of goods by CD to AB and management fee payable by CD and GH) are not relevant.

17 Earnings per share

17.1 D The denominator of the earnings per share ratio is the weighted average number of ordinary shares outstanding during the period

The other answers are incorrect because:

- Only an entity whose shares are traded in a public market (ie. listed entity) is required to disclose earnings per share.

- Earnings per share only represents the return for ordinary shareholders **not** all capital providers.

- Preference dividends must also be deduced from profit after tax to arrive at earnings and the weighted average not the year end total of ordinary shares should be used.

17.2 The correct answer is: 17.7.

To restate comparatives, apply the reciprocal of the bonus fraction to the prior year.

$$\text{Bonus fraction} = \frac{\text{No. of shares after bonus issue}}{\text{No. of shares before bonus issue}} = \frac{3}{2}$$

EPS: $26.5 \times 2/3 = 17.7$

17.3 B 5.1 million

Calculate the shares that are treated as being issued for nil consideration:

No. of shares under option		500,000
No. of shares that would have been issued at the average market price	$\dfrac{500,000 \times \$2.80}{3.50}$	(400,000)
No. of shares treated as issued for nil consideration		100,000

Shares used in EPS calculation = 5,000,000 + 100,000 = 5.1m

17.4 The correct answer is: $1.33.

EPS = $120,000/90,476 (W1) = $1.33

Workings

1 Weighted average number of shares

Date Narrative	No. of shares	Time	Bonus Fraction	Weighted average
1.1.X6 B/f	80,000	8/12	1.5/1.4 (W2)	57,143
1.9.X6 1 for 4 rights issue	20,000			
	100,000	4/12		33,333
				90,476

2   Bonus fraction

= Fair value before rights issue/theoretical ex rights price = $1.5/$1.4 (W3)

3   Theoretical ex-rights price

	$
4 shares × $1.50	6
1 share × $1	1
5 shares	7

TERP = $7/5 shares = $1.4

17.5 A 35.2 cents

$$\text{Diluted EPS} = \frac{\$2,852,964 \,(\text{W1})}{8,100,000 \,(\text{W2})} = 35.2 \text{ cents}$$

Workings

1   *Diluted earnings*

	$
Basic earnings	2,763,000
Interest saving net of tax ($1,836,000 × 7% × 70%)	89,964
Diluted earnings	2,852,964

2   *Diluted number of shares*

	No. of shares
Basic	6,000,000
Maximum no. of shares on conversion (2m/100 × 105)	2,100,000
Diluted number of shares	8,100,000

17.6 The correct answer is: 7.8 cents

$$\text{EPS} = \frac{8,200,000}{10,500,000} = 7.8 \text{ cents}$$

Weight average number of shares:

Date	Narrative	Number of shares	Time	Weighted average
1 January 20X3	B/f	10,000,000	9/12	7,500,000
1 October 20X3	FMP issue	2,000,000		
		12,000,000	3/12	3,000,000
				10,500,000

17.7 The correct answer is: $1.17.

EPS is restated to take account of the rights issue for comparability:

Without the rights issue EPS	= $100,000 /80,000
	= $1.25
The theoretical ex-rights price is:	= ((4 shares at $1.50 each) + (1 share at $1))/5
	= $1.40
Adjusting for the rights issue:	= $1.25 × (1.40/1.50)
	= $1.17

Remember that the original EPS for the corresponding period must be multiplied by: Theoretical ex-rights price / Fair value before the rights issue

17.8 B 9.8 cents per share.

Earnings = ($180,000 − $60,000) = $120,000.

Weighted average number of shares = 1,000,000 × 3/12 + 1,300,000 × 9/12 = 1,225,000

EPS = $120,000/1,225,000 = 9.8c.

17.9 The correct answer is: 17.9 cents.

$$\text{Diluted EPS} = \frac{\$966,000 \ (W1)}{5,400,000 \ (W2)} = 17.9 \text{ cents}$$

Workings

1 Diluted earnings

	$
Basic earnings (1,040,000 − 270,000)	770,000
Interest saving net of tax (4,000,000 × 7% × 70%)	196,000
Diluted earnings	966,000

2 Diluted number of shares

	No. of shares
Basic	3,000,000
Maximum no. of shares on conversation	2,400,000
Diluted number of shares	5,400,000

17.10 C 72.7 cents.

$$\text{Diluted EPS} = \frac{\$3.8m}{5m + 225,000 \ (W1)} = 72.7 \text{ cents}$$

Workings

1 *Number of shares issued at nil consideration*

Number of shares under option	1,000,000
No. that would have been issued at full market price (1,000,000 × $3.10)/$4	775,000
No. of shares for nil consideration	225,000

18 Ethics

18.1 C It is the responsibility of the directors to prepare the financial statements in an ethical manner and hence the shares should be classified as liabilities.

The directors as a whole are responsible for the financial statements and should all act ethically, the burden does not fall on just one director.

18.2 B Explain to the managing director that under IAS 17 *Leases*, this lease should be treated as a finance lease.

If the finance director were to treat the lease as an operating lease, this would constitute non-compliance with IAS 17 which requires leases were the risks and rewards are substantially transferred to the lessee to be treated as finance leases. As a result, the finance director would not be complying with the principle of professional competence under the CIMA Code of Ethics.

However, both resigning with immediate effect and calling the CIMA Ethics Helpline are both rather extreme actions when explaining the rules of the relevant accounting standard to the managing director would be likely to convince him of the correct accounting treatment.

18.3 B,C,D,E The correct answers are:

- The IFRS 10 definition of control has been met. Therefore, ZZ should consolidate RR in its group financial statements.

- The $400 million has been incorrectly recognised as dividends paid. Instead it would be more accurate to record it as a loan.

- There is an ethical risk that the finance director has deliberately set up RR to keep the investment activities of ZZ off balance sheet.

- If the finance director does not consolidate RR, there is a risk that the finance director is associated with a report that omits or obscures information.

As ZZ does not own any shares directly in RR, at first glance RR does not look like a subsidiary. However, the IFRS 10 definition of control as been met as ZZ has power over RR due to the operating guidelines that have been set up; ZZ has exposure to the variable returns of RR in the form of 95% of the profits and 100% of the losses; and ZZ has the ability to use its power of RR to affect the amount of their returns. Therefore, RR should be consolidated into ZZ's group accounts. The treatment of $400 million as dividends paid is incorrect because RR is not a shareholder of ZZ. In substance, it is a loan which will be repaid in 4 years.

There is a risk that the finance director has set up RR to deliberately keep the investment activities which are inherently risky off balance sheet.

The CIMA Code of Ethics states that accountants should not be associated with reports that omit or obscure information. If RR is not consolidated, the group financial statements of ZZ will be omitting information.

18.4   B,C,D   The correct answers are:

- There is a self-interest threat here as if the proceeds of the loan are recorded as an operating cash flow the target needed for the directors to receive extra income is more likely to be met.

- IAS 7 *Statement of Cash Flows* allows some flexibility in classification of cash flows but the proceeds from a loan should always be recorded as a financing cash flow.

- If the proceeds of the loan are recorded as an operating cash flow, the directors of JJ will not be complying with IAS 7 and will be failing to comply with the CIMA Code of Ethics' principle of professional competence.

IAS 7 does allow some flexibility in classification of items within the statement of cash flows. For example, dividends paid may either be presented within operating or financing activities. However, loan proceeds should always be presented as a financing cash flow. As the directors receive extra income if the operating cash flow exceeds a certain target, there is a self-interest threat here. The CIMA Code of Ethics' principle of professional competence is only adhered to if financial statements are prepared according with international accounting standards which would not be the case if the proceeds were to be recorded as an operating cash flow.

18.5   B   It would be unethical just to treat the loan as 'cash and cash equivalents' purely to improve the perceived liquidity of the company.

In the absence of an IFRS covering a specific transaction, other event or condition, IAS 8 *Accounting policies, changes in accounting estimates and errors* requires management to use its judgment to develop an accounting policy which results in information that is **relevant** to the economic decision-making needs of users and **reliable**, considering *in the following order*:

1   IFRSs dealing with similar and related issues;

2   The *Conceptual Framework* definitions elements of the financial statements and recognition criteria; and

3   The most recent pronouncements of other national GAAPs based on a similar conceptual framework and accepted industry practice (providing the treatment does not conflict with extant IFRSs or the *Conceptual Framework*).

If the loan were shown as cash, it would breach the *Conceptual Framework's* qualitative characteristics as follows:

- Understandability - it would hide the true nature of practices of the company, making the financial statements less understandable to users.

- Relevance - the director's loan should be disclosed separately as users of financial statements need to be made aware of the director being made a loan under favourable terms

- Faithful representation - this means complete, neutral and free from bias. If the loan is shown in cash, the financial statements will be biased by hiding the true nature of the loan and overstating the liquidity position.

- Comparability - if the loan is not outstanding year on year, the financial statements would not be comparable. The directors would not be acting in the shareholders' best interests by recording the loan in cash and cash equivalents.

The directors would not be acting in the shareholders' best interests by recording the cash in cash and cash equivalents. This is because the shareholders are not usually involved in the day to day running of the company and would therefore not be aware of the loan unless it were disclosed separately.

18.6   B,C   The correct answers are:

- To align its accounting policies to the industry norm.

- To provide information that is more relevant to the economic decision-making needs of the users of financial statements.

It would be unethical to follow a specific accounting treatment simply to reduce the tax liability or improve the perception of the entity's financial performance. IAS 8 *Accounting policies, Changes in accounting estimates and Errors* requires the entity to consider relevance, reliability and industry practices when determining their accounting policies.

18.7   The correct answer is:

CIMA's Code of Ethics clearly states that a professional accountant should not be associated with reports believe that the information contains a materially false or **misleading** statement; contains statements or information furnished **recklessly**; or **omits** or obscures information.

18.8   D   Governance.

The other principles are professional competence and due care and professional behaviour.

18.9   D   Try to persuade the finance director to change his mind and follow the required accounting treatment of IAS 17 *Leases*.

At this stage, the chief executive has not been threatening toward the finance director, he has merely promoted his own viewpoint. Therefore, it would be a bit extreme to resign or report the chief executive for acting unethically. A proportionate response and first port of call would be to try and persuade the chief executive to change his mind.

18.10 C   IAS 27 requires the entity to apply the same accounting for each category of investments making this proposed policy unacceptable.

Accountants should not pick and choose which accounting policy makes their financial statements look best. They should select accounting policies which result in information that is most relevant to the economic decision-making needs of users and reliable. There is no need to call the Ethics Helpline at this stage. The finance director should study IAS 27 in more detail before determining the accounting policy.

19 Analysis of financial performance and position I

19.1   B   1.26:1.

(Receivables + short term investments) are divided by (trade payables, overdraft, taxes payable + deposits in advance):

(158,000 + 18,000)/(61,000 + 64,000 + 10,000 + 5,000) = 1.26.

19.2   B   13%.

The formula for calculating return on capital employed is:

(Profit before interest and tax)/(Equity + long term debt – investments)

= $600/$4,550

= 13%

19.3   D   PQ moved to an out of town location where the rent and employment costs were less than in the previous year.

Reclassifying expenses from administrative expenses to cost of sales will make gross margin fall but will have no impact on operating margin as whether the expenses are in cost of sales or administrative expenses, they will still need to be deducted in calculating the operating profit and therefore margin.

Rent and employment costs are operating costs, so reducing these costs will improve the operating margin.

Interest is a finance cost and therefore has no impact on operating profits.

Increasing trade discount will reduce gross profit margins and therefore operating profit margins also.

19.4   The correct answers are:

- TH made an unusually large sale immediately prior to the year end at a good profit margin
- TH paid its payables earlier than usual out of a positive cash balance

Sale on cash or credit terms at a good profit margin just before year end would increase cash or receivables in excess of the reduction in inventories and would therefore increase current assets.

Paying payables earlier than usual out of a positive cash balance would reduce cash (current assets) but would also reduce payables (current liabilities) by the same amount. Since current liabilities are lower than current assets the decrease would be proportionately greater thus boosting the current ratio.

Incorrect answers

- Goods purchased for cash - current assets remain the same

- Payables paid out of an overdraft - current liabilities remain the same

- Machine purchased on credit - a machine is a non current asset so would have no impact on current assets but as it was purchased on credit, it would increase current liabilities which would cause the current ratio to decrease not increase.

- Reduction in customers' credit period - this would result in a decrease in receivables but an increase in cash so no change in current assets overall nor the current ratio.

19.5   The correct answer is: 25.

EPS = $300,000 / 5 million shares = 6c

PE ratio = 150 / 6 = 25

19.6   C   X has a smaller proportion of productive assets than its competitor

Carrying its non-current assets at historic cost would make X's asset turnover higher than its competitor as X would have a lower asset balance.

X embarked on a programme of capital investment in the previous year which should result in extra revenue in the current year thus making X's asset turnover ratio higher than its competitor's. Recruiting additional production staff would also make X's asset turnover ratio higher than its competitor's.

19.7   A,B,E   The correct answers are:

- In accordance with IAS 16 the company revalued its properties which resulted in a significant increase in the carrying value as compared to three years ago.

- Towards the end of the current year SL made major investments in plant and machinery financed by borrowing.

- Asset turnover has reduced as compared to the previous year.

Revaluations decrease profits and increase capital employed and will therefore decrease return on capital employed. A year end investment in plant and machinery financed through additional capital will increase the capital employed without increasing profits in the current year, and will therefore reduce ROCE.

ROCE can be expressed as: asset turnover x operating margin. Therefore, when asset turnover falls, this causes ROCE to decrease.

The other answers are incorrect for the following reasons:

Where loan notes are issued to replace shares and vice versa will have no impact on operating profits or total capital employed and will therefore have no impact on ROCE. And as explained above, if asset turnover increases, it will cause ROCE to increase.

19.8   B,C   The correct answers are:

- During the current year, a revolutionary product has been launched and sales have exceeded all expectations.

- During the previous year, RS discontinued one of its loss making activities which resulted in a significant drop in reported basic earnings per share, although the alternative earnings per share based on continuing operations showed above average growth.

The introduction of a revolutionary product would cause market confidence in RS to increase and the share price to rise, making its P/E ratio higher than the sector average.

Discontinuing a loss making operation and focusing on continuing operations with an above average growth is likely to increase market confidence in RS and cause the P/E ratio to increase.

The other options are incorrect for the following reasons: Profit warnings would reduce market confidence in RS and make the share price and P/E ratio fall. Low market expectations for the sector would impact all entities in the sector including RS and would not make RS's P/E ratio significantly higher than the sector average.

If RS's competitors had invested in innovative new technology, this should make RS's P/E ratio lower than it is competitors rather than higher.

19.9   C   The cake shop has a higher level of wastage of inventory than the electrical store.

Given that both entities charge the same mark up on cost per unit when they arrive at their selling price, wastage can be the only reason for the cake shop having a lower gross margin that the electrical store.

The other answers are incorrect for the following reasons:

- Although a trade discount would allow the electrical store to have a lower cost base, as both entities apply the same mark up on cost, this should have no impact on the gross margin.

- The cake shop's higher inventory turnover just means that the cake shop is selling goods more quickly than the electrical store but as both stores charge the same mark up on cost, this will have no impact on the gross margin.

- The level of volume does not impact margins. Margins are affected by change in prices and costs not volume.

19.10 D   The current ratio would decrease, the quick ratio would decrease

Using some numbers to help, let's say:

Sales   = $20 per month

GP   = $5 (25% × $20)

Cash   = $10 (1/2 × $20 sales)

Inventory   = $15 ($20 sales - $5 profit)

Payables   = $15 (1 month's worth of inventory)

Now:

CA   = 10 + 15 = 25

CL   = 15

Current ratio 1.67:1 (25/15) and quick ratio 0.67:1 (10/15)

After adjustment (if inventory were increased to 1.5 month's sales, it would be $15 × 1.5 = $22.5)

CA   = 10 + 22.5 = 32.5

CL   = 22.5

Current ratio 1.44:1 (32.5/22.5) and quick ratio 0.44:1 (10/22.5)

20 Analysis of financial performance and position II

20.1 A   An increase in revenue.

An increase in revenue will probably lead to an increase in operating profit. There will be no increase in capital employed.

Decreasing the level of dividends has no effect on ROCE in the short term. In the long term it would increase retained earnings and capital employed and therefore reduce ROCE.

Revaluing land and buildings upwards decreases ROCE, because it increases capital employed and reduces profits.

Issuing ordinary shares increases capital employed and decreases ROCE in the short term, although the issue proceeds can be used to generate additional profit and this may help to increase ROCE in the longer term.

20.2 D   The entity has purchased a property for cash.

This reduces current assets without a corresponding reduction in current liabilities.

The other answers are incorrect because:

Poor credit control would increase receivables and reduce cash so no impact on current assets.

Inventory is excluded from quick ratio so no impact.

Reducing the allowance for receivables would increase current assets and thus increase the quick ratio.

20.3   C   Make a rights issue of ordinary shares.

This would increase both cash and share capital, increasing current (liquid) assets but without incurring any additional liabilities.

Offering a settlement discount to customers would make cash received lower than receivables which would cause the current ratio to decrease rather than increase.

Making a bonus issue of shares would generate no cash at all and would only affect QR's reserves, not its current ratio.

Selling current asset investments would just replace the investments with cash, having no effect on the current ratio.

20.4   D   2.22 times.

Dividend cover = Earnings / Dividends

We have earnings but we need to work out dividends. Playing with the numbers we are given in the question, we can work out the following.

P/E = 15

We have E (in this case, earnings per share), so rearranging we get P = PE ratio × E, i.e.:

Share price = 15 × $0.36
                  = $5.40

We also know the dividend yield, or D/P, = 3%. Since we now know P (share price) to be $5.40, we have the equation:

D / $5.40 = 3%

Which we can rearrange as:

D = 3% × $5.40
   = $0.162 per share

We now have the figures for both earnings and dividends, and can work out the dividend cover as:

Dividend cover = E / D
                     = $0.36 / $0.162
                     = 2.22 times

This means that RS's earnings cover its dividend payout 2.22 times.

20.5   A $53,333.

Revenue = $800,000

Revenue : Total assets = 2.5:1

Therefore Total assets = $800,000/2.5 = $320,000

Total assets = Non-current assets + current assets = $320,000

Non-current assets: Current assets = 1:1

Therefore, Non-current assets and Current assets = $160,000 each

Current assets: Current liabilities = 1.8:1

Therefore Current liabilities = 160,000/1.8 = $88,889

Current assets – Inventory : Current liabilities = 1.2:1

Therefore Current assets – Inventory = $88,889 × 1.2 = $106,667

So Inventory = $160,000(Current assets) – $106,667 (Current assets – Inventory) = $53,333

20.6   A,D,E   The correct answers are:

- Return on capital employed will decrease
- Net profit margin will decrease
- Non-current asset turnover will decrease

A revaluation will increase the revaluation surplus therefore equity and capital employed, making ROCE decrease. As the assets are larger, the depreciation will increase making profit lower and the net margin decrease. Non-current asset turnover is calculated as revenue/non-current assets, therefore, it too will decrease.

A revaluation will have no effect on the current ratio and will make gearing (debt/equity) decrease as equity has increased. Interest cover is likely to decrease because profit before interest and tax will fall due to the higher depreciation.

20.7   C   Non-current asset turnover.

A manufacturing company will have high assets (factory, plant and machinery, inventories etc.). Therefore non current asset turnover (revenue / non current assets) will be a measure of how efficiently an entity is using its non current assets to generate revenue.

The P/E ratio is a measure of the market confidence in the future of an entity. Gearing relates to long term solvency and the current ratio relates to liquidity.

20.8   B   Decrease in return on capital employed; increase in gearing.

A lease liability would be recognised and therefore capital employed would increase, while there would probably be relatively little impact on PBIT (depreciation charges would replace lease rentals). Hence ROCE would decrease.

The recognition of a lease liability would cause debt and therefore gearing to increase.

20.9   B   Gearing and interest cover.

Although all these ratios could be of interest to the bank, as a long term loan creditor the bank will be particularly interested in factors that affect the company's ability to pay interest.

These include: whether it is getting into further debt or improving its situation; and the level of profit in relation to interest expense.

20.10   D   A manufacturer

ABC has a relatively high operating profit and a relatively low asset turnover. This suggests that it is capital intensive.

An architect and an insurance broker would not normally have high levels of non-current assets.

A food retailer is more likely to have significant non-current assets, but this type of business normally has low operating profit share margins.

Therefore a manufacturer is the most likely option.

21 Analysis of financial performance and position III

21.1 D 1.00.

This is the ratio of current assets excluding inventories to current liabilities. (Receivables + Cash) / Payables

= (600,000 + 200,000) / 800,000

= 1

The other answers are incorrect for the following reasons:

0.75 is incorrect as it is calculated as receivables/payables i.e. cash has been wrongly excluded. 0.50 is incorrect as the loan notes should be excluded as they are non-current liabilities. 1.50 is the current ratio rather than the quick ratio.

21.2 C $32,400.

Cost of sales per month = $36,000.

	Current	Proposed	Change
Inventory	(1.5 × $36,000) = $54,000	(1.1 × $36,000) = $39,600	-$14,400
Payables	(1.0 × $36,000) = $36,000	(1.5 × $36,000) = $54,000	+$18,000
Reduction in working capital			-$32,400

Working capital = Inventory + receivables − payables.

Therefore, if inventory decreases working capital decreases. And if payables increase, working capital decreases.

21.3 The correct answer is: D

Proposal 1	Proposal 2
decrease ratio	increase ratio

Proposal 1 will cause the acid test ratio to fall, because although receivables will convert into cash more quickly, the amount of cash received (net of the discount) will be less than the amount of the receivables. Current assets will fall, without any change in current liabilities, so the acid test ratio will fall.

Proposal 2 will cause the acid test ratio to rise, by delaying the reduction in cash that would occur by paying suppliers. Since the acid test ratio is less than 1.0, anything that prevents an equal fall in current assets above the line and current liabilities below the line will boost the ratio.

This solution can be demonstrated with simple numbers. Suppose receivables = 200 and cash = 100, so payables must be 750 (since the acid test ratio is currently 0.4).

Proposal 1: If all the receivables take the 2% discount, there will be receivables of 0, cash of (100 + 98% of 200) = 298 and payables of 750. Acid test ratio = 298/750 = 0.397 = lower.

Proposal 2: If payment of 100 is delayed to payables, cash will rise by 100 and so too will payables. Cash 200, receivables 200 and payables 850. Acid test ratio = 400/850 = 0.47 = higher.

21.4 B,D,E The correct answers are:

- Published financial statements contain estimates such as depreciation

- Accounting policies may vary between companies, making comparisons difficult

- The nature and character of a business may change over time, making strictly numerical comparisons misleading.

Published financial statements are frequently unreliable as a result either of fraud or of error on the part of management - may be the case, but this is offset by the statutory requirement for them to

BPP
LEARNING MEDIA

represent a true and fair view, and by the fact that most investment decisions (for example) would involve an element of due diligence work to ensure that the accounts could in fact be relied upon.

There are no prior year figures to compare to current year figures is incorrect because in published financial statements comparatives must be shown.

The following are problems associated with inter-temporal analysis (ie analysis of the same company, over time):

*   Changes in the nature of the business
*   Unrealistic depreciation rates under historical cost accounting
*   The changing value of the currency unit being reported
*   Changes in accounting policies

The following are problems associated with cross-sectional analysis (ie analysis of different companies, at the same time):

*   Different degrees of diversification
*   Different production and purchasing policies
*   Different financing policies
*   Different accounting policies
*   Different effects of government incentives

Although the nature of the business being volatile will impact the accounts the volatility will affect all companies within the industry and thus ratio analysis will still be useful/meaningful to assess relative performance.

21.5   C   The correct answer is: 69.7%.

Gearing   = Debt/(Debt + Equity) × 100%
            = (100,000 + 475,000) / (30,000 + 20,000 + 200,000 + 575,000)
            = 69.7%

The preference shares are treated as debt because they are redeemable meaning that they contain an obligation (to repay the principal) and therefore meet the IAS 39 definition of financial liability.

21.6   A,D,F   The correct answers are:

*   Gearing of RF has decreased due to the increase in total equity.
*   Shares were issued at a premium to nominal value.
*   RF may have paid a dividend to shareholders in 20X8.

Retained earnings may have fallen due to other factors such as dividends, not only due to a loss. Long term borrowings may have increased due to a reclassification from short-term debt. Long term borrowing could also have increased due to amortisation and effective interest in the year. Share capital may have increased due to a market share issue, not only a bonus issue.

21.7   A   Increase sales.

An increase in sales will probably lead to an increase in operating profit. There will be no increase in capital employed.

Restructuring its long term finance would have no impact on ROCE as overall capital employed will remain the same. Revaluing land and buildings upwards decreases ROCE, because it increases capital employed (revaluation surplus) and reduces profits (higher depreciation). Issuing ordinary shares increases capital employed and decreases ROCE in the short term, although the issue proceeds can be used to generate additional profit and this may help to increase ROCE in the longer term.

21.8   A,C,D   The correct answers are:

- One entity revalues its properties and the other entity holds its assets under the historical cost model

- One entity has assets nearing the end of their useful life whilst the other entity has recently acquired new assets

- One entity depreciates its assets over a much shorter useful life than the other entity

All of these would cause the value of non current assets to be comparatively higher in one of the entities thus causing a difference to the asset turnover ratio.

Whether an entity buys assets for cash or under a finance lease has no impact on the non-current asset turnover ratio because in both instances, the entity will record an asset in their statement of financial position. If one entity had purchased their assets for cash and the other under operating leases, that would impact asset turnover as under an operating lease, no asset is recorded in the statement of financial position.

Neither interest or borrowings feature in the asset turnover ratio so the rate of interest an entity pays is not relevant this year.

To help with questions like this, think of the formula and what impacts the items on the top and bottom half:

$$\frac{\text{Revenue}}{\text{Non} - \text{current assets}}$$

The ratio of debt to equity does not feature in the asset turnover ratio so has no impact.

21.9   B,D,E   The correct answers are:

- Access the entities P/E ratio from the financial press and compare this with other entities in the sector to assess the market's view of the risk of LP.

- Review the narrative reports within the financial statements that give details of recent investment and related financing to assess if the business is undergoing expansion and likely to bring additional future returns.

- Review the financial report to establish the dividend per share paid over the last few years and to identify whether increased gearing has negatively impacted on investor returns.

It is unlikely that the individual would be able to gain access to board minutes or have direct discussions with the CFO due to issues of confidentiality.

It is also unlikely the individual would be given access to management forecasts.

21.10   B,C,E   The correct answers are:

- Entity B is controlling its overheads better than entity A but acquisition of either would cause LOP's net profit margin to fall.

- The market confidence in the future of LOP is greater than in either of the two targets.

- Acquisition of both entity A and entity B would cause LOP's gross and net margins to fall.

Entity A is operating its core activities better than entity B as entity A has the higher gross margin. The other two statements are correct but do not relate specifically to financial performance (gearing relates to financial position and the size of the entity has nothing to do with financial performance).

22 Analysis of financial performance and position IV

22.1   D   Paying a supplier and taking an early settlement discount.

Working capital is calculated as current assets less current liabilities. Paying a supplier and taking an early settlement will reduce cash less than payables so will cause working capital to increase. Therefore this is the correct answer.

The other answers are incorrect for the following reasons:

Delaying a payment to trade payables would cause trade payables to increase and therefore working capital to decrease.

Reducing the credit period given to customers would cause receivables to fall and cash to rise with a nil effect on current assets and working capital.

Purchasing inventory on credit will cause current assets and current liabilities to increase by the same amount resulting in a nil effect on working capital.

22.2   B,C   The correct answers are:

- Increased inventory obsolescence
- Slow down in trading

If inventory is becoming obsolete then sales may fall, leading to a build up of old inventory.

A slow down in trading would probably affect inventory levels because the level of purchases would take a while to adjust to the lower levels of sales, leading to a build up of inventory.

The following two options would NOT cause inventory days to increase:

- A marketing decision to reduce selling prices - a reduction in selling price would not directly affect either the purchase price or the level of inventory. If anything, it would be more likely to reduce inventory days, as the entity moves towards more of a low-margin, fast-turnover approach.

- Seasonal fluctuations in sales orders - this would affect inventory days, but it would not affect it from year to year (on the assumption that the 'seasonality' in question does not take place over more than one year!).

Changing supplier may change payables days etc but is unlikely to impact on average inventory days if the same inventory lines/products are being purchased/sold.

22.3   B   TR moved to an out-of-town office location where rent and employment costs were lower than they were in 20X8.

Rent and employment are both operating costs, so reducing them would improve the operating margin.

Interest is a finance cost, and would not be included within operating profit.

Increasing the trade discounts offered would actually reduce the operating margin because it would increase the cost of discounts allowed.

Increased public awareness of the company might help to explain eg a higher level of sales activity, but this would not have any impact on the operating profit margin.

22.4 C,D The correct answers are:

- GH made an unusually large sale just before the year end
- GH paid its payables earlier than usual, because it had a positive cash balance

Making a large sale before the year end would cause inventory to fall and trade receivables to increase. This will cause the current ratio to increase because inventory will fall by the cost of the goods but trade receivables will increase by the selling price which will be higher.

Paying payables earlier than usual out of a positive cash balance will cause current assets (cash) and current liabilities (payables) to fall by the same amount. However, as current liabilities are less than current assets (due to a current ratio of 1:2:1 prior to the transaction), this will have a greater impact on current liabilities than current assets causing the current ratio to increase.

The other answers are incorrect:

If GH paid its payables earlier than usual by making use of its bank overdraft facility, current liabilities would remain the same and there would be no impact on the current ratio.

Buying inventory for cash would have no overall impact on current assets or the current ratio because one current asset (cash) would fall and another current asset (inventory) would increase by the same amount.

22.5 A,D,F The correct answers are:

- Towards the end of 20X9, major investments were made in plant & machinery that were financed by borrowing - capital will be increased but earnings will not, so ROCE will fall.

- In line with IAS 16, SK revalued its properties, resulting in a significant increase in their carrying value - profit will fall due to higher depreciation but capital employed (the revaluation reserve) will rise, so ROCE will fall.

- Asset turnover is down in comparison with 20X8 - asset turnover and ROCE are closely linked; so any rise/fall in one will go along with a rise/fall in the other

The incorrect answers are:

- SK converted $10m 10% loan notes into $10m share capital halfway through 20X9 - neither will affect PBIT or capital employed, so ROCE should not be affected.

- Asset turnover has increased in comparison with the prior year - this would indicate an increase in ROCE, not a decrease.

- SK issued $5m loan notes to redeem $5m redeemable preference shares (at par) - neither will affect PBIT or capital employed, so ROCE should not be affected.

22.6 The correct answer is:

Entity **B** would make the better investment as it has the **better** net profit margin, is **less** risky and the market has greater confidence in its **future**.

22.7 A,B,D The correct answers are:

- Entity A and B may have different accounting policies causing lack of comparability between their ratios

- The indicators only cover profitability and gearing. There are no measures of efficiency or liquidity, both of which are very important for an entity's survival.

- Entity A and B operate in different geographical areas which will impact tax rates, interest rates and share prices and cause lack of comparability

The other statements are incorrect because not all the ratios relate to past performance (P/E ratio relates to the market confidence in the future of an entity). P/E is an investor ratio so one investor ratio has been calculated. There is no evidence to suggest the three entities operate in different business sectors.

22.8 A CD operates at the luxury end of the market and is able to charge a higher price for its goods sold compared to AB.

It may be possible that CD's management exercises greater control over overheads, but this is less likely than the other options.

If AB received goods at a significant discount they would have a higher gross profit margin, not a lower gross profit margin.

Cheaper interest rates on borrowings could result in smaller overheads and therefore bigger profit /revenue margins, but this would not explain the big difference in gross profit margin and is less likely than the other options,

22.9 B Receivable days.

Supermarkets do not offer customers a credit period. Immediate payment is required on checkout. Therefore, there will be few trade receivables making receivable days a pointless ratio to calculate.

22.10 D Construction

For an entity operating in the construction sector, the buildings are their key assets and as they are for resale, they will be recorded in inventory rather than property, plant and equipment. However, an entity investing in properties for rental, would record their assets in non-current assets rather than inventory.

This is unlikely to be a retail store as you would expect higher property, plant and equipment and lower inventory as the entity would just stock enough to fill its shelves. An insurance broker would have much higher trade receivables and payables as they are the middleman between the customer and the insurer.

23 Analysis of financial performance and position V

23.1 B The correct answer is: 19.

Workings:

EPS = $400,000 / 5,000,000 shares = 8c
P/E ratio = 150/8 = 19

23.2 A The failure of QW's to raise long term finance to fund its investing activities has resulted in a deterioration QW's financial adaptability and liquidity.

It is good financial management to finance long term assets (investing activities) with long term finance (financing activities). However, whilst QW has managed to finance some of its investing activities from its operating activities, it has failed to raise long term finance to cover the remainder. Instead it has relied on an overdraft which is both expensive and risk.

The other statements are incorrect for the following reasons:

A negative cash flow in investing activities is indicative of expansion rather than decline. QW has not show competent stewardship by financing long term assets with an overdraft. As no prior year figures are given, it is not possible to conclude on whether QW's working capital management has improved or deteriorated.

23.3 The correct answer is:

Return on capital employed

$$\frac{\text{Profit before interest and tax}}{\text{Equity} + \text{Debt} - \text{Investments}}$$

Operating profit margin

$$\frac{\text{Profit before interest and tax}}{\text{Revenue}}$$

23.4	D	Increase by less than 30%.

Say current assets are $75,000

Current liabilities are $50,000

A 30% decrease in both will be $15,000.

Current assets will then be $60,000, current liabilities $35,000, and current ratio will be 60:35 = 1.71.

This is an increase of less than 30%.

23.5	B	Insurance broking

MNO has no inventories, moderate levels of land and property, low levels of other non-current assets and very high trade receivables and trade payables.

This suggests that MNO operates in a service industry. An insurance broker is the only one of the four that fits this profile. The insurance broker is effectively the middleman between the customer and the insurer. The high receivables and payables relate to premiums and claims being passed between the customer and the insurer by the insurance broker.

23.6 The correct answer is: 2.6%

Dividend per share = $10m/100m = 10 cents

$$\text{Dividend yield} = \frac{\text{Dividend per share}}{\text{Market price per share}}\ 100\%$$

$$= \frac{10}{390} \times 100\%$$

$$= 2.6\%$$

Note: to calculate the dividend per share, you must use the number of shares rather than par value (100m × 0.5 = $50m).

23.7 The correct answer is: 57.4.

Gearing = long term debt /equity = (100 + 40)/244.

23.8	A	Current ratio	Quick ratio
		3.25	2.88

$$\text{Current ratio} = \frac{\text{Current assets}}{\text{Current liabilities}}$$

$$= \frac{145 + 247 + 50}{99 + 37}$$

$$= 3.25$$

$$\text{Quick ratio (or acid test)} = \frac{\text{Current assets} - \text{inventories}}{\text{Current liabilities}}$$

$$= \frac{145 + 247}{99 + 37}$$

$$= 2.88$$

23.9	D	P/E ratio.

This is calculated as the current market price of an entity divided by its earnings per share. The share price takes into account the market's view of the entity's future performance and the EPS takes into account the entity's past performance.

Therefore, a high P/E ratio indicates greater confidence in the future of an entity compared to its past performance. Dividend yield calculates the cash return on an investment. Earnings per share is simply a measure of past profitability (per share). Return on capital employed is a measure of profitability and efficiency.

23.10 C   XX is suffering from a worsening liquidity situation in 20X9.

This is true because the current ratio has fallen, customers are taking longer to pay, inventory is taking longer to sell and XX is paying its suppliers more quickly.

24 Analysis of financial performance and position VI

24.1   The correct answer is: 10.9.

Price/EPS = 2.62/0.24.

24.2   D   WX's share price may be relatively lower than that of ST and UV because of an adverse effect such as a profit warning.

If ST were regarded by the market as the riskiest entity or had the highest earnings, its P/E ratio would be the lowest. An average P/E ratio is not indicative of a safe investment. The higher the P/E ratio, the greater confidence the market has in the future of the entity.

24.3   C

P/E ratio	Dividend yield
Increase	Decrease

Think of the ratio formulae to help you.

$\text{P/E ratio} = \dfrac{\text{Current market price per share}}{\text{EPS}}$ so an increase in share price will cause the P/E ratio to increase

$\text{Dividend yield} = \dfrac{\text{Dividend per share}}{\text{Market price per share}} \times 100\%$ so an increase in share price will cause the dividend to fall.

24.4   B,C,E   The correct answers are:

- Increase in payroll costs due to staff bonuses.
- Major investment in property, plant and equipment shortly before the year end.
- A revaluation of property in the year resulting in a significant uplift in value.

ROCE will fall when profit before interest and tax falls or when capital employed increases. Increases in the average interest rate and a large tax bill do not affect ROCE as they affect profit after interest and tax. A repayment of the long term loan would improve ROCE as it will cause capital employed to fall.

24.5   The correct answer is: 3.24.

$\text{Interest} = \dfrac{\text{profit before interest}}{\text{interest}}$

136/42 = 3.24

24.6   C   The analysis of financial statements using ratios provides useful information when compared with previous performance or industry averages.

This is correct because ratios are only useful if they can be compared to other information so relative performance and position can be considered.

The other statements are incorrect for the following reasons:

Ratios are a useful tool to all stakeholders (including management) not just investors. Ratios based on past performance are not necessarily indicative of what will happen in the future - for example, the general economy might change, a new competitor might enter the market, an entity might introduce a new product.

24.7   The correct answer is: 24%

Return on capital employed $= \dfrac{\text{Profit before interest and tax}}{\text{Equity} + \text{long term debt} - \text{investments}} \times 100\%$

$= (10{,}200/42{,}500) \times 100\%$

$= 24\%$

24.8   C   S is less likely to be benefiting from economies of scale since its revenue is significantly lower.

It would not be possible to determine the effects of a control on admin expenses alone, as the ratios do not identify the impact of just admin expenses. If Y had secured better supply discounts than the other entities it would have the biggest gross profit margin. It would not be possible to determine the effects of the tax rate alone, as the ratios do not identify the impact of just tax.

24.9   B,C,F   The correct answers are:

- S's high gearing is likely to be a deliberate strategy to take advantage of low borrowing rates.
- S would be the riskier investment for AB because it has high gearing.
- Y would give AB greater benefit in terms of additional borrowing capacity.

The P/E ratio can be used to compare the relative return on an investment, it is not a measure of risk. The market is more confident about the performance of Y, as evidenced by the higher P/E ratio. The P/E ratio is a measure of return and the impact of acquiring an entity with a lower P/E ratio would not automatically cause the acquiring company ratio to fall.

Y has lower relative borrowing than S and thus there would be more scope for further debt finance to be raised in the future.

24.10   B   S and Y may be subject to different tax rates which would reduce comparability of their operating profit margins.

This is because operating profit is before interest and tax do different tax rates would have no impact on operating margin.

The other options are true for the following reasons:

- As S and Y are listed on different stock exchanges, one market might be more active than the other resulting in a higher share price and high P/E ratio.
- Different levels of finance costs will affect the comparability of the P/E ratio as it affects profits which are a component of EPS, an input to the P/E ratio.
- Different accounting standards can make it difficult to compare entities.

25 Mixed Bank 1

25.1   A,C,E   The correct answers are:

- They rank before ordinary shares in the event of a liquidation
- If the entity makes higher profits than expected, the dividend will not rise.
- The entity cannot claim tax relief on the dividends paid.

Non-cumulative preference shares do not have any rights if the company is unable to make the dividend payment in a particular year - this would only apply if the preference shares were *cumulative*.

25.2   The correct answer is: $311,000.

Convertible debt must be split into its liability and equity component parts. The liability element (which is given here) is calculated as the present value of future cash flows (interest and capital), discounted at the market rate of non-convertible debt. The equity component is the residual (i.e. the proceeds less the liability component).

	$
Proceeds	4,000,000
Liability component (given)	(3,689,000)
Equity component (residual)	311,000

25.3   A,D,G   The correct answers are:

- V has a present obligation
- A provision for $60,000 should be created
- V will incur an expense of $60,000 in the profit or loss for the current year

This is an onerous contract, the costs of fulfilling the contract are greater than the benefits that V can gain from it. The full cost of future rentals under the contract (£60,000) should be provided for at the date on which the contract becomes onerous.

25.4   C $345.

The amount to be included in the statement of profit or loss in the year ended 20X8 is the difference between the liability required at the end of 20X7 and 20X8. The liability is calculated by spreading the expected cost of the rights, but adjusting the fair value of the share option at the end of each period as the options are cash settled:

20X6: $150 \times \$4.50 \times 1/3 = \$225$

20X7: $150 \times \$4.20 \times 2/3 = \$420$

20X8: $150 \times \$5.10 \times 3/3 = \$765$

Journal in 20X8:

Dr Staff costs $345

Cr Liability (765-420) $345

25.5   A $400,000.

	$
Jennifer	250,000
Juniper	180,000
Intra-group trading	(30,000)
	400,000

25.6   A,B,E   The correct answers are:

- The consolidated statement of financial position will no longer include 100% of the asset and liabilities of DR.

- The consolidated profit or loss will include its share of the associate, DR, from 1 November 20X8.

- A gain or loss on the deemed disposal of DR will be included in consolidated profit for the year.

25.7   C $291,350.

DYQ and EZR became members of the CXP group on 1 November 20X5. Therefore post-acquisition profits are taken from that date.

CXP has an effective interest in EZR of 48.75% (75% × 65%).

	$
CXP	266,000
DYQ (178,000 – 152,000) × 75%	19,500
EZR (214,000 – 202,000) × 48.75%	5,850
	291,350

25.8   The correct answer is:

	Attributable to owners of the parent $000	Non-controlling interest $000
Balance at the start of the year	X	X
Total comprehensive income for the year	X	X
Dividends paid	(X)	(X)
Adjustment to NCI for sale of shares in UV	**BLANK**	**72**
Adjustment to parent's equity for sale of UV shares	**43**	**BLANK**
Balance at the end of the year	X	X

The adjustment to equity is calculated as:

	$'000
Consideration received	115
Increase in NCI on disposal (180 × 8%/20%)	(72)
Adjustment to equity	43

The journal to record this would be:

Dr (↑) Cash	$115,000
Cr (↑) Parent's retained earnings (in consolidated retained earnings working)	$43,000
Cr (↑) Non-controlling interests	$72,000

The percentage sold is calculated as the 20,000 shares sold divided by the 250,000 total shares in UV i.e. 8%. This is a subsidiary to subsidiary disposal so in substance no disposal has occurred. Instead it should be treated as a transaction between group shareholders (the parent is selling shares to the NCI) and recorded in equity with an increase to NCI and an adjustment to the parent's equity.

25.9   A,C,D   The correct answers are:

- KL – an entity in which the controlling shareholder of HJ has a 30% shareholding and significant influence

- Mr Smith – the domestic partner of Ms Wilson who is a director of HJ

- WX - the defined benefit pension plan for the employees of HJ

Ms Green is not a related party of HJ as she is not key management personnel.

Trade unions do not qualify as related parties under IAS 24.

Under IAS 24 Related parties, parent and subsidiaries, fellow subsidiaries, parent and associates, associates and joint ventures are all related. However, two associates in the same group are not related to each other as common significant influence is not considered sufficient.

Where a person who has control of the entity (and also their close family) has significant influence in another entity, that second entity is related to the first entity. This means that KL qualifies as a related party.

Key management personnel and their close family which includes domestic partners are considered to be related parties. This means that Mr Smith is a related party of HJ.

Post-employment benefit plans are also considered to be a related party to the entity. This means that WX would also be considered to be a related party.

25.10   A $1.5m.

Revenue: current assets	= 5:1
Therefore current assets	= $30m/5
	= $6m
Current ratio (current assets: current liabilities)	= 2:1
Therefore current liabilities	= $6m/2
	= $3m
Acid test ratio (current assets - inventory: current liabilities)	= 1.5:1
Therefore current assets – inventory	= $3m × 1.5
	= $4.5m
Hence, Inventory =	$6m – $4.5m
	= $1.5m

$3.0m is the difference between current assets and current liabilities.

$4.5m is the quick assets total.

$10.5m adds the current assets to the quick assets rather than deducting one from the other.

26 Mixed Bank 2

26.1   A,B   The correct answers are:

- Underwriters are paid a fee for guaranteeing that the shares will be purchased
- Lower gearing

The process of producing a prospectus and organising underwriting for a share issue takes time – a bank loan is quicker to arrange.

Interest cover is profit before interest and tax divided by the interest payable; neither are directly affected by a share issue in a project that will not deliver profits in the short-term.

26.2   D

Dr Finance costs	$142,800	
Cr Financial liability		$142,800

	$000
Net proceeds (6,000 – 120)	5,880,000
Finance costs (6% × 5,880)	352,800
Interest paid (3.5% × 6,000)	(210,000)
Balance at 31 December 20X3	6,022,800

The effective interest of $352,800 should have been recorded in profit or loss rather than the interest paid of $210,000. Therefore an extra $142,800 needs to be added to the finance costs and the financial liability needs to be increased by the same amount.

26.3   A,B,D   The correct answers are:

- Provisions should be made for constructive obligations (those arising from a company's pattern of past practice) as well as for obligations enforceable by law.

- Discounting may be used when estimating the amount of a provision if the effect is material.

- A restructuring provision may only be made when a company has a detailed plan for the reconstruction and a firm intention to carry it out.

IAS 37 specifically excludes retraining and relocation of continuing staff from restructuring provisions. The provision for an onerous contract should at the lower of the cost of fulfilling the contract and penalties from failure to fulfill it. Contingent assets where an inflow of economic benefits is probable should be disclosed not recognised.

26.4 B

Dr Staff costs $86,400

Cr Other components of equity $86,400

The journal is calculated to increase the amount included in equity from the amount calculated at the end of 20X5:

$10 \times \$18 \times 1,200 \times 1/2 = \$108,000$

To the amount that should be included in equity at the end of 20X6:

$10 \times \$18 \times 1,200 \times 90\% \times 2/2 = \$194,400$

26.5   The correct answer is: $265,500.

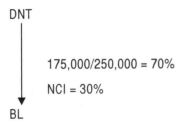

DNT

175,000/250,000 = 70%

NCI = 30%

BL

Acquisition was on 31 May 20X8, so only 3 months' of BL's profits arose post acquisition.

	$
NCI at acquisition (fair value)	262,500
NCI share of post acquisition retained earnings(30% × 40,000 × 3/12)	3,000
NCI at 31.8.20X8	265,500

26.6 B

Consolidated statement of profit or loss and other comprehensive income

Consolidate for a full year and pro-rate non-controlling interests

Consolidated statement of financial position

Consolidate assets and liabilities

Reduce non-controlling interests by $55,000

Record an adjustment to equity of $40,000 in consolidated retained earnings

Before the disposal AMY owned 80% of BNZ, making BNZ a subsidiary. AMY then sold 10,000 of their 40,000 shares in BNZ i.e. a quarter of their shareholding = ¼ × 80% = 20%. After the disposal, BNZ owned a 60% shareholding (i.e. 30,000 of BNZ's 50,000 shares) so BNZ was still a subsidiary. Therefore BNZ must be consolidated for a full year in the statement of profit or loss and other comprehensive income, pro-rating NCI (20% for the first 6 months; 40% for the next 6 months). BNZ must also be consolidated in the statement of financial position. The disposal is treated as a transaction between group shareholders with a reduction in NCI of $55,000 ($275,000 × 20%) and an adjustment to the parent's equity:

	$'000
Consideration received	95
Increase in NCI (275 × 20%)	(55)
Adjustment to equity	40

26.7 A,B,C The correct answers are:

- XC is the parent
- The NCI in G is 48%
- XC has control of both F and G

XC owns 60,000 of the 100,000 shares in F i.e. 60% making F a subsidiary (not a sub-subsidiary).

F owns 90,000 of the 150,000 shares in G i.e. 60%. XC also owns 24,000 of the 150,000 shares in G directly i.e. 16%, making this a D-shaped group. G is a sub-subsidiary because XC controls more than 50% of G's shares (16% directly and 60% indirectly).

The effective interest in G is calculated as the 16% owned directly plus the 36% owned indirectly (60% × 60%), giving a total effective interest of 52% and therefore a NCI of 48%.

26.8   The correct answers are:

	Non-controlling interests $
Balance at 1 January 20X4 (10% × 100,000 × $2.20)	22,000
Total comprehensive income for the year (10% × $25,000)	2,500
Dividends paid (10% × $5,000)	(500)
Balance at 31 December 20X4	24,000

26.9   A   A close family member of the Chief Executive of NV purchased an asset from NV.

The Chief Executive of NV is a related party as he is key management personnel and close family of a related party is also considered to be a related party in their own right.

However, providers of finance (XYZ Bank), departments and agencies of a government that do not control/jointly control/significantly influence the reporting entity (government of Country X) and a supplier with who an entity transactions a significant volume of business (YU) are not considered to be related parties.

26.10   B   0.84:1.

The quick ratio is current assets excluding inventory, divided by current liabilities:

(70,000 + 10,000)/(88,000 + 7,000) = 0.84

27 Mixed Bank 3

27.1   The correct answer is:

- A bond will be issued at the **market price** and redeemed at the **nominal value**. Bonds are normally **redeemable** and the interest payments will normally be **less than** an equivalent bank loan because of their marketability.

The issue price of a bond will be close to its nominal value – but the exact price paid will be determined by market demand for the bond. Most bonds are redeemable.

Bonds are normally cheaper than an equivalent bank loan because investors can sell the bonds on the market at any point prior to redemption i.e. they are marketable.

27.2   The correct answer is:

	Statement of financial position	Statement of profit or loss and other comprehensive income	Statement of changes in equity
Heading	Non-current liability	Finance cost	BLANK
Amount (in $)	1,211,642	61,642	BLANK

As these preferred shares are redeemable and cumulative, they contain an obligation to repay the principal and to pay the dividends. Therefore they should be treated as a financial liability rather than equity. As the redemption date is not until 31 March 20Y8, the liability should be non-current. The classification of the dividends should be consistent with the classification of the shares themselves and therefore a finance cost should be recorded in profit or loss rather than a dividend in the statement of changes in equity. As the shares are not held for trading, the liability should be measured at amortised cost. It is the effective interest (which includes the dividend paid and part of the issue costs/premium on issue/premium on redemption) which should be recorded in profit or loss, rather than the dividend paid.

27.3 C

Legal action against DH	Legal action taken by DH
Make a provision	Disclose as a note

The legal action against DH is a potential provision. The filing of the action prior to the year end is the past event and as the legal advisers believe the liability will materialise, it can be concluded that there is a legal obligation and a probable outflow. The amount given of $700,000 implies a reliable estimate therefore all three criteria for a provision have been met.

The legal action taken by DH is a potential contingent asset. As the inflow is probable, it should be disclosed in a note to the accounts.

27.4

The correct answers are:

	Account reference	$
Dr	Staff costs	356,400
Cr	Liabilities	356,400

The cost of the arrangement is spread over the vesting period (3 years) being $120 \times 900 \times 9.90 \times 1/3 =$ $356,400 in 20X8.

The transaction is cash-settled, so the amounts are included in liabilities, not equity.

27.5

The correct answer is: $32,500

Acquisition was on 31 May 20X8, so 9 months' of BL's profits arose pre acquisition.

	$	$
Consideration transferred		700,000
NCI at acquisition (fair value)		262,500
Net assets at acquisition		
Share capital	250,000	
Pre-acquisition retained earnings		
At 1.1.20X7	650,000	
To 31.5.20X8 (40,000 × 9/12)	30,000	
		(930,000)
		32,500

27.6 B

$190,000.

	$
Fair value of investment on date control achieved	340,000
Original cost of 18% investment	(150,000)
Profit on de-recognition of investment	190,000

27.7

The correct answer is: $355,000

	JG	TR
	$'000	$'000
Per statement of profit or loss	725	450
Less: Impairment of goodwill	(25)	–
	700	450
NCI share	× 25%	× 40%
	175	180

Total NCI = $175,000 + $180,000 = $355,000

PH owns 75% of JG (75/100). JG owns 80% (64/80) of TR. Therefore, the effective interest in TR is 60% (75% × 80%), making NCI in TR 40%.

27.8 D

$105,880,000

The equity attributable to the owners of the parent at the year end is calculated as:

	$'000
Share capital (parent's only)	2,900
Consolidated retained earnings (see below)	102,980
	105,880

Consolidated retained earnings is calculated as:

	P $'000	S $'000	A $'000
At 31 December 20X7	78,200	38,500	16,000
PUP [($1.4m - $1m) × ¼ in inventory]		(100)	
Less: Pre-acquisition		(12,300)	(3,000)
		26,100	13,000
Group share of S post acquisition (80% × 26,100)	20,880		
Group share of A post acquisition (30% × 13,000)	3,900		
	102,980		

27.9 C   53.2c.

Profit for the year $1,000,000 – $200,000 – $100,000 – $20,000 = $680,000

680,000/1,278,376 = 53.2c

EPS is calculated using the weighted average number of ordinary shares in issue during the year.

Profits are calculated after tax, NCI and preference dividends (i.e. on what is available for the ordinary shareholder).

27.10 C   9.3%

ROCE = PBIT/(Equity + long term debt - investments)

= $450,000 / $4,850,000 = 9.3%

---

28 Mixed Bank 4

28.1   The correct answer is:

Investors in preference shares require a **lower** level of return than ordinary shareholders because they face less **uncertainty** over the level of their return, and therefore face **less** risk.

28.2 B   Gain to OCI $9,856.

An available for sale financial asset should be measured initially at fair value plus transaction costs. Subsequent measurement is at fair value with gains or losses in other comprehensive income.

Initial measurement (1.1.X2)

	$
Fair value (40,000 × $2.12)	84,800
Commission (3% × $84,800)	2,544
	87,344

Revaluation gain at 31.12.X2

	$
Fair value (40,000 × $2.43)	97,200
Previous value	(87,344)
	9,856

28.3 C   II only.

1   As the board decision had not been communicated to customers and employees there is assumed to be no legal or constructive obligation therefore no provision should be made.

2   As refunds have been made in the past to all customers there is a valid expectation from customers that the refunds will be made therefore the amount should be provided for.

3   There is no present obligation to carry out the refurbishment therefore no provision should be made under IAS 37.

28.4 B

Estimated no. of employees entitled to benefits	×	No. of instruments per employee	×	FV per instrument at grant date	×	Proportion of vesting period elapsed at year end

The FV of the instrument is adjusted at each year end for cash settled transactions whereas it is always at the fair value at the grant dated for equity settled share based payments. The cost is never spread over the exercise period. It is always spread over the vesting period.

28.5 A $10,080,000.

	$
Cash 80% × 3,000,000 × $1.20	2,880,000
Shares 80% × 3,000,000 × 2 × $1.50	7,200,000
	10,080,000

The fair value of cash consideration is straightforward. For consideration given in the form of shares, the fair value as at the acquisition date should used. IFRS 3 (revised) requires that any costs related to the acquisition, such as professional fees, are written off immediately to profit or loss, so these are not included in the consideration figure.

28.6 The correct answer is: $33,000.

	$
NCI in profit for the period to 1 October 20X5 (30% × 9/12 × 120,000)	27,000
NCI in profit for the period from 1 October 20X5 to 31 December 20X5 (20% × 3/12 × 120,000)	6,000
	33,000

28.7 B $1,194,000.

	PH $'000	JG $'000	TR $'000
At 31 Dec 20X5	1,200	360	500
Retained earnings at acquisition		(480)	(360)
		(120)	140
Group share:			
JG (75% × (120))	(90)		
TR (60% × 140)	84		
	1,194		

The effective interest in TR is (75% × 80%) = 60% and TR was acquired on 1 Jan 20X5.

28.8 B,D The correct answers are:

- Decreasing the shareholding in a subsidiary from 75% to 60%
- Total comprehensive income for the year of a subsidiary (multiplied by the NCI share)

Decreasing a shareholding in a subsidiary from 75% to 60% will make NCI increase from 25% to 40%. 100% of the subsidiary's total comprehensive income (TCI) will be added across in the consolidated statement of profit or loss and other comprehensive income to show control but the NCI share of that TCI does not belong to the group so must be added to the NCI 'liability' in the consolidated statement of changes in equity.

Increasing the shareholding in a subsidiary from 80% to 90% would result in a decrease in NCI from 20% to 10%.

Dividends paid by the subsidiary cause NCI to decrease not increase.

A share issue by the parent has no impact on NCI.

28.9 B,D The correct answers are:

- A bonus issue will have no effect on RS's capacity to generate earnings in the future
- A rights issue is a combination of an issue of shares at full market price with a bonus element

28.10 D,E   The correct answers are:

- The P/E ratio will move according to how the market reacts to the majority of the holders converting to ordinary shares.

- Gearing will decrease and profit available for distribution will be allocated over a greater number of ordinary shares.

Interest cover will increase as there is less interest (no more interest payable once the bonds convert) that needs to be covered by profits. EPS and the P/E ratio may increase or decrease depending on the relative sizes of the interest expense no longer payable to the shares issued. Gearing will decrease as there is less debt and more equity (gearing = debt/equity).

29 Mixed Bank 5

29.1   The correct answer is: 4.74%

An undated bond is irredeemable so the correct approach to use is $K_d = I (1-t) / P_0$

$I = 6$

$(1-t) = 0.75$

$P_0 = 95$

$K_d = 6 \times 0.75 / 95 = 0.0474$ or **4.74%**

29.2   D $1,000.

$$\text{Sum of digits} = \frac{n(n+1)}{2}$$

Where n = number of interest bearing instalments. Here as payments are in advance so the first of the four instalments does not include any interest. This makes n = 3.

$$\text{Sum of digits} = \frac{3 \times 4}{2}$$

$$= 6$$

The year ended 31 December 20X5 is the second year of the lease so interest is calculated as:

$2/6 \times \$3,000 = \$1,000$ (the first year of the lease would be calculated as $3/6 \times \$3,000$).

29.3   The correct answer is: $287,500

	$
Taxable temporary differences b/f	850,000
Accelerated tax allowances (500,000 – 450,000)	50,000
Revaluation surplus	250,000
Taxable temporary differences c/f	1,150,000
Deferred tax liability at 25%	287,500

29.4   B   Debit cash $6,000, credit revenue $1,000 and credit deferred income $5,000.

This is revenue from services which must be recognised on a stage of completion basis. Therefore, revenue for the month of June (one-sixth of the $6,000 received) will be recognised in the statement of profit or loss and other comprehensive income, and the remainder will be credited to deferred income.

29.5   The correct answer is: $'000 135

Investment in associate:		$'000
Cost of associate		60
Share of post-acquisition reserves	(40% × [220 – 30])	76
Unrealised intra-group profit	(40% × 10 × 25%)	(1)
		135

Note: The unrealised profit is deducted from the investment in the associate rather than inventory as the associate holds the inventory at the year end.

29.6   The correct answer is: $414,000.

	$
NCI at acquisition (30% × (1,000,000 + 500,000))	450,000
NCI share of post acquisition reserves to 1 October 20X5	
30% × [(950,000 + 9/12 × 120,000) – 500,000]	162,000
	612,000
Decrease in NCI on second acquisition (10%/30% × 612,000)	(204,000)
NCI share of post acquisition reserves to year end (20% × 3/12 × 120,000)	6,000
	414,000

Note: the fair value of NCI at acquisition of $600,000 is not relevant here as it is group policy to measure NCI at acquisition at their proportionate share of the net assets.

29.7   The correct answer is: 204,000.

Goodwill is retranslated at each year end:

B$510,000 / 2.5 = A$204,000.

29.8   The correct answer is:

On disposal of a subsidiary, the proceeds from the sale of the **shares** are recorded as a cash **inflow** in the **investing** section of the statement of cash flows. The cash balance of the subsidiary at the disposal date is **deducted from** the sales proceeds (or for an overdraft, **added to**) and the **net** figure is shown in the statement of cash flows.

An investor in a company owns shares not net assets. Therefore, on disposal, shares are sold. This is an inflow in the cash flow as the sales proceeds are a cash receipt. The 'investing' section of the cash flow is where purchases and sales of non-current assets (including subsidiaries) are recorded. IAS 7 *Statements of cash flows* requires the sales proceeds to be shown in the statement of cash flows net of the subsidiary's cash balance at the disposal date.

29.9   A   50.7c.

$$\text{Basic EPS} = \frac{\$320,000 - \$20,000}{(\text{W1})\,591,667} = 50.7c$$

(W1)   *Weighted average number of shares*

Date	Narrative	No. of shares	Time	Bonus Fraction	Weighted Average
1.1.X3	B/f	500,000	2/12	(W2) 11/10	91,667
1.3.X3	Rights issue (1 for 5)	100,000			
		600,000	10/12		500,000
					591,667

(W2)   *Bonus fraction*

$$= \frac{\text{Fair value per share immediately before rights issue}}{\text{Theoretical ex} - \text{rights price}}$$

$$= \frac{\$11}{\$10}$$

(W3)   *Theoretical ex-rights price*

	$
5 shares × $11	55
1 share × $5	5
6 shares	60
TERP = $60/6 =	$10

29.10   The correct answer is:

The market has **greater** confidence in the **future** performance of KL and it is likely that KL has been established for a longer time and has a proven track record for success. Investing in GH is likely to be **more risky** than investing in KL.

30 Mixed Bank 6

30.1   The correct answer is: 6.3%.

An internal rate of return approach needs to be used to assess the cost of redeemable debt.

IRR = NPVa + [NPVa / (NPVa-NPVb) × (b-a)]

Where a = the lower % rate (5%) and b = the higher % rate (10%).

IRR   = 5 + [3.21/(3.21 − - 9.51)] × (10 − 5)

= 5 + [3.21 / (3.21 + 9.51) × 5]

= 5 +1.3= **6.3%**

30. 2   The correct answer is: $9,600.

Operating lease – spread the rent-free period over the term of the lease

Total rent payable =   4 years × $12,000   = $48,000

Over five years = $48,000/5 years   = $9,600 per annum

$9,600 charged to profit or loss for year ended 30 April 20X8.

30.3   A   Accrued expenses nil, interest receivable nil.

The accrued expenses will all be deductible for tax purposes, so the tax base is nil.

When the interest is received it will all be subject to tax, so the tax base is nil.

30.4   B   Include $6,000 in revenue for the year and create a current liability for $6,000

$12,000 was received in the current year on 1 July 20X2. This represents 6 months' worth of sales but only 3 of these months relate to the year ended 30 September 20X2 ie July/August/September 20X2. Therefore revenue of $12,000 × 3/6=$6,000 must be recognised. The remaining $6,000 relates in sales in the next accounting period (October/November/December 20X2) and therefore should be recorded as deferred income within current liabilities.

30.5   D   Dr Share of profit of associate $8,750 Cr Inventories $8,750

Provision for unrealised profit = $500,000 × 25/125 = $100,000 × ¼ = $25,000

Adjust for the parent share in the associate = $25,000 × 35% = $8,750

Reduce the profit in associate (as they have made the profit on the sale) and reduce the inventory in the parent (included in the consolidation) as the inventory held by the parent is overvalued.

30.6   The correct answer is:

When the shares in Q are disposed of, its resources cease to be **controlled** by the group on 1 November 20X6. The consolidated statement of profit or loss will include the income and expenses for the **10 months** to 1 November 20X6, the non controlling interest of 20% will be calculated on the profits for the same period and the group profit or loss on disposal of the shares should be included in the results. The profit or loss is calculated as the fair value of the **consideration** received less the net assets and goodwill on 1 November 20X6 plus the non controlling interest on 1 November 20X6.

30.7 B $5,099,000.

	$000
HM	3,200
OS (3000 ÷ 1.58)	1,899
	5,099

The consolidated statement of profit or loss and other comprehensive income of the foreign subsidiary is translated at the average rate.

30.8 B $125,000

	$'000
Balance b/d	515
Revaluation gain	50
Depreciation	(60)
Acquisition of subsidiary	90
	595
Cash paid to buy PPE (balancing figure)	**125**
Balance c/d	720

30.9 A It is a deliberate attempt to mislead potential acquirers who might rely on D's financial statements and as a result the directors are acting unethically.

There appears to be no commercial reason for the transaction therefore it would be reasonable to assume that the directors had entered into the transaction purely to manipulate the results of D at the year end.

30.10 A,B,E The correct answers are:

- Gearing
- Return on capital employed
- Interest cover

Revaluing property, plant and equipment will impact on the value of net assets and increase the revaluation reserve, which will increase equity. The additional depreciation charges on the revalued assets will reduce profits.

Gearing will be affected by the increased equity.

Return on capital employed will be impacted by the change to operating profit and the higher equity within capital employed.

Receivable days will not be affected as the revaluation does not impact receivables or revenue.

Dividends per share will not be impacted as the revaluation will not impact dividend policy or the number of shares.

Interest cover will be affected due to the change in profit from the extra depreciation.

Quick ratio will not be impacted as the revaluation will not affect cash, receivables or current liabilities.

31 Mixed Bank 7

31.1 C 8%.

Cost of the preference shares is 8%.

$$K_{pref} = \frac{d}{P_0}$$

There is no growth in the dividend (and no tax relief) as preference shares pay a fixed dividend (here 6%).

So 6 / 0.75 = 8%

If this company issued new preference shares today on these terms then they would cost 8%.

The other answers are obtained by using the nominal value as the share price and / or by applying tax relief i.e. multiplying by (1-t).

31.2 The correct answers are:

Current lease liability $16,547 (W2)

Depreciation charge $17,660 (W3)

Workings

1 Finance charge

	$'000
Total lease payments (5 × $21,000)	105,000
Fair value of asset	(88,300)
Total finance charge	16,700

Finance charge allocation

SOD = (5 × 6)/2 = 15

(n = 5 as payments are in arrears so all instalments are interest bearing)

	$
20X1 5/15 × 16,700	5,567
20X2 4/15 × 16,700	4,453

2 Lease liabilities

	$
Fair value	88,300
Finance charge (W1)	5,567
Instalment	(21,000)
Balance at 31 December 20X1	72,867
Finance charge	4,453
Instalment	(21,000)
Balance at 31 December 20X2	56,320

Non-current liability	= $56,320
Current liability	= $72,867 - $56,320 = $16,547

3 Depreciation

Depreciate over shorter of useful life (6 years) and the lease term (5 years).

Depreciation = $88,300/5 years

= $17,600

31.3 A Receipt of a non-taxable government grant.

Receipt of a government grant creates a permanent difference between accounting and taxable profits as it will never be taxed. The other options all create temporary differences and so give rise to deferred tax liabilities.

31.4 D $21,500

First check if the contract is profitable:

	$'000
Total revenue	60
Total expected costs (21+3+19)	(43)
Overall profit	17

Then calculate cost of sales based on the stage of completion given in the question:

Cost of sales = 50% × Total expected costs of $43,000=$21,500

If you forgot to include the $3,000 paid for next year's inventory in total costs, you would have reached the incorrect answer of $20,000. All costs relating to the contract must be recorded in the total costs figure used to calculate cost of sales. And if your selected answer was $21,000, you have incorrectly recognised cost of sales on a costs incurred basis rather than a stage of completion basis. You would have arrived at $18,500 if you had treated the $3,000 as closing inventory and deducted it - but this is not a normal sale of goods - cost of sales must be calculated as total costs multiplied by the stage of completion.

31.5 C Include 25% of the assets and liabilities of UV and 25% of the revenue and expenses generated by UV.

If UV was a joint venture then it would be included at either cost or as an available for sale financial asset. On consolidation no further entries are required as the 25% share of UV has already been included in the accounts of T.

31.6 B $364,500.

	$	$
Consideration transferred		670,000
Non-controlling interests (22% × (500,000 + 280,000 + 6/12 × 95,000))		182,050
Fair value of acquirer's previously held investment		340,000
Less: Net fair value of identifiable assets acquired and liabilities assumed		
Share capital	500,000	
Retained earnings (280,000 + 6/12 × 95,000)	327,500	
		(827,500)
		364,550

31.7 The correct answers are:

	$'000
On translation of net assets	
Closing net assets at closing rate	**10,691**
Opening net assets at opening rate	**9,814**
	X
Less profit	**285**
	X
Translation difference on goodwill	54
	X

	$'000
On translation of net assets	
Closing net assets at closing rate (15,800,000 + 450,000)/1.52	10,691
Opening net assets at opening rate (15,800,000/1.61)	(9,814)
	877
Less profit (450,000/1.58)	(285)
	592
Translation differences on goodwill (see working)	54
	646

	$'000
Goodwill at acquisition (1,680,000/1.61)	1,043
Impairment [(1,680,000 × 20%)/1.58]	(213)
Exchange gain to OCI (bal)	54
Goodwill at 31 December 20X1 [(1,680,000 × 80%)/1.52]	884

31.8 C $375,000.

	$
B/ d	4,550,000
SPLOCI - TCI	425,000
Acquisition of subsidiary	
25% × 1,100,000)	275,000
Dividend paid (balancing figure)	**(375,000)**
C/ d	4,875,000

31.9 B,C,D The correct answers are:

This proposed treatment results in non-compliance of IAS 7 *Statement of cash flows* which requires these proceeds to be treated as 'investing' rather than 'operating'.

As these cash flows are one-off rather than recurring, it would be misleading to the users of financial statements to classify them as 'operating'.

There is a self-interest threat here as the motivation for this accounting treatment is the job security of the directors.

Whilst it is true that IAS 7 offers some flexibility in the classification of cash flows (e.g. dividends may be presented as 'operating' or 'financing'), it is clear in its treatment of buying and selling non-current assets which must be presented in 'investing activities'. Even if the directors think they are acting in the shareholders' best interests, they would not be considered to be acting ethically nor demonstrating professional competence as their proposed accounting policy does not comply with IAS 7.

31.10 C LM's management has shown competent stewardship of the entity's resources by increasing long term finance to partly fund investing activities.

The management of LM have generated funds from daily operations, but have invested a large amount in the continuing business, as seen by the large outflow in investing activities. This may be through the acquisition of property, plant and equipment, purchase of shares as a strategic investment or through investing in intangible assets. This demonstrates strong stewardship and investment in the future of the business. A small net cash outflow is not a sign of a company in decline or of insolvency, it must be considered against the components of the cash flows.

32 Mixed Bank 8

32.1 D

Cost of debt = 4.0%,

Cost of equity = 9.1%.

The cost of debt is calculated using $K_d = I(1-t) / P_0$

$I =$	$5(1-t)$	$= 0.75$
$P_0 =$	94% of 100	$= 94$
So $K_d =$	$5 \times 0.75/94$	$= 0.04$

Cost of equity = $d_1 / P_0 + g$

$d_1 =$	0.2 and P	$= 2.40 - 0.20 = 2.20$ ex div and $g = 0$
So $K_e =$	0.2/2.2	**= 9.1%**

32.2   The correct answers are:

	Account reference	$
Dr	Property plant and equipment	74,000
Cr	Finance lease liability	74,000

The lease is initially recorded at the lower of the PVMLP (74,000) and the fair value (80,000).

32.3 D   Asset which will be included in the statement of financial position at the amount that is expected to be able to be recovered from future expected profits.

Tax losses can be carried forward to reduce current tax on future profits, representing a tax saving and thus a deferred tax asset (less tax payable in the future). These can only be recognised to the extent that it is probable the losses can be used before they expire.

32.4 B $20 million.

Here the outcome of the contract cannot be estimated reliably. Therefore prudence dictates that no profit should be recognised. IAS 11 allows revenue to be recognised to the extent of recoverable costs incurred. Here $20 million of costs have been incurred and as the customer has been invoiced for and paid progress billings of $23 million, all of these costs can be deemed recoverable. Therefore revenue of $20 million should be recognised.

It is incorrect to recognise no revenue here as that would imply that no work had been done when the contract is 25% complete. It is also incorrect to recognise the amount invoiced of $23 million as revenue as that would mean recording a profit of $3 million when it is uncertain if a profit will be made on this contract. Finally, recognising revenue of $25 million is incorrect - you only recognise revenue based on stage of completion when the outcome of the contract can be measured reliably.

32.5 B,C,E,F The correct answers are:

- The significant judgments and assumptions made in determining whether the entity has control, joint control or significant influence of the other entities, and in determining the type of joint arrangement.

- Information to understand the composition of the group and the interest that non controlling interests have in the group's activities and cash flows.

- The nature, extent and financial effects of interests in joint arrangements and associates, including the nature and effects of the entity's contractual relationship with other investors

- The nature and extent of interests in unconsolidated structured entities.

The disclosure of entries to remove intragroup transactions is not required in the group financial statements by any of the international financial reporting standards. IFRS 10 *Consolidated Financial Statements* does require disclosure of this elimination. IAS 24 *Related Party Disclosures* does consider a parent and its subsidaries to be related parties, however, intragroup transactions are exempt from disclosure in the group financial statements as they are eliminated on consolidation.

The requirement to disclose the fair value of each class of financial assets and financial liabilities comes from IFRS 7 *Financial Instruments: Disclosures* **not** IFRS 12. Interests in another entity accounted for in accordance with IAS 39 *Financial Instruments: Recognition and Measurement* are outside the Scope of IFRS 12.

32.6 B,E,F   The correct answers are:

- In substance the 15% investment has been sold

- A profit or loss on de-recognition of the 15% shares is calculated as the fair value of the 15% at the date control is achieved less original cost

- Previous revaluation gains on the available for sale investment are reclassified out of other comprehensive income

As the control boundary has been crossed, in substance a 15% investment has been sold and a 95% subsidiary acquired. The 15% investment is revalued to its fair value and this fair value is included in the goodwill calculation. The investment is then de-recognised from the consolidated statement of financial position as in substance it has been sold.

A profit or loss on de-recognition results from the revaluation of the 15% investment to its fair value and this is calculated as fair value on the date of acquisition of the 15% less the original cost.

The profit or loss on de-recognition must be recognised in profit or loss (not other comprehensive income).

On de-recognition of an available for sale financial asset, IAS 39 requires previous revaluation gains to be reclassified out of other comprehensive income into profit or loss.

32.7   C $1,155,000.

	Group	Owners of HM	NCI (20%)
	$'000	$'000	$'000
HM	580	580	–
OS (450/1.58)	285	228	57
Impairment [(1,680 × 20%)/1.58]	(213)	(170)	(43)
Exchange gains	646	517	129
	1,298	1,155	143

32.8   The correct answer is: $120,000

	$'000
Balance b/d	6,600
Share of profit for the year (700 × 30%)	210
Share of other comprehensive income (200 × 30%)	60
	6,870
Dividends received (balancing figure)	**(120)**
Balance c/d	6,750

32.9   E   Intimidation.

The other threats are defined as follows:

Self-interest	Accountant's personal or other interest may inappropriately influence their judgment or behaviour
Self-review	Where accountant evaluates previous judgments made by themselves
Advocacy	Threat that accountant promotes client's position to the point that their objectivity is compromised
Familiarity	Risk that accountant is too trusting or accepting of information provided by a client or employer because of a long or close relationship with them

32.10   The correct answers are:

Dividend cover   Dividend yield

$$\frac{\text{Earnings per share}}{\text{Dividend per share}}$$ $$\frac{\text{Dividend per share}}{\text{Share price}}$$

Mathematical tables and exam formulae

PRESENT VALUE TABLE

Present value of 1.00 unit of currency, that is $(1+r)^{-n}$ where r = interest rate; n = number of periods until payment or receipt.

Periods (n)	Interest rates (r)									
	1%	2%	3%	4%	5%	6%	7%	8%	9%	10%
1	0.990	0.980	0.971	0.962	0.952	0.943	0.935	0.926	0.917	0.909
2	0.980	0.961	0.943	0.925	0.907	0.890	0.873	0.857	0.842	0.826
3	0.971	0.942	0.915	0.889	0.864	0.840	0.816	0.794	0.772	0.751
4	0.961	0.924	0.888	0.855	0.823	0.792	0.763	0.735	0.708	0.683
5	0.951	0.906	0.863	0.822	0.784	0.747	0.713	0.681	0.650	0.621
6	0.942	0.888	0.837	0.790	0.746	0.705	0.666	0.630	0.596	0.564
7	0.933	0.871	0.813	0.760	0.711	0.665	0.623	0.583	0.547	0.513
8	0.923	0.853	0.789	0.731	0.677	0.627	0.582	0.540	0.502	0.467
9	0.914	0.837	0.766	0.703	0.645	0.592	0.544	0.500	0.460	0.424
10	0.905	0.820	0.744	0.676	0.614	0.558	0.508	0.463	0.422	0.386
11	0.896	0.804	0.722	0.650	0.585	0.527	0.475	0.429	0.388	0.350
12	0.887	0.788	0.701	0.625	0.557	0.497	0.444	0.397	0.356	0.319
13	0.879	0.773	0.681	0.601	0.530	0.469	0.415	0.368	0.326	0.290
14	0.870	0.758	0.661	0.577	0.505	0.442	0.388	0.340	0.299	0.263
15	0.861	0.743	0.642	0.555	0.481	0.417	0.362	0.315	0.275	0.239
16	0.853	0.728	0.623	0.534	0.458	0.394	0.339	0.292	0.252	0.218
17	0.844	0.714	0.605	0.513	0.436	0.371	0.317	0.270	0.231	0.198
18	0.836	0.700	0.587	0.494	0.416	0.350	0.296	0.250	0.212	0.180
19	0.828	0.686	0.570	0.475	0.396	0.331	0.277	0.232	0.194	0.164
20	0.820	0.673	0.554	0.456	0.377	0.312	0.258	0.215	0.178	0.149

Periods (n)	Interest rates (r)									
	11%	12%	13%	14%	15%	16%	17%	18%	19%	20%
1	0.901	0.893	0.885	0.877	0.870	0.862	0.855	0.847	0.840	0.833
2	0.812	0.797	0.783	0.769	0.756	0.743	0.731	0.718	0.706	0.694
3	0.731	0.712	0.693	0.675	0.658	0.641	0.624	0.609	0.593	0.579
4	0.659	0.636	0.613	0.592	0.572	0.552	0.534	0.516	0.499	0.482
5	0.593	0.567	0.543	0.519	0.497	0.476	0.456	0.437	0.419	0.402
6	0.535	0.507	0.480	0.456	0.432	0.410	0.390	0.370	0.352	0.335
7	0.482	0.452	0.425	0.400	0.376	0.354	0.333	0.314	0.296	0.279
8	0.434	0.404	0.376	0.351	0.327	0.305	0.285	0.266	0.249	0.233
9	0.391	0.361	0.333	0.308	0.284	0.263	0.243	0.225	0.209	0.194
10	0.352	0.322	0.295	0.270	0.247	0.227	0.208	0.191	0.176	0.162
11	0.317	0.287	0.261	0.237	0.215	0.195	0.178	0.162	0.148	0.135
12	0.286	0.257	0.231	0.208	0.187	0.168	0.152	0.137	0.124	0.112
13	0.258	0.229	0.204	0.182	0.163	0.145	0.130	0.116	0.104	0.093
14	0.232	0.205	0.181	0.160	0.141	0.125	0.111	0.099	0.088	0.078
15	0.209	0.183	0.160	0.140	0.123	0.108	0.095	0.084	0.079	0.065
16	0.188	0.163	0.141	0.123	0.107	0.093	0.081	0.071	0.062	0.054
17	0.170	0.146	0.125	0.108	0.093	0.080	0.069	0.060	0.052	0.045
18	0.153	0.130	0.111	0.095	0.081	0.069	0.059	0.051	0.044	0.038
19	0.138	0.116	0.098	0.083	0.070	0.060	0.051	0.043	0.037	0.031
20	0.124	0.104	0.087	0.073	0.061	0.051	0.043	0.037	0.031	0.026

Cumulative present value of 1.00 unit of currency per annum, Receivable or Payable at the end of each year for n years $\frac{1-(1+r)^{-n}}{r}$

Periods (n)	Interest rates (r)									
	1%	2%	3%	4%	5%	6%	7%	8%	9%	10%
1	0.990	0.980	0.971	0.962	0.952	0.943	0.935	0.926	0.917	0.909
2	1.970	1.942	1.913	1.886	1.859	1.833	1.808	1.783	1.759	1.736
3	2.941	2.884	2.829	2.775	2.723	2.673	2.624	2.577	2.531	2.487
4	3.902	3.808	3.717	3.630	3.546	3.465	3.387	3.312	3.240	3.170
5	4.853	4.713	4.580	4.452	4.329	4.212	4.100	3.993	3.890	3.791
6	5.795	5.601	5.417	5.242	5.076	4.917	4.767	4.623	4.486	4.355
7	6.728	6.472	6.230	6.002	5.786	5.582	5.389	5.206	5.033	4.868
8	7.652	7.325	7.020	6.733	6.463	6.210	5.971	5.747	5.535	5.335
9	8.566	8.162	7.786	7.435	7.108	6.802	6.515	6.247	5.995	5.759
10	9.471	8.983	8.530	8.111	7.722	7.360	7.024	6.710	6.418	6.145
11	10.368	9.787	9.253	8.760	8.306	7.887	7.499	7.139	6.805	6.495
12	11.255	10.575	9.954	9.385	8.863	8.384	7.943	7.536	7.161	6.814
13	12.134	11.348	10.635	9.986	9.394	8.853	8.358	7.904	7.487	7.103
14	13.004	12.106	11.296	10.563	9.899	9.295	8.745	8.244	7.786	7.367
15	13.865	12.849	11.938	11.118	10.380	9.712	9.108	8.559	8.061	7.606
16	14.718	13.578	12.561	11.652	10.838	10.106	9.447	8.851	8.313	7.824
17	15.562	14.292	13.166	12.166	11.274	10.477	9.763	9.122	8.544	8.022
18	16.398	14.992	13.754	12.659	11.690	10.828	10.059	9.372	8.756	8.201
19	17.226	15.679	14.324	13.134	12.085	11.158	10.336	9.604	8.950	8.365
20	18.046	16.351	14.878	13.590	12.462	11.470	10.594	9.818	9.129	8.514

Periods (n)	Interest rates (r)									
	11%	12%	13%	14%	15%	16%	17%	18%	19%	20%
1	0.901	0.893	0.885	0.877	0.870	0.862	0.855	0.847	0.840	0.833
2	1.713	1.690	1.668	1.647	1.626	1.605	1.585	1.566	1.547	1.528
3	2.444	2.402	2.361	2.322	2.283	2.246	2.210	2.174	2.140	2.106
4	3.102	3.037	2.974	2.914	2.855	2.798	2.743	2.690	2.639	2.589
5	3.696	3.605	3.517	3.433	3.352	3.274	3.199	3.127	3.058	2.991
6	4.231	4.111	3.998	3.889	3.784	3.685	3.589	3.498	3.410	3.326
7	4.712	4.564	4.423	4.288	4.160	4.039	3.922	3.812	3.706	3.605
8	5.146	4.968	4.799	4.639	4.487	4.344	4.207	4.078	3.954	3.837
9	5.537	5.328	5.132	4.946	4.772	4.607	4.451	4.303	4.163	4.031
10	5.889	5.650	5.426	5.216	5.019	4.833	4.659	4.494	4.339	4.192
11	6.207	5.938	5.687	5.453	5.234	5.029	4.836	4.656	4.486	4.327
12	6.492	6.194	5.918	5.660	5.421	5.197	4.988	4.793	4.611	4.439
13	6.750	6.424	6.122	5.842	5.583	5.342	5.118	4.910	4.715	4.533
14	6.982	6.628	6.302	6.002	5.724	5.468	5.229	5.008	4.802	4.611
15	7.191	6.811	6.462	6.142	5.847	5.575	5.324	5.092	4.876	4.675
16	7.379	6.974	6.604	6.265	5.954	5.668	5.405	5.162	4.938	4.730
17	7.549	7.120	6.729	6.373	6.047	5.749	5.475	5.222	4.990	4.775
18	7.702	7.250	6.840	6.467	6.128	5.818	5.534	5.273	5.033	4.812
19	7.839	7.366	6.938	6.550	6.198	5.877	5.584	5.316	5.070	4.843
20	7.963	7.469	7.025	6.623	6.259	5.929	5.628	5.353	5.101	4.870

FORMULAE

Divided growth model	Cost of Irredeemable debt
$P_0 = \dfrac{d_1}{k_e - g}$ $k_e = \dfrac{d_1}{P_0} + g$ $g = r \times b$	$K_d = \dfrac{1(1-t)}{P_0}$
WACC $WACC = k_e \left[\dfrac{V_e}{V_e + V_d} \right] + k_d [1-t] \left[\dfrac{V_d}{V_e + V_d} \right]$